What Really Happened

HOW DONALD J. TRUMP SAVED AMERICA FROM HILLARY CLINTON

Howie Carr

Howie Carr

To the deplorables, all of them.

ACKNOWLEDGMENTS

FIRST, I WOULD LIKE TO THANK PRESIDENT DONALD J. TRUMP FOR RUNNING for president and, against all odds, sparing the nation the nightmare of a Hillary Clinton presidency.

Closer to home, as they say, thanks to my wife Kathy, who has worked hard to see this latest book through to completion, and to my radio staff—especially executive producer Steve Robinson. Operations manager Jared Goodell handled many details, and associate producer Grace Curley was always there.

Also, thanks to Ian Wilson, who runs my network's fulfillment center—I hope the orders for this volume keep you busy for months, Ian.

Our printer, Bookmasters, always does a great job, and Jennifer Welsch was again willing to go above and beyond the call of duty to get this book into your hands. And in case you were wondering, this book you are holding was printed by Americans in America—specifically, at Bookmasters' factory in Ohio.

Chris Wrona is an old-style proofreader—that means she actually catches errors before they get into print and embarrass the author.

Once again, my thanks to the *Boston Herald*, where I have worked for so long, for providing the photographs. Pat Purcell deserves kudos from everyone in New England, especially me, for keeping Boston a two-newspaper town all these years. Like President Trump, Pat always faced long odds, but nevertheless he persisted, to coin a phrase. Thanks also to *Herald* photo editor Jim Mahoney and Gwen Gage, the paper's vice president of promotions and marketing.

I can't express my gratitude enough to my radio affiliates, who have been such great partners with me since I went out on my own in 2014. In 2018, I particularly look forward to working with iHeart in Boston, after their much-appreciated takeover of WRKO.

And finally, thanks once again to all of you who listen to my radio show every weekday afternoon, in whatever medium—broadcast, internet, podcast, app or Newsmax TV.

I hope you enjoy this book.

PROLOGUE

I NEVER THOUGHT HE'D REALLY RUN.

Like a lot of people, I figured it was just a gag, a tease to get some free publicity before he called NBC and told them he'd changed his mind and really did want to come back for another season of *The Apprentice*.

I mean, he'd been talking about running for president as far back as 1988. In 2011, he actually flew up to Nashua and delivered a speech to the New Hampshire Chamber of Commerce. We booked him for a post-speech interview on my show, but he cancelled at the last minute and soon announced, much to the relief of Mitt Romney, that he would be passing up the race.

That was, like, the fourth time he'd gotten cold feet.

But when he made his astonishing announcement speech in June 2015, I knew we had to get him on the show. By the time he was scheduled, Trump-mania had already become a national phenomenon—companies like Macy's were cancelling their contracts with him, Univision was up in arms and the mainstream media were bizarrely obsessing about him. (Did he really hire actors to pad the announcement crowd at Trump Tower—how dare he!)

After we booked him, I went to the Federal Elections Commission (FEC) website and pulled his contributions. What I wanted to hit him on were all the New York Democrats he'd given money to. So I asked him, what's up with all this… Hillary Clinton? Chuck Schumer? Eliot Spitzer?

"Look, it's pretty simple," he told me matter-of-factly, without apology. "I do business in New York. Sometimes I need these guys to make calls for me. And when I give them money, they do what I tell them to do."

In other words, Trump was saying, he bought politicians, a dime a dozen. He wasn't bribing them, he was just buying, or at least renting them. It was "honest graft," as another New York politician, Plunkitt of Tammany Hall, had put it at the turn of the 20th century, as opposed to "dishonest graft."

But Trump felt no obligation to explain such fine distinctions. He assumed his audience had as little regard for Hillary and Client No. 9 and Carlos Danger and the rest of the hacks he'd duked cash to as he did. And he was right.

When it came to politicians, Trump believed in the golden rule—he who has the gold, rules.

Amazing—I considered how, say, a Mitt Romney would have answered such a question. Probably, after breaking into a cold sweat, and looking desperately over at his handlers, Mitt would have stammered out some lame response about how while he didn't necessarily agree with Chuck Schumer on every issue, he certainly supported a robust two-party democracy blah-blah-blah....

Trump, on the other hand, just told the truth. He didn't try to bullshit his supporters. He and they both understood the system was corrupt, but Trump wanted to make it clear, he was the one calling the shots. He was the alpha male.

And that's the way it was with every issue. Illegal immigration—build the wall! ISIS—bomb the shit out of them! Unvetted Muslim immigration—no more until "we figure out what the hell's going on."

Before he took over Bill O'Reilly's time slot on Fox in 2017, Tucker Carlson wrote a piece for POLITICO about the bracing effect of Trump's blunt honesty on the national dialogue.

"In a country where almost everyone in public life lies reflexively," Carlson wrote, "it's thrilling to hear someone say what he really thinks, even if you believe he's wrong. It's especially exciting when you suspect he's right."

In the days after my first radio interview with Trump, I heard back from so many people who'd been listening. They all told me the same thing—get him back on! Like everybody else in the media, I quickly realized that this guy was ratings gold.

Then I got a phone call from Ernie Boch Jr., the billionaire car dealer. He too was fascinated by Trump's latest reality TV show, and he wanted to throw what we in Boston call a "time" for Trump, at his estate off the Auto Mile in Norwood.

I put Ernie together with Corey Lewandowski and pretty soon it was announced that Trump would be flying in on a Friday night in August. He had to borrow Ernie's private jet to get up from New York, because his 747 was too big to land at the Norwood airport. That was the kind of problem the other candidates didn't have.

As the big day approached, I began getting calls from people I hadn't heard from in years. They were begging me to get them inside. It was like having a fistful of Super Bowl tickets when the Pats are playing. I was Mr. Big.

When Trump arrived, it was like the Beatles in 1964. The crowds ran after him as he made his way to the tent, trying to touch his coat, or grab a selfie with him. All the cable news networks covered first his press conference—he insulted CNN—and then his speech, live.

Wherever he went on Ernie's estate that night, he was surrounded and swept along by a throng of beefy security guards and adoring fans. At one point I got close enough to hand him a copy of the 1996 Democratic party platform, which I'd promised him, so he could read for himself Bill Clinton's tough talk on illegal immigration. But then he was gone, and I never got within eyeshot of him again that night.

Later, after the event was over and Trump was flying back to New York, I checked my voicemails and heard Trump's voice.

"Howie," he was yelling. "Where the hell are you?"

All in all, it was perhaps the most amazing campaign in American political history. And the greatest irony of all was that this *sui generis* candidate, this product of the new media, this lifelong Democrat, would find himself the last obstacle standing in the way of the final "fundamental transformation" of the Republic into a Third World hellhole, or maybe I should say shithole, the word that has lately been sending all the usual suspects into the usual paroxysms of fake outrage.

It was John Adams who said, "Our Constitution was made only for a moral and religious people. It is wholly inadequate to the government of any other."

And now it would be up to a thrice-married, potty-mouthed, onetime casino-owning billionaire from Queens to defend Adams' moral and religious people, to be the last conservative standing athwart the tide of history, as William F. Buckley once wrote, yelling "Stop!"

He may have been an imperfect vessel, but Trump was the only Republican candidate who could have possibly halted the seemingly inevitable slide into statism, the soft despotism of Political Correctness.

In his POLITICO piece, Carlson mentioned how evangelicals were willing to overlook Trump's shortcomings, but he could have also been describing all the other groups whom Hillary would describe a few months later as "deplorables."

"What they're looking for is a bodyguard," Carlson wrote, "someone to shield them from mounting (and real) threats to their freedom of speech and worship."

This book is the story of that campaign—of *What Really Happened.*

Are you listening, Hillary?

Chapter One

Last Call

THE STUDIO HOTLINE LIT UP.

"Is this the man?" I asked my producer.

It was Donald J. Trump, and it was 6:30 pm EST on Election Day.

This would be the last interview he did before the final results started coming in. I was anxious. Everyone in the studio was. The fate of the country was hanging in the balance. I was curious to see what kind of mood he was in. Guests who were close to the campaign had come on the show earlier that day with funerary tones that inspired little confidence.

Ann Coulter, whose 2015 book *Adios America* foreshadowed much of Trump's immigration policy and rhetoric, sounded glum.

"How ya feeling today, Ann?" I asked.

"No idea. We'll see," she said. "I'm voting and praying."

It was a stark change from just 11 days earlier. Coulter had been with me for a big event at the Kowloon Restaurant in Saugus, Massachusetts, and the tone had been joyous.

"So often on Friday afternoons we get these dumps of information and it's always depressing," I told the crowd. "Today, though, is the exception that proves the rule… FBI to take new investigative steps on the Clinton emails. The investigation has been re-opened!"

The crowd roared.

FBI Director James Comey, who had earlier in the year exonerated Hillary Clinton for criminal mishandling of classified information on her private email server, had stunned the nation.

In a letter to Congress, Comey revealed that the FBI had "learned of the existence of emails that appear to be pertinent to the investigation" into Clinton's private server. Those emails were located on a laptop computer used by disgraced former New York Congressman Anthony Weiner a/k/a Carlos Danger, husband of top Clinton aide Huma Abedin. Weiner was yet again under investigation for sending illicit messages, this time to an underage girl. His perversion became our political lifesaver.

Eleven days before Election Day and there was a glimmer of hope that Clinton might yet suffer the consequences of her corruption. But that hope faded in subsequent days. The overwhelming consensus of the political media was that Trump was finished. So, Coulter wasn't in high spirits on Election Day, and neither was former New York Mayor Rudy Giuliani, who had spent the last year battling with the liberal media as a top Trump surrogate. He had given us a gloomy report from New York an hour earlier. He sounded even more dispirited than Coulter. I must admit that I, too, was increasingly becoming resigned to a future with President Hillary Rodham Clinton.

That was a bleak prospect.

Clinton had admitted her desire to stack the Supreme Court with Justices who would gut the First Amendment by overturning *Citizens United v. FEC*—a decision which established, among other things, that the federal government couldn't prohibit criticism of Hillary Clinton. How long would it be before the Federal Communications Commission, at the direction of President Clinton and her band of liberal sycophants, came after conservative talk radio? I kept these concerns to myself. Privately I feared that another Clinton presidency threatened my own livelihood.

The First Amendment wasn't my only worry.

While Clinton made no effort to conceal her contempt for free speech and *Citizens United*, she took pains to conceal her agenda when it came to guns. But she had been caught on mic at a private event admitting her true intentions. At a fundraiser in New York, Clinton told donors that "the Supreme Court is wrong on the Second Amendment."

"And I am going to make that case every chance I get," she said. "We've got to go after this."

With the late Justice Antonin Scalia's seat awaiting the next president, Clinton would have gotten her wish—the abolition of genuinely free political speech and severe new restrictions on the right to bear arms.

It was the first presidential election of my lifetime where the Bill of Rights itself was on the chopping block.

Clinton's immigration policies were the mirror opposite of the hardline stances that had propelled Trump to the GOP nomination. She wasn't shy about wanting open borders, increased immigration, and millions more unvetted refugees from the Middle East. Although she had previously voted in favor more border security, including a physical barrier, she now mocked the wall. She parroted the Democrat talking points that the refugees were all widows and orphans. Who could be afraid of widows and orphans?

It was insanity. America was carrying a foreign load of as many as 30 million illegal aliens. Low-skilled immigration, legal and illegal, had for decades undermined the wages of low-income Americans, especially black and Hispanic Americans. Heroin and fentanyl trafficked across the southern border by Mexican cartels were killing more U.S. citizens than traffic accidents. But the Democrat nominee wanted to double down on the same failed immigration policies that were destroying the country.

Clinton's political platform was national suicide.

But the fate of the country didn't matter so long as she could continue the breathtaking corruption, the open and gross looting of the federal treasury for her tax-dependent vassals, and the massive, international RICO conspiracy that was the Bill, Hillary and Chelsea Clinton Foundation.

All of this was front and center in my mind throughout Election Day. I'd seen plenty of my candidates lose elections—I'm a conservative in Massachusetts—but this one felt ominously unique. This felt like America's last chance to reverse the fundamental transformation of the nation that started with Massachusetts Sen. Ted Kennedy's Immigration and Naturalization Act of 1965 and had been almost brought to completion by President Barack H. Obama.

The stakes couldn't have been any higher, and I was anything but optimistic. But when Trump came on air, he was confident and unwavering.

"I'm doing good." he said. "I feel great. It looks like it's going to be a beautiful, tight, long night."

From his perch in Trump Tower in New York City, Trump had monitored the news networks all day. And he was eager to get information from wherever he could, any bit that might inform him as to the fate of his unlikely presidential campaign.

"We seem to be doing well. How are we doing in New Hampshire? How is that all going?" he asked. "Our whole theme, Howie, as you know, from the beginning, was Make America Great Again. And we're going to do that. We're going to repeal and replace Obamacare, which has just been decimating our country and our businesses and our jobs. That has to go. We're going to have strong borders. We're going to rebuild. We have no choice. We have to replenish our military. Our military is in such serious trouble. We're going to build it up and we're going to take care of our veterans. We're going to save the Second Amendment. We're going to do a lot of great things for the country."

I asked him if he would contest the results of the election.

"We're going to see what happens. Hopefully I won't have to. The numbers are going to start to come out pretty soon and we'll see what happens. Hopefully I won't have to," he said.

"We'll have maybe a victory and maybe a big one."

Any regrets, I asked?

"No. You know, it's been amazing. I started off against 17 talented people and we end up with one, and one that shouldn't even be able to run based on what happened with her. We'll see what happens, but I have no regrets."

I asked him about South Carolina Sen. Lindsey Graham saying he would be voting for the Never Trump candidate, Evan McMullin—or as I had been calling him, Evan McMuffin. Even on the cusp of one of the most important evenings of his life, Trump was still fighting, still counter-punching against "Sen. Gramnesty."

"It's absolutely insane. All he's doing is giving up the Supreme Court," he said. "Look, I beat him very badly in the primaries. People forget that. He didn't even register in the primaries. He was terrible. He was so terrible. He was easy pickings. And rather than manning up, he goes and does a thing like that. But people forget that he even ran in the primaries!"

I asked him what the mood was like in Trump Tower.

"It's very exciting. All these states are very close. We're really in play in Michigan, which was hardly ever in play for a Republican. Not since Ronald Reagan. And Michigan is doing well—we have a lot of states that are doing well. It's a very exciting time. And we're going to see, Make America Great Again, Howie."

Then he added, "We'll see at the end of a few hours, I guess. The time is fast approaching."

If Trump was sweating the impending results, it didn't show. He was comfortable enough in these late hours to revel in an old attack on Massachusetts Sen. Elizabeth Warren, a.k.a. the Fake Indian.

"Look, she's Pocahontas because I think you have more Indian blood in you than she does," he said. "I think she's a total phony."

Trump talking a good game, but I still wasn't convinced. My last segment before the show ended on Election Day was not a happy one.

"Don't get down," I told my listeners.

"If you're feeling depressed, just turn off the TV."

Chapter Two
Very Fake News

As he began his long march to the White House, Donald J. Trump faced a host of implacable foes, but none more dangerous, or treacherous, than the mainstream media. It was another of the campaign's many ironies, because Trump had for so many years been a member in good standing of the chattering classes, a bona fide Beautiful Person.

That is, until June 16, 2015, the day he started running for president.

As a Republican.

Until his fateful trip down the escalator on Fifth Avenue, Trump possessed all the credentials not just for lionization by, but also immunity from any attacks by the elite media.

He was a billionaire. He lived in a penthouse on the Upper East Side of Manhattan. He had an Ivy League degree. He wrote checks to all the right Democrats. At his resorts, he comped all the right people.

And most importantly, Donald was a good earner, as they say in the Mob. He sold newspapers, and his broadcast appearances guaranteed high ratings, and not just for his own reality TV shows. Howard Stern loved having Trump as a guest on his radio show because he would say anything. When his then-girlfriend Marla Maples appeared on Diane Sawyer's prime-time TV show in 1990, she generated the show's highest ratings ever.

You don't kill the golden goose. Which was why NBC sat on the *Access Hollywood* tapes for 11 years, until Trump was closing in on their beloved Hillary in the home stretch of the fall campaign. Only then did someone at NBC leak the *Access Hollywood* tape to a *Washington Post* reporter who had gone to Harvard with NBC "News" president Noah Oppenheim.

The elite media comprise a very small world, as Trump always knew, although it seems likely he never realized how quickly his old friends would turn on him. During the first few months of the campaign, in fact, they not only tolerated Trump, they egged him on, as he kneecapped the GOP frontrunners, one after another.

But once the media grandees perceived him as a genuine threat to their PC hegemony, they took off the gloves. Every shot below the belt! Ready, fire, aim!

At age 69, Trump entered the race as a veteran of the New York media wars. As a young man, Trump's mentor, celebrity Manhattan lawyer Roy Cohn, had advised him to court the city's tabloid gossip columns, and he did. Trump was endlessly in the headlines. When the New York City government proved incapable of getting an ice-skating rink built in Manhattan, Trump stepped in and completed the job, under budget and ahead of schedule.

When Ed McMahon, Johnny Carson's longtime late-night sidekick, was in deep financial trouble late in life, Trump offered to buy his LA home and then let him live in it rent-free. Trump was always taking out full-page ads in the *Times* to promote this cause or that. He was so ubiquitous on the media landscape that he became a running joke in that quintessentially Eighties magazine, *Spy*. The editor of *Spy*, Graydon Carter, always called Trump a "short-fingered vulgarian."

His greatest splash in the tabloids came when his first marriage to Ivana Trump disintegrated. The city's two biggest tabs picked sides. The *Post* was with The Donald, and all the anti-Ivana inside dirt was funneled to Cindy Adams. Ivana spilled the dirty laundry on her cheating husband to Liz Smith of the *Daily News*.

Back and forth they battled. During one stretch, the Trumps were the "wood"—the front-page splash headline—12 days running in the *Daily News*. In the *Post* they were page-one eight days in a row. One day the big news was that during a getaway to Palm Beach, the estranged couple slept in separate beds at Mar-a-Lago. Another day, the *Post* splash was, "Trump: Fire Liz Smith!"

The most memorable headline—or at least Trump's favorite—ran in the *Post* in 1990. It was over a story about Marla Maples' supposedly dishing to her friends about her love life with Trump. The headline:

"Best Sex I've Ever Had"

For years, a framed copy of that *Post* front page hung in Trump's New York office.

Sometimes he made the cover of magazines like *Time*. Those covers would be framed and prominently displayed in his various properties. At Mar-a-Lago, arriving guests could see a framed story from a trade paper about how *The Apprentice* was topping the TV ratings.

But by the time Trump announced his candidacy for president, the media landscape had undergone a drastic transformation. Until the 1970's, journalism had been a trade, not a profession. Most of the great newspapermen came out of the lower middle classes. Mike Royko grew up over a barroom in Chicago. Jimmy Breslin in New York was throttled by the Goodfellas gangsters he drank with in Queens.

Even journalists from the more prestigious newspapers like the *New York Times* never forgot their blue-collar roots. Abe Rosenthal, the longtime executive editor of the *Times*, got the tip on the infamous Kitty Genovese murder in 1964 from a cop friend he was having lunch with.

Even the owners of the *Times* understood that future publishers had to learn the business from the bottom up. If you wanted to run a newspaper, you had to first cover fires and county commissioners and the state legislature. The Sulzberger scions would be farmed out to papers run by *Times* alumni—Arthur "Pinch" Sulzberger put in his apprenticeship at the now-defunct *Raleigh Times*.

A generation later, even Pinch's pampered son had to do a stretch in the tank towns, as it were. But by the time A.G. Sulzberger's elevation to publisher was announced at the end of 2017, a wire story noted that his best-known work as a *Times* writer was a "whimsical" piece he tossed off about his stint in Kansas City and "his struggles to survive as a vegetarian in a 'mecca of meat.'"

How Brooklyn hipster, how Millennial is that?

The get-me-rewrite! era of American journalism sputtered to an end around the time of the Watergate scandal in 1972. Suddenly a generation of pampered Baby Boomers were interested in journalism. Being a reporter was cool, edgy, fashionable, romantic.

The "college boys," as they were derisively called in the old-school city rooms, wanted to be, not Bob Woodward and Carl Bernstein, but Robert Redford and Dustin Hoffman. Overnight, it seemed, newspapers were teeming with trust-funded rich kids, products of second- and third-tier private colleges who weren't quite bright enough to get into Ivy League law schools, but whose fathers were on a first-name basis with the blue-blooded patrician publishers and editors—the Grahams and Bradlees in Washington, the Taylors and Winships in Boston, the Knights in Philadelphia, the Binghams in Louisville and so forth.

Between that phenomenon and affirmative action, by the 1970's there weren't many slots left in newsrooms for the next generation of Roykos and Breslins.

Now reporters had to have masters' degrees. Pulitzer Prizes were awarded for "public service," i.e., unreadable tut-tutting series written by the smug, self-important types Tom Wolfe once described as "paralyzing snoremongers."

An even more ominous trend developed in the early 1980s—the farm system that funneled young reporters from small- and mid-market media to the big cities began to fail. Under the new feeder system, if you wanted a big job—especially in TV—you didn't waste your time covering the police beat in Cleveland (as Joe Eszterhas did before going first to the *Rolling Stone* and then to Hollywood). No, you became an aide to a politician on Capitol Hill—a Democrat politician, naturally—and then you migrated straight to network TV.

Tim Russert was one of the first Beltway Democrat hacks to make the jump—from digging up oppo research on the would-be opponents of his boss, Sen. Daniel Patrick Moynihan, to hosting *Meet the Press*. Russert was pals with Mike Barnicle, who went from running an elevator on Capitol Hill during the Vietnam war to writing a fiction-heavy column for the *Boston Globe*.

By 2015, the Beltway media and the Democrat establishment had become one and the same.

For example, George Stephanopoulos, the former Bill Clinton flack, was hired by ABC "News," along with neoconservative Bill Kristol, allegedly to provide balance. Kristol was soon kicked to the curb, but Stephanopoulos quickly rose to become host of *Good Morning America*, lobbing interview softballs at his old Democrat bosses while framing "gotcha" questions for GOP politicians.

Before the election, Stephanopoulos' wife told the *Hollywood Reporter*, "If Trump wins, we'll start looking at real estate in Sydney, Australia. No crime, no guns."

ABC's crack reporting staff included Claire Shipman, who was married to Jay Carney, Obama's press secretary. Then there was Brian Ross, who falsely reported that the Aurora movie-theater shooter was a member of the Tea Party. After Trump became president, Ross again scooped the world—with news that candidate Trump had directed Gen. Michael Flynn to reach out to the Russians *before* the election. That would have been "collusion," except of course that it had never happened. Nonetheless, even though it was fake-news Brian Ross with the scoop, the stock market immediately tanked 350 points, costing investors billions of dollars before ABC "News" retracted the story.

Ross was briefly suspended for his latest excursion into fiction, but like Brian Williams at NBC, he would not be fired. Making stuff up is not a fireable offense unless it harms a Democrat, and few in the mainstream media would ever dream of writing a negative story about any of their fellow travelers.

Then there was *Meet the Press* on NBC—after Russert's death, the show was taken over by one David Gregory. During the brooming of the Hillary Clinton email-server non-probe by the FBI in 2016, four of Hillary's top aides were represented by a lawyer named... Mrs. David Gregory. All of Mrs. Gregory's clients were granted immunity from prosecution.

Gregory married his wife on Nantucket. Presiding over the ceremony was federal appeals court judge Merrick Garland, whom Obama unsuccessfully tried to appoint to the Supreme Court after the death of Antonin Scalia in 2016.

Gregory tanked the ratings of *Meet the Press* so he was fired (and then picked up by CNN—the Clinton News Network). He was replaced by Chuck Todd, a career Democrat coatholder who once worked for Iowa Sen. Tom Harkin, who falsely claimed to have been a combat Air Force pilot in Vietnam.

Todd is married to still another Democrat operative, whose employers have included a former Florida House speaker who went to prison for tax evasion, ex-US Rep. Gary Condit, who was investigated in the brutal murder of an intern with whom he was having an affair, and ex-Sen. Ernest "Fritz" Hollings, who as governor of South Carolina began flying the Confederate flag above the state capitol in Columbia.

Later Mrs. Todd worked for a PAC set up by Sen. John Edwards, the one-time ambulance chaser from North Carolina whose scandalous affair with a campaign volunteer he impregnated was totally ignored by the mainstream media until his federal indictment on campaign-finance charges.

Before he became a "journalist," Jake Tapper of CNN was a coatholder for Chelsea Clinton's mother-in-law, Rep. Marjorie Margolies-Mezvinsky of Pennsylvania. Her husband, Edward Mezvinsky, a Congressman from Iowa, spent five years in federal prison after being convicted of bank, mail and wire fraud in a $10-million scam.

Savannah Guthrie is married to Al Gore's former chief of staff. Susan Rice, Obama's former national security adviser and a serial prevaricator, wed a former ABC producer. The sister of Ben Sherwood, the president of ABC Television Group, was a deputy secretary of energy under Obama.

The list goes on and on, but one person I used to work with in Boston sums up the incestuousness of the Washington/Democrat media establishment. When I first met Martha Raddatz Bradlee, she was a reporter for Channel 5 in Boston.

She was married to the son of Ben Bradlee, the former editor of the *Washington Post* to whom JFK had handed the delicate assignment of spiking the story about his scandalous first marriage to a twice-divorced Protestant socialite in Palm Beach in 1947. The senior Bradlee's sister-in-law, Mary Pinchot Meyer, was one of JFK's last girlfriends before her mysterious unsolved murder on a canal path in 1964.

In her Boston days, Martha was far from the credulous PC cheerleader she has since become. Like her, I was a local TV reporter, and she had a saying about our business:

"We are not reporters, we are TV reporters. We are not in news, we are in TV news."

To paraphrase an old Hollywood saying, I knew Martha Raddatz before she was a virgin.

After divorcing Bradlee *fils*, Martha reclaimed her maiden name and got a job with NPR, where seldom is heard a discouraging word, about liberals anyway. (In 2017 both NPR and PBS were revealed to be dens of liberal sexual predators and perverts, including Charlie Rose, Garrison Keillor and a former *Times* man named Michael Oreskes, among many others.) Her second husband was Julius Genachowski, a classmate of Obama's at Harvard Law School. Obama later appointed him to the FCC, and even attended his wedding to Raddatz.

No wonder Martha Raddatz was so crestfallen on the evening of Nov. 8, 2016.

On Beacon Hill and elsewhere, nepotism laws purportedly prohibit politicians from hiring their offspring. They may be only sporadically enforced, but at least they're on the books. No such rules exist in the alt-left media. Democrat nepotism is rampant, starting at the top.

With absolutely no experience in journalism or television, Chelsea Clinton was hired in 2011 as a $600,000-a-year correspondent for NBC News. She "worked" there, basically as an intern, for three years. Chelsea was not only the world's highest-paid intern, she was also the only intern in the history of television with her own producer.

After his father's death, Luke Russert was hired by NBC News. He had the same experience as his father did when he was brought on board—zero.

Chris Cuomo, the son and brother of New York governors, cohosts CNN's abysmal morning show. He is daily shocked by Donald Trump's outrages, including his alleged homophobia, even though when his father was first running for governor in 1986 in the Democrat primary against the bachelor mayor of New York City, Ed Koch, the Cuomo campaign's whispered slogan was: "Vote for Cuomo, Not the Homo."

Like his fellow New Yorker Trump, Koch learned the hard way about the double standards of the media. After leaving office, he bitterly described the press as "Democrat operatives with press passes."

Nancy Dickerson was the first female TV network correspondent. Her son John Dickerson succeeded sexual harasser Charlie Rose as male host of *CBS This Morning*. Dickerson's ratings may be low, but his credentials as a Beltway pundit are impeccable: he once wrote a magazine story saying that Obama "can only cement his legacy if he destroys the GOP."

John Harwood of CNBC and the *New York Times* is yet another Thanks-Dad legacy hire. His father, Richard, worked for the *Times* during Watergate.

Parroting the official Nixon party line, Harwood *père* poo-pooed the break-in as a third-rate burglary. Harwood *fils*, whose girlfriend at one time was a Democrat US senator, threw "gotcha" questions at Trump in an early GOP debate and surreptitiously sent memos to the Clinton campaign advising them on how to destroy their rivals. In short, the Harwoods are the quintessential Washington family—they kiss the asses of whomever is in power.

Laura Jarrett is the daughter of Valerie Jarrett, Obama's top confidante. When the Obamas vacated 1600 Pennsylvania Avenue on Jan. 20, 2017, the Iranian-born Valerie Jarrett actually moved into the Obama's spacious rented digs in the exclusive Kalorama neighborhood in Northwest Washington. Daughter Laura now covers Trump's Justice Department for CNN.

Carl Bernstein, one of the original Watergate reporters, in his dotage published a slobbering hagiography of Hillary. Then he was hired by CNN to join the amen chorus. His gay son Jacob is a *New York Times* reporter. A few weeks after Bernstein *père* spent hours on the CNN set breathlessly recounting the bogus allegations against Trump in the dodgy dossier that the Clintons and the DNC paid for, at a party in New York Bernstein *fils* called Melania Trump a "hooker."

Jacob Bernstein was not fired, nor even suspended. Imagine if he had called Michelle Obama a hooker....

Perhaps the only legacy hire who has ever amounted to anything in journalism lately is Ronan Farrow, the son of Mia Farrow and (take your pick) Woody Allen or Frank Sinatra. He was briefly given a show on MSNBC, but it didn't last long. He went to work investigating Harvey Weinstein, but NBC got cold feet. After all, this was the network that in 1999 refused to run the story of Juanita Broaddrick's alleged rape by Bill Clinton in 1978.

As Farrow began interviewing Weinstein's rape victims, NBC refused to allow him to use a network camera crew. Farrow had to pay for his own. Then, with the story well in hand, NBC "News" president Noah Oppenheim spiked it. Oppenheim is an aspiring screen writer who had been seen weeks earlier having a sit down in a Manhattan restaurant with the pervy producer. Farrow had to take the story to *The New Yorker*, which was only too happy to print what turned out to be the catalyst of perhaps the biggest news story of 2017.

As for Weinstein, when he issued his inevitable *mea culpa* before fleeing to "rehab," he specifically mentioned that as part of his penance, he would work to destroy… Donald Trump. Say what you will about Weinstein, he knew his audience.

Ethical problems in the Washington press corps are nothing new. As early as 1924, in his famous essay, "Journalism in America," H.L. Mencken described the average DC newspaper correspondent:

"What ails him mainly is that he is a man without sufficient force of character to resist the blandishments that surround him from the moment he sets foot in Washington... His willingness to do press work for the National Committees in campaign time and for other highly dubious agencies at other times is not to be forgotten."

Mencken wrote that 92 years before *Wikileaks* showed how many Beltway navel-gazers were getting their copy edited—and in at least one case actually written—by the DNC. The more things change....

Just as the Beltway's elite media were abandoning any vestigial pretenses of objectivity, the internet was wreaking havoc on the business models of mass media, especially newspapers. In the early 2000's, the print media's two major sources of revenue—display and classified advertising—dried up. Why buy an expensive classified ad when you can just post your listing on Craig's List?

Next, newspaper circulation imploded. Why worry about getting a paper delivered every morning when you can read the entire edition online—at midnight, for free?

By 2010, all newspapers were reeling, and many metropolitan sheets began shuttering the Washington and foreign bureaus they had always maintained. This made it even easier for the Democrats inside the Beltway to control the narrative.

Ben Rhodes was a typical Obama aide, a rich preppy from Manhattan whose older brother David was the president of CBS "News." The White House put the aspiring novella writer in charge of managing the coverage of the Iranian nuclear deal. In an interview with the *New York Times* magazine in 2016, Rhodes confessed how easy it had been to create an "echo chamber" to manipulate the new breed of DC reporters.

"The average reporter we talk to is 27 years old," Rhodes said, "and their only reporting experience consists of being around political campaigns. That's a sea change. They literally know nothing."

Actually, they did know one thing: they hated Donald Trump. Overnight, as the campaign heated up, Trump's media image morphed from that of a glad-handing New York billionaire into that of a racist, homophobic, even anti-Semitic monster. It was preposterous—his beloved daughter Ivanka had converted to Judaism after her marriage to Jared Kushner. Trump's mentor, Roy

Cohn, was a gay Jew who died of AIDS. Trump was so close to Cohn that in January 2018, it was reported that when the president became angry with his attorney general, Jeff Sessions, he once yelled in frustration, "Where's my Roy Cohn?" As for gay marriage, Trump was for it before Hillary Clinton (but then, so was Dick Cheney).

When Trump bought Mar-a-Lago in 1985, he opened the membership rolls to Jews, blacks and gays. That didn't go over well at the island's then "restricted" clubs like the Everglades, the Sailfish and, most significantly, the Bath and Tennis Club, across South Ocean Boulevard from Mar-a-Lago.

There goes the neighborhood—that was the B&T's outraged response to the arrival of the parvenu from Queens and his *déclassé* posse. In one famous incident, two Mar-a-Lago guests—rapper Puff Daddy and his then-girlfriend Jennifer Lopez—commenced what the Palm Beach newspaper called "the horizontal rhumba" on a beach chair under the B&T's picture window, in broad daylight.

The WASPy Old Guard in Palm Beach hated Trump. The town sued him when he erected a huge pole in his front yard and began flying the kind of giant American flag most often seen outside Sun Belt auto dealerships. Once again the B&T was appalled.

But those old stories were never mentioned in the mad rush to tar Trump as a throwback to the bad old days of Jim Crow, *Gentlemen's Agreement* and *Mad Men*.

Eugene McCarthy, the late senator from Minnesota, once compared political reporters to birds on a telephone wire. When one bird flies onto the wire and perches, McCarthy said, the rest of the flock follows him. Then, when one bird flies off, they all fly off.

Fifty years later, even more than birds, the Washington press corps resembled lemmings stampeding over a cliff. The Center for Public Integrity recently researched the 2016 presidential campaign contributions of donors who described themselves as journalists, reporters, editors or anchors.

Hillary Clinton received $382,000 from the Fourth Estate, Donald Trump $14,000. Put another way, Trump got 4 percent of their contributions, which, oddly enough, is according to other studies approximately the percentage of network-news stories about his new administration that have been favorable.

In the run-up to the 2016 election, Victor Davis Hanson described the anti-Trump tone of the campaign coverage by the Beltway elite media:

"(They) sound quite clever without being especially bright, attuned to social justice without character. Their religion is not so much progressivism as appearing cool and hip and 'right' on the issues… Well-connected and mediocre… They write and sound off about the buffoon Trump and preen in sanctimonious moral outrage."

Alienating half the country—the "deplorable" half—might not seem a good business model. But the left-wing media gleefully went after Trump's throat, even if it hurt their bottom line. The *Daily News* in New York was a prime example. Long the top-selling daily in America—its circulation in 1947 topped 2.4 million—"New York's Picture Newspaper" had almost gone out of business several times since the early 1980's.

In 2015 its owner had unsuccessfully tried to sell the troubled tabloid, but got no offers. So the traditional newspaper of New York's blue-collar white ethnics decided to go all in, all anti-Trump, all the time.

I knew that Trump had read the *Daily News* every day of his life, and I understood how pissed off he must have been about its sudden lurch to the left. One day on my radio show I mentioned to him that one of my prep schoolmates, Jimmy Finkelstein, whom Trump also knew, had been trying to buy the tabloid.

"You tell Jimmy not to do it!" Trump told me. "There's nothing left to that paper. It's a sinkhole. It's failing. It's going under!"

Day after day for a year, the *Daily News* printed screaming anti-Trump headlines and photo-shopped graphics. One day he was pictured chopping off the head of the Statue of Liberty. On the Saturday after the story about the *Access Hollywood* tapes broke, the *Daily News*' headline was "GRAB THEM BY THE P***Y."

That night the *Daily News* was prominently waved around on the set of *Saturday Night Live*. Morning Joe and his crew of sexual predators and plagiarists likewise held up the front page many mornings. But there was a downside to all that "buzz," as they call it.

The paper's circulation in the outer boroughs—Staten Island, Brooklyn, the remaining Archie Bunker neighborhoods in Queens—began plummeting. Newsstand sales utterly collapsed. Three weeks before the election, the editor behind the anti-Trump crusade was summarily fired.

But it was too late. In the fall of 2017, the *Daily News* was finally sold—for $1. Its circulation had dipped to under 200,000. Trump had once again called the shot.

The media's anti-Trump hysteria—their "echo chamber," as Ben Rhodes would say—was most evident after those *Access Hollywood* tapes that so mesmerized the *Daily News* and *Saturday Night Live*, along with all the rest of the anti-Trump media.

What would become known as the alt-left media immediately went into 24/7 attack mode. The same pompous moralists who had dismissed Bill Clinton's perjury and obstruction of justice as "just sex," who had laughed off his references to "pussy" while in the golf cart with Vernon Jordan on Martha's Vineyard—now they were claiming to be shocked, shocked over Trump's use of the p-word with Billy Bush on the bus.

Ironically, some of the pundits most angry about Trump's alleged misogyny would a year later be outed as sexual predators themselves. Others would claim that they had no idea that their coworkers at CNN or NBC or NPR or PBS or the *Times* had been serial sexual predators.

Christiane Amanpour of CNN is married to Bill Clinton's former State Department spokesman, Jamie Rubin. Her boss at CNN is Jeff Zucker, who was the executive producer of *The Today Show* during the time Matt Lauer was touching everything but the third rail. None of that shocked her, apparently, but on November 8, Amanpour got the shock of her life.

"I was shocked—very few of us ever imagined that so many Americans… would be angry enough to ignore the wholesale vulgarity of language, the sexual predatory behavior, the deep misogyny…."

As distraught as the media's sexual predators and harassers and enablers were by the evil of Donald Trump, the departure of their hero from the White House was even more traumatic for them.

This was Matt Lauer on January 13, 2017 after Obama gave the Medal of Freedom to Joe Biden, another prominent Democrat with wandering hands:

"I'm glad there were no cameras in my apartment yesterday 'cause I was sitting there just weeping. I just burst out crying when I saw that moment. It was incredible!"

Comrade Chris Matthews was an MSNBC host who had followed what has become the traditional media career path—he parlayed a hack job with former Democrat House Speaker Tip O'Neill into a TV gig as a liberal pundit who never, ever veered from the party line. He may be best known for saying that listening to a Barack Obama speech gave him a tingle up his leg. More recently he has also become known for the fact that his network had to pay $40,000 to a woman who claimed he was sexually harassing her.

As Obama left office, Comrade Chris swooned again:

"Is there a husband, a father that we would wish more as a model for our sons, for our sons-in-law to have and raise our grandchildren? Is there anyone who carries himself better?"

Certainly not… Donald J. Trump.

This was the sanctimonious, arrogant, self-satisfied wrecking crew that Trump would be up against, first in the campaign, and later during his presidency. Story after scurrilous screaming-headlined story, many of which never panned out, some of which later had to be retracted. Once upon a time the "facts" would have been checked out before the story went to press, or online. But with Trump, there was no need to nail anything down—not if the story could be used to damage him, not if it could be used as clickbait for the millions of trolls in the blue states infected with Trump Derangement Syndrome.

Fake news, Trump would eventually come to call the entire phenomenon of the modern, post-fact media. Fake news was the phrase he used, until he came up with an even better one.

Very fake news.

Chapter Three

Contenders...or Pretenders?

IN EARLY 2015, THE REPUBLICAN PRESIDENTIAL PRIMARY WAS LOOKING LIKE business as usual. The growing size of the field of candidates was unprecedented, but the nature of the candidates was pretty routine. Most of the prospective GOP nominees were current or former elected officials, and all of them had harbored obvious White House ambitions from the moment they entered politics. There were a few outsiders flirting with the race, but that was nothing new for the party of Herman Cain.

The primary campaign seemed destined to be like all the others in the modern history of the GOP. Conservative candidates would try to tack right to earn the support of the party's base, while the moderate candidates would make the case that they were more electable. Highly-paid Beltway bandits, er, consultants would cut ads criticizing some elected official for a vote he cast 10 years earlier. Opposition research would be unveiled at just the right moment. Republicans would battle throughout the entire primary season and then fall in line, even if begrudgingly, behind the victor.

That all changed on June 16, 2015 when Donald Trump and his wife, Melania, descended the escalator at Trump Tower in New York City to announce his candidacy.

From the beginning, Trump turned Republican Party politics on its head and fundamentally changed how the game is played. He was not bound by the wonkish white papers of the Heritage Foundation. He didn't care what the Club for Growth thought. He wasn't enamored with the "smart" entitlement reforms Paul Ryan was always advancing, like Sisyphus rolling his stone. He wasn't cribbing talking points from the *National Review* or *The Weekly Standard* or the *Wall Street Journal* editorial page. Far from a doctrinaire conservative or party-line Republican, Trump was a non-partisan pragmatist who was not afraid to attack the orthodox views of the American right.

Trump's stances on some mainstay Republican positions were radical. He challenged the bipartisan consensus that several decades of free trade agreements had worked to the benefit of the American middle class. He ripped the North American Free Trade Agreement (NAFTA), the Clinton era granddaddy of all free trade agreements, as well as the emerging Trans-Pacific Partnership (TPP). He attacked America's political elite as well as the leaders of our trading partners. Mexico, Japan, China—they were all killing us on trade because they have smart leaders and our leaders are stupid, not to mention poor negotiators. He delivered the same message, day after day, until it finally sunk in.

On foreign policy, Trump was pugnacious in his rhetoric while maintaining an America First vision of avoiding other nations' problems. Some neocon Republicans were still promoting Bush era nation-building. Not Trump. He felt no such obligation to defend stupid, costly wars. And that message resonated with a war-weary American middle class that was fed up with the Middle East quagmire that had festered under Obama.

In many ways, Trump was a heretic in the modern Republican Party. His position on abortion had "evolved" over the years. The Clintons had attended his most recent wedding in Palm Beach. He was fond of eminent domain property seizures. He didn't get worked up over longstanding culture wars, including the debate over transgender bathrooms. He was thoroughly a New Yorker, originally from Queens, although now, as a billionaire, he lived in Manhattan.

Early on, before Trump's quixotic campaign became a powerful national movement, most Republicans operatives thought Trump's various heresies would eventually cause him to crash and burn. These were the Karl Rove types who comprised the GOP Establishment, or GOPe, for short. You see them on TV every night.

They came to D.C. after college for an internship that their rich uncle helped set up and they never left. Maybe they rose to become a Chief of Staff, or perhaps they briefly left mid-level Capitol Hill for law school or a job at a think-tank or a lobbying firm or some GS-13 bureaucratic post in the federal government. At their cocktail parties, they prattle on about political inside baseball and brag about their various connections. They inhabit a bubble—the D.C. bubble—and they all walk and talk alike. Few of them understood the political and economic realities facing Americans outside of the Beltway or the Acela corridor. Think Bill Kristol or George Will.

The GOPe's connection to, and understanding of, the American people was entirely restricted to public-opinion polling and focus groups, so it's no surprise that these Establishment-types lost touch with the electorate. Voters didn't care that the libertarian Cato Institute was critical of the methods Trump used to acquire land for a casino in Atlantic City; they were worried about stagnant wages and mortgages that were getting harder to pay. Voters didn't mind that Trump deviated from traditional Republican stances; they were tired of the political class's systemic, bipartisan corruption.

What they wanted was a fighter—and not just someone who would fight for lower taxes. They wanted someone who would go to battle for their culture and their way of life in the face of sweeping societal upheaval.

Two words: America First.

When Trump entered the presidential race, political correctness was at its zenith. Its enforcers, the PC Police, had never been more powerful. *Happy Holidays* was the *de rigueur* December greeting. Ninth-graders weren't freshmen; they were first-years. Diversity training wasn't a prescription for an employee who had somehow crossed Human Resources; it was mandatory for everyone.

Columbus Day was being replaced by Indigenous Peoples Day. Even Halloween was on the way out—all costumes must now eschew "cultural appropriation," comrades. Pronouns were not rooted in biology or historical linguistic uses, but were instead decided on a case-by-case basis, with heavy fines threatened against those who declined to follow the new rules of sex and gender in America. What's that, you say? Creating a wedding cake for a gay couple would violate your sincerely held Christian beliefs? Get ready for the full force of the federal government to come crashing down on you. One off-color quip or tweet, one stray deviation from leftist cultural dogma, and mobs of rage-filled liberals would descend upon you. Social, political, and economic ostracism awaited those who dared defy the transient and ever-changing edicts of political correctness.

Outside of New York City, Hollywood, and Washington, D.C., Americans were fed up with it.

Conservatives, and probably a good number of political independents, didn't like what was happening in the media and on college campuses. They were put off by the overt politicization of ESPN and other traditionally apolitical parts of life. Late-night comics and glitzy award shows they had once enjoyed had become virtue-signaling spectacles, with semi-literate millionaire celebrities lecturing the working classes about global warming, Third World poverty and "sustainable" lifestyles. American culture was changing, rapidly, and not for the better. Only one candidate captured this cultural fury and channeled it into a transformative political movement.

Donald Trump would become the bellicose iconoclast of the working classes, fearlessly shattering the orthodoxies of political correctness that had been forced upon Joe Sixpack by the elite masters of American culture. But before he could win a lasting victory against political correctness, Trump had to secure the GOP nomination. The old saying is that politics ain't bean bag, that it is blood sport. Once Trump became the front-runner, he had a target on his back. One by one, a challenger would rise to take a swipe at Trump. One by one, each would fall victim to his fearsome counter-punch.

THE GOVERNORS

Scott Walker

Wisconsin's Republican Gov. Scott Walker was toeing the party line. He had won three hard-fought state elections, including a 2012 union-backed recall election. The public-sector unions, irked by Walker's support for right-to-work laws, dumped $20 million into the effort only to see Walker win by six points. Despite unhinged attacks from the left, including an outrageous, illegal politically motivated special investigation of his donors, Walker's state was economically on the rebound, benefitting from the governor's free-market reforms and conservative policies. Walker was a model Republican governor, uncowed by his liberal foes and committed to enacting a pro-business agenda.

Walker had genuine blue-collar appeal. He rode a Harley, and when the Green Bay Packers were playing, he'd regularly tweet out pictures of himself watching the game while quaffing a Leinenkugel or a Point Special. In addition to his record as a conservative who could win tough elections, Walker's aptly named Unintimidated PAC was flush with as much as $40 million in cash very early in the campaign. But that cash advantage dried up quickly. By the end of September, Walker's campaign was struggling to keep the lights on.

The Wisconsin governor was hobbled by a string of cringe-worthy gaffes. There was the time he wrote to a Jewish constituent around Hanukkah: "thank you again and Molotov." I'm sure he meant *Mazel tov*. And then the time Walker took a trip to Europe, a rite of passage for aspiring presidential candidates looking to show their foreign policy chops. Walker's foreign foray took a turn south when he refused to answer some basic questions.

"I just think for me, commenting on foreign policy, or in this case economic policy, in a country where you're a visitor is not the politest," Walker said at a London-based think tank.

Walker was also ill-prepared for a predictable gotcha question on evolution from BBC journalist Justin Webb.

"Do you believe in evolution?" asked Webb.

"I'm going to punt on that one," answered Walker. "I'm here to talk about trade, not to pontificate on other issues. I love the evolution of trade in Wisconsin and I'd like to see an even bigger evolution as well."

Memo to would-be politicians: when you're punting on the question, you don't say you're punting on the question.

Walker tripped again at the Conservative Political Action Conference in Washington, D.C. He was a hero to that crowd because of his no-holds-barred fight with labor union bosses and mobs of their unruly, pinky-ring thugs at the state capitol in Madison. But he took his war-time reminiscing a little too far in order to boost his credentials to be Commander-in-Chief of the American military. When it came to ISIS, Walker said, "If I can take on 100,000 protesters, I can do the same across the world."

Look, Governor, we're all glad you beat the unions, but AFL-CIO President Richard Trumka is no Abu Bakr al-Baghdadi.

Walker stepped in it again during an August 2015 interview with NBC's Chuck Todd. Like the other GOP candidates, Walker was struggling with how to respond to questions about Trump's vow to build a wall on the southern border. He told Todd he agreed with Trump that more should be done to secure not just the southern border, but the northern border as well.

Todd asked, tongue-in-cheek, whether that meant building a wall on the Canadian border.

"They have raised some very legitimate concerns," Walker replied. "Including some law enforcement folks that brought that up to me at one of our town hall meetings a week and a half ago. So that's a legitimate issue for us to look at."

His communications staff spent the rest of the week mopping up after widespread mockery on social media.

Walker's most substantive gaffe came on the question of birthright citizenship. As was the case with the wall, Trump's boisterous, fast-paced campaign had his opponents always responding, constantly on the defense. Before they had even had time to process Trump's latest speech, rally, or pronouncement, Trump had already moved on. For a traditional candidate, it would be an almost impossible environment to survive in, but Trump had no interest in running the usual kind of boring Republican campaign. Walker, on the other hand, was a traditional GOP candidate, a career politician with well-paid Beltway consultants trying to create the perfect, focus-grouped message. Too many cooks spoil the broth, and they quickly spoiled Walker's candidacy.

When it came to birthright citizenship, Trump had come out fiercely opposed, but Walker and his handlers couldn't quite figure out where he stood. After Trump suggested repealing the policy, which allows illegal aliens to get protected status—and welfare—in the U.S. via their anchor babies, Walker agreed with the idea. "Yeah, absolutely, going forward," he said at the Iowa State Fair.

A few days later he went on CNBC and shanked another Wisconsin punt. "I'm not taking a position on it one way or the other," he said.

About one week later he came full circle, telling ABC News he would not support changes to the U.S. Constitution that would prohibit birthright citizenship. "Well, I said the law is there. And we need to enforce the laws, including those that are in the Constitution."

But gaffes and waffling and flip-flops weren't the only things that did Walker in. He was not spared the hurricane of criticism and insults that Trump dished out with such relish to his growing crowds.

Trump was at a high school in Oskaloosa, Iowa, near the end of July, and he'd caught wind of some negative attacks Walker allies were whispering to reporters. The *Wall Street Journal* had reported that a prominent Walker backer named Gregory Slayton called Trump "DumbDumb" in an invitation to a fundraising event. Trump, who frequently spoke of his counter-punching abilities, struck back with glee.

"Today," Trump began, "I read this horrible statement from his fundraiser guy about Trump, and I say, 'Finally, I can attack. Finally.'"

The crowd knew he was just warming up.

"Wisconsin's doing terribly. It's in turmoil. The roads are a disaster because they don't have any money to rebuild them. They're borrowing money like crazy. They projected a $1 billion surplus, and it turns out to be a deficit of $2.2 billion. The schools are a disaster. The hospitals and education are a disaster. And he was totally in favor of Common Core, which I hate, I hate!"

The crowd booed and hissed at the mention of the controversial federal education standards, so Trump went in for the kill.

"I've been nice to Scott Walker," said Trump, referring to the $10,000 he had given to Walker's re-election campaign the previous year. "He's a nice guy. He came up to my office three or four months ago and presented me with a plaque because I helped him with his election." After conjuring the image of Walker kneeling before a generous donor with a beautiful plaque, Trump suggested that maybe "Wisconsin paid for it."

Walker entered the race the morning of July 13, 2015, and suspended his campaign ten weeks later on September 21, following two dismal debate performances and a collapse in his poll numbers. His campaign burned through $7.9 million while Unintimidated PAC raised over $24 million to support his candidacy. With his exit speech, Walker lobbed more than a few shots at Trump, a trend that would continue as the GOP also-rans started piling up. Walker called on the low-polling GOP candidates to drop out of the race, "so that the voters can focus on a limited number of candidates who can offer a positive conservative alternative to the current front-runner."

Jeb Bush

Scott Walker's biggest obstacle early on in the race was former Florida Gov. John Ellis "Jeb" Bush. Pre-Trump, Bush and Walker were dueling for the top spot in opinion polls, with each candidate garnering around 16 percent of GOP primary voters' support, according to the *Real Clear Politics* average of polls. Bush brought to the primary fight not only the elaborate political network the Bush family had developed and then nurtured through more than three decades of federal patronage, but also a campaign war chest of more than $100 million. I remember thinking at the time that I liked Walker, but I wasn't sure how anyone could surmount the cash advantage Bush had at his disposal. It seemed inevitable, early on, that Republicans were going to nominate another Bush. Inevitable, and depressing.

Fortunately, "Juan" Ellis Bush took care of undermining himself—with plenty of help from Trump.

Bush's struggles began in May 2015, a full month before he had officially entered the race, during an interview with Megyn Kelly on Fox News. Kelly asked Bush the most obvious question you could possibly ask George W. Bush's younger brother, the question to which he should have devoted many hours rehearsing an answer.

"On the subject of Iraq, obviously very controversial. Knowing what we know now, would you have authorized the invasion?" asked Kelly.

Bush didn't skip a beat.

"I would have," he said. "And so would have Hillary Clinton, just to remind everybody."

In other words, Bush said he would have invaded Iraq even if he knew intelligence reports suggesting Saddam Hussein was in possession of weapons of mass destruction were bogus. He would wage war without a rationale. Bush later claimed he misunderstood the question and assured voters that he, like them, now believed the war had been a terrible mistake. But the damage was done.

Trump had a knack for taking those small "misstatements" and turning them into vicious attacks on Bush's competence. In a July appearance on my radio show, Trump ridiculed Bush's botched interview with Kelly.

"Bush didn't even know if Iraq was a good thing. It took him five days to get it out of his mouth," Trump told me. "He couldn't answer the question!"

I pointed out to Trump that Bush was the only candidate then leading him in the New Hampshire polls.

"Well, that's embarrassing to be honest with you," he said, "because I don't get him."

In a television interview around the same time, Trump kept up the attack.

"He's stumbling. I don't know, I don't understand this man," Trump said. "He's stumbling like he's not even a smart person—on simple questions. What's going to happen when it's complicated?"

Bush struggled throughout the primary debates in the face of withering attacks from Trump. But his worst debate moment came when he decided to attack Florida Senator Marco Rubio, who was once a protégé of sorts when Bush was governor of the Sunshine State and Rubio was the young House Speaker in Tallahassee. In the third primary debate in late October, Bush delivered an obviously well-rehearsed attack on Rubio for missing Senate votes to campaign, saying Rubio should "campaign or resign." Bush looked uncomfortable delivering the line, which was nothing new, but it was Rubio's devastating retort that left him deeply damaged.

"I don't remember you ever complaining about John McCain's vote record. The only reason why you're doing it now is because we're running for the same position and someone has convinced you that attacking me is going to help you," said Rubio, to great applause from the Colorado audience. A sullen Bush never recovered during the debate.

A certain awkwardness characterized everything Bush did.

His campaign signs used just his first name—Jeb—and added an exclamation point—Jeb!

Why? "It connotes excitement," Bush told late-night host Stephen Colbert.

"You find a Democrat that's for cutting taxes—cutting spending ten dollars, I'll give 'em a warm kiss," he said incoherently during one debate.

"Please clap," he begged an audience in New Hampshire that failed to recognize a well-hidden applause line.

Asked about gun control following a mass shooting at Umpqua Community College in Roseburg, Oregon, Bush said, among other things, "stuff happens."

Following his disastrous debate performance in October, Bush revamped his campaign with a new message, "Jeb Can Fix It."

It was almost as if he was trying to become an object of mockery on social media and in the tabloids.

At a Rotary Club lunch in Nashua, New Hampshire, Bush was in midsentence droning on about some wonky policy issue when his host pulled the plug and said, "Thank you, governor."

"That's it?" Bush asked incredulously.

"They're kicking me out the door," he said, shrugging awkwardly, "They're kicking me out the door." The Rotary official explained to the governor that the campaign schedule had a hard stop. But the C-SPAN cameras showed a sullen, dejected Bush walking back to his table and finishing his rubber chicken lunch, utterly alone.

Bush on the campaign trail was a disaster—awkward, impersonal, nerdy. He couldn't connect with an audience. He came across as stilted and confused.

"I have a lot of really cool things that I can do other than sit around and be miserable listening to people demonize me and me feeling compelled to demonize them," Bush told a South Carolina town hall. "That is a joke. Elect Trump if you want that."

Bush was a flawed candidate from the outset—his brother's baggage hurt him in the primaries and would have destroyed him in the general election. Ultimately, however, as was the case with Gov. Walker, the coroner handling Bush's campaign autopsy must list the cause of death as Trump.

Trump famously nicknamed Bush "Low-energy Jeb." It was a moniker that haunted him the entire campaign and will no doubt appear in his real, as well as his political, obituary. Trump added to the low-energy nickname a blizzard of attacks against Bush, capitalizing on his brother's political baggage and his moderate policies, especially on immigration.

Bush entered the election with well-known positions on immigration—positions that were anathema to the Republican base, a fact he and his top-heavy, overfunded campaign appeared oblivious to.

At Iowa Rep. Steve King's Freedom Summit in January 2015, when Trump's candidacy was still regarded as a Trump Tower machination to promote the new season of *The Apprentice*, Bush signaled that he would not shy away from the liberal, permissive immigration policies outlined in his 2014 book, *Immigration Wars*. Indeed, Bush's immigration platform was identical to the New York Sen. Chuck Schumer's infamous comprehensive immigration reform legislation, dubbed the Gang of Eight deal.

"We need to find a way, a path to legalized status for those that have come here and have languished in the shadows," said Bush. "There's no way that they're going to be deported. No one is suggesting an organized effort to do that."

Even before Bush went to Iowa with his don't-deport-the-illegal-alien-criminals message, he'd already committed his worst gaffe—at least when it came to immigration. But this wasn't a gaffe in the style of Joe Biden, it was more of a Michael Kinsley gaffe, where a politician accidentally reveals what they really believe.

"Yes, they broke the law, but it's not a felony," said Bush. "It's an act of love. It's an act of commitment to your family."

An act of love—a line that would haunt him throughout the campaign as report after report surfaced of illegal aliens, those plucky little fellows Jeb said were languishing in the shadows, committing heinous acts of violence against U.S. citizens. Given the opportunity to walk-back his "Act of Love" line, Bush stood by the comment.

"I believe that the great majority of people coming here illegally have no other option," said Bush. (What about the option of, I don't know, respecting the laws of the United States and staying in Mexico?)

"They want to provide for their family," he said.

Yes, they want to come here and get on food stamps, Medicaid, WIC and Section 8 while working under the table and not paying taxes.

The more he spoke about his "valedictorians," as he described MS-13 gangbangers and Dominican fentanyl dealers, the further he cratered in the polls. Internet trolls changed his campaign name to ¡Jeb! Bush's support for broad amnesty for illegal aliens was an absolute deal breaker he could never talk his way out of. But he never clearly divorced himself from his brother's dismal record either. At the September 2015 GOP debate in Simi Valley, California, Bush sought to clarify his brother's legacy.

"When it comes to my brother," he said, "there's one thing I know for sure. He kept us safe."

According to the *Washington Examiner*'s Byron York, the Bush campaign poll-tested that message rigorously before deploying it at the Ronald Reagan Library that evening. The messaging poll of more than 1,500 likely primary voters in New Hampshire, Iowa and South Carolina found Republicans agreed with the he-kept-us-safe sentiment and generally liked the former president. But then Trump delivered his counter-punch, on Bloomberg TV.

"When you talk about George Bush, I mean, say what you want, the World Trade Center came down during his time," said Trump. "He was president, okay? Blame him or don't blame him, but he was president. The World Trade Center came down during his reign."

By the time Iowa rolled around, Bush got just 2.8 percent of the vote in the caucuses. All told, Bush's campaign and super PAC spent $2,800 per Iowa vote. His aides later insisted this was because the campaign did not invest much time and energy in the state, focusing instead on New Hampshire and South Carolina.

Combined with his PAC, Bush would go on to spend $1,150 per vote in New Hampshire—more than any other candidate—only to finish fourth. Bush's campaign spending was so lavish in New Hampshire that we received reports his allies were sending out electronic tablets to voters that came pre-programmed with campaign literature. I joked at the time that Bush would have been better off sending out a nice bottle of single-malt scotch to every GOP voter.

Bush dropped out of the race on Feb. 20, 2016, after failing to win 10 percent of the vote in South Carolina, finishing well behind Trump.

Months after Bush had departed the race to focus on those other "cool things," columnist Matthew K. Lewis wrote a campaign obituary for Mike Murphy, the Beltway political consultant who ran Bush's Right to Rise PAC. Murphy was supposed to be some vaunted campaign genius who was going to ensure Jeb took his rightful place as the third Bush in the White House. Instead, Right to Rise PAC burned through $118.3 million in establishment donor money. Murphy insists he didn't cash in on the usual 15 percent commission media buyers collect, but I hope he did. It's going to be hard for him to ever find work again after the Right to Rise fiasco.

As wretchedly as Murphy managed the Bush family's runt of the litter, he did offer up the best post-mortem analysis of the 2016 primary fight and Bush's ultimate demise

"[Jeb!] was the guy who was handing out policy papers when Trump was handing out broken bottles."

John Kasich

The other chief executive in the race was Ohio Gov. John Kasich, whose father, he'll have you know, was a mailman.

Kasich entered the race as a darling of the mainstream media. As they always do, the fake conservative columnists for the *New York Times* and the *Washington Post*, and even many lefty commentators, trotted out a familiar canard. If Republicans nominate the centrist, the moderate, the milquetoast, non-confrontational candidate, then surely they will win the election with ease. We saw this with Arizona Sen. John McCain in 2007 and 2008. The so-called "Maverick" was beloved by the mainstream media—right up until he won the nomination, at which point he became an ultra-right-wing radical who needed to be destroyed. Overnight, he went from a principled maverick on his campaign bus, the Straight Talk Express, to a deranged Captain Queeg on the Straitjacket Express. Anything to elect Obama.

The same m.o. would have been used against Kasich had he prevailed in the primaries. The RINO class loved Kasich, but his track record as governor alienated most conservatives. Kasich was one of the few Republican governors who wholeheartedly embraced Obamacare, opting to expand his state's medical welfare program, Medicaid, after the Supreme Court ruled that expansion was optional rather than mandatory. He partnered with Democrats, adopted their talking points, and even pushed out their bogus statistics about the impact and cost of the decision to expand. Just a few years after opening the Medicaid rolls to able-bodied, childless adults, Ohio was spending far more on the welfare program than Kasich had ever predicted, owing in part to higher than forecasted enrollment. It turns out, a lot of people will take the free stuff if the government offers it to them. Shocking, isn't it?

But whereas embracing Obamacare's Medicaid expansion made Kasich a villain in the conservative movement, it made him a "reasonable" Republican for the anchors at CNN. So, much of the campaign analysis from left-wing pundits concluded that Kasich was perhaps the only candidate moderate enough to beat Hillary Clinton. Unfortunately for the son of a mailman—but fortunately for the rest of us—Kasich was almost as dreadful at modern campaigning as ¡Jeb!

Kasich's debate performances were some of the worst in the race. Unlike some of the other candidates, there was no single glaring gaffe that brought him down. Instead, it was his personality, his fake "aw shucks" routine, his Kung fu ninja hands, and his repeated reminders that his father was a mailman. (Have I told you, by the way, that Kasich's father was a mailman?) Kasich also couldn't stop talking about the fact that he once served in Congress. "I was on a subcommittee once that…" was a frequent refrain. In an election where political outsiders were enjoying an unusual degree of success, Kasich was continually reminding voters that he was, despite his humble Midwestern roots, a career politician.

Like his comrades in the GOP establishment, Kasich often found himself on the losing side of exchanges with Trump. Kasich had a mean streak, and Trump exposed it. "He was such a nice guy," Trump explained during a debate. "And he said, 'Oh, I'm never going to attack.' But then his poll numbers tanked. He's got very little—that's why he's on the end—and he got nasty. And he got nasty."

The front-runner's mockery of Kasich also extended to the Son of a Mailman's eating habits on the campaign trail. It's an unspoken rule of presidential campaigning that you're supposed to go to local restaurants and sample the local fare, whether it's pork on a stick in Iowa or cheesesteaks in Philadelphia. But Kasich took it too far. As he campaigned from state to state, news cameras invariably caught him gorging himself like a ravenous beast, half-eaten food hanging down his chin as he chewed with his mouth open while simultaneously trying to answer questions. Pancakes, Italian subs, kielbasa, it didn't matter. He wanted it super-sized with a doggy bag to go, and throw in a couple of cannolis for the road. His gluttonous campaign feasts became so common that more than a few pundits suggested he was only keeping his campaign alive for the free eats.

In late April 2016, when rumors were brewing that Kasich and Sen. Ted Cruz were forming an alliance aimed at forcing a brokered convention, Trump lampooned Kasich's culinary habits at a rally.

"Now you look at Kasich, did you see him?" Trump said. "He has a news conference all the time when he's eating. I've never seen a human being eat in such a disgusting fashion. I'm always telling my young son Barron, always with my kids, all of them, I'd say 'children, small, little bites.' This guy takes a pancake and he's shoving it in his mouth.

"It's disgusting," he said. "Do you want that for your president?"

"NOOOO!" the crowd roared.

The Ohio governor never broke five percent in public opinion polling until February 2016, when other credible GOP candidates began dropping out and the field narrowed. He peaked at around 22 percent in late April, but by that time the math was becoming more difficult for Trump's opponents. Nonetheless, Kasich remained in the race through the Indiana primary. He dropped out on May 4, a day after Cruz had suspended his campaign.

By then Kasich had become an embarrassment. He was like the man who came to dinner, a party guest who stuck around way too long, hoping to get a free sandwich and a beer. In an earlier time, the mailman's son might have been picked up by local cops on one of those vague statutes the Warren court eventually declared unconstitutional—failure to give a good account of one's self or, my favorite, being abroad in the night. He was a loiterer, a political vagrant. No one really knew what Kasich was doing, least of all himself. Making a moral stand? Hardly. He was merely positioning himself for the future, taking advantage of the moment to keep himself in the public eye. Even though the convention was in Cleveland, in his home state, Kasich boycotted, proving that he would not back the GOP nominee.

How much did Kasich's lack of support matter? Not that much on Election Day. But at the beginning of the general election, Kasich's obstinacy was just another hurdle Trump would have to overcome in order to clinch the pivotal swing state of Ohio.

Chris Christie

New Jersey Gov. Chris Christie entered the presidential race just two weeks after Donald Trump. Christie had developed a reputation as a hard-nosed straight talker, unafraid of confrontation. He rose to national attention during his first term when he sparred, often and at length, with the liberal Democrat machine that dominated the state's politics. Political commentators were noting as early as 2012 that Christie would be a credible force in the 2016 Republican primary. He delivered a somewhat self-indulgent keynote address at the RNC convention in 2012. After President Obama won reelection, we learned that the Romney campaign had vetted Christie as a potential running mate. However, the Romney campaign insisted that Christie resign his governorship if he wanted to join the ticket. So-called "pay to play" laws would have restricted political contributions from companies doing business in his state. Not willing to risk his governorship, Christie was out of the running.

Christie had two huge advantages when it came to fundraising. For starters, he was in New Jersey, home to some of the wealthiest political donors in the country, right next to New York, where other well-heeled Wall Street types could be solicited. Throughout his governorship, Christie had cultivated these relationships, and he put them to use in 2013-2014 as chairman of the Republican Governors Association. Leading the RGA provided Christie with a fundraising advantage, and it allowed him to campaign across the country under the pretense of helping other Republicans. The RGA tour put Christie into the local news cycles of various states and earned him the loyalty of politicians and party leaders across the country.

Christie launched his campaign on June 30, 2015, at his old high school in New Jersey, but one of his first campaign stops was in Maine with Gov. Paul LePage. LePage had been a top beneficiary of Christie's RGA stewardship in 2014. The brash conservative would repay that favor by endorsing Christie and sticking with him until the bitter end.

"To receive an endorsement from someone who knows what it's like to run a blue state," said Christie. "who knows what it's like to make tough decisions, who knows what it's like to engage in hand-to-hand combat to try to get things done for the people who elect you—to get an endorsement from Paul LePage today is an incredible honor."

LePage's support for Christie came despite the obvious stylistic similarities between him and Trump. LePage even bragged on my radio program that he was "Little Trump."

"I was Donald Trump before Donald Trump became popular," LePage told me during a remote broadcast in Augusta, Maine. When I offered him a Make America Great Again hat, he gladly donned it and posed, grinning, for a picture that likely irritated Christie's staff. (LePage would later endorse Trump on my radio show on February 26, 2016 and would host the candidate at a handful of rallies in Bangor and in southern Maine.)

Looming over Christie's entire campaign—and his entire career, really—was his infamous hug of Barack Obama in the wake of Hurricane Sandy in the run up to the 2012 election. It wasn't an endorsement of Obama, but that's what it looked like. But what really doomed Christie was the now-infamous George Washington Bridge closure scandal. In the fall of 2013, Christie appointees and staffers colluded to create traffic jams in Fort Lee, N.J., by closing access lanes to the toll booths. Christie's opponents alleged the closures were an act of retribution against the Democrat mayor of Fort Lee, who had declined to endorse Christie's 2013 re-election bid. The feds launched an investigation that resulted in the indictment of three key Christie aides.

The media, especially MSNBC, feasted on the scandal, which was dubbed Bridgegate. What did Christie know and when did he know it? The governor maintained that he was not involved with the bridge closure, but most political observers were unconvinced. The scandal marked an historic decline in Christie's approval rating among New Jersey voters and probably contributed to his poor performance in the GOP primaries. However, by the time I booked Christie for an interview on my radio program, Bridgegate wasn't the issue I was interested in talking about.

One month before he came on my show in early May, Christie had proposed a massive set of entitlement reforms. While I understand that U.S. entitlement programs are the primary driver of our national debt and must be reformed, Christie's plan was tantamount to stealing from millions of hardworking Americans who had paid into the system their entire lives. The Social Security payments that millions of Americans, including me, had made to Uncle Sam came with a promise that we'd benefit during retirement. Christie was proposing to take that away with means-testing. Under the Christie plan, seniors earning more than $80,000 a year would see benefits reduced and those making more than $200,000 would lose their benefits entirely. It was outrageous.

"You're proposing what amounts to a bait-and-switch, aren't you? I mean, what's the difference between this and Bernie Madoff?" I asked, referring to Madoff's billion-dollar Ponzi scheme.

"I'm older than you are," I told him. "I started paying into this program when Lyndon Johnson was president, right? Nobody said anything about means-testing."

Christie didn't back down.

"What's your solution, Howie? What's your solution?" he asked. The audience, including listeners across the Granite State, were unconvinced.

In a crowded field of candidates, Christie never caught fire. In Iowa, where the governor had spent considerable time and resources, he placed tenth in a field of 12 candidates, finishing forth among the governors in the contest. Christie spent even more time in New Hampshire—70 days, all told—vying for a win in the first-in-the-nation primary. But he finished sixth in a field of nine in the Feb. 9 primary.

Seventeen days later Christie endorsed Trump.

The endorsement sent the political class into convulsions. New Hampshire's *Union Leader*, which had endorsed Christie, claimed the governor had promised he would never endorse Trump. The paper's legend-in-his-own-mind publisher Joe McQuaid wrote in an editorial that he had been wrong to have endorsed Christie in the first place.

The *New York Times* editorial board called the new political alliance a "Bully Bromance."

"Consistency has never been Mr. Christie's strong suit, and that showed in his endorsement on Friday," the *Times* sniffed. "If Mr. Trump should win the presidency, he might want to consider Mr. Christie for transportation secretary, since he already knows so much about traffic patterns on commuter bridges."

Massachusetts Gov. Charlie "Tall Deval" Baker, who also had endorsed Christie after pocketing millions from the RGA in 2014, quickly started backpedaling. "I don't believe that his endorsement of Donald Trump says much of anything of why I chose to endorse him," Baker told the *Boston Herald*.

Christie would prove to be a fierce surrogate for Trump. Whether it was on the stump or over the airways, Christie advocated for Trump and prosecuted a hard case against Clinton. There was a lot of talk about Christie joining the ticket as Trump's running mate. Some thought that would be too much New Jersey and New York for the rest of the country outside the metro area. But I thought, and still do, that Christie lost out on the VP spot because Trump still had lingering concerns about Christie's role in Bridgegate.

Trump reads the New York papers, and they covered Bridgegate rigorously. The federal trial of his aides, which took place in Newark during the fall campaign, was devastating to Christie. I'm told Trump was appalled by the portrayal of Christie by the witnesses—a preening egomaniac hurling full water bottles at a female aide, a single mother of four who wept first as she recounted how Christie had treated her, and then later, when the jury convicted her of fraud and conspiracy.

Christie's political skill was on full display at the GOP convention in Cleveland where he dissected Hillary Clinton's lack of qualifications, her misguided politics, and her astonishing corruption. The governor told the crowd to play the jury while he read out the charges against Clinton.

"Hillary Clinton," he intoned, "as a failure for ruining Libya and creating a nest for terrorist activity for ISIS, answer me now, is she guilty or not guilty?"

"Guilty!" came the uproarious reply.

"Hillary Clinton," he asked next, "as an inept negotiator of the worst nuclear arms deal in American history, is she guilty or not guilty?"

"Guilty!" the crowd bellowed.

On and on, Christie indicted Clinton, and the crowd loved it. The speech was a clever bit of theater—one of the best of the convention. It was obvious to everyone that Christie was auditioning for a plum position in the Trump administration. Attorney General or Chief of Staff, perhaps? But when the *Access Hollywood* tape with Billy Bush blew up that Friday evening in October, Christie failed a crucial test of loyalty. That weekend, Christie backed out of campaign appearances with Trump, another move that would count against him as he sought a plum job in the Trump administration.

THE OUTSIDERS

Carly Fiorina and Ben Carson

Trump wasn't the only outsider in the GOP primary race. Former Hewlett Packard CEO Carly Fiorina and retired neurosurgeon Ben Carson also sought the GOP nomination without having held prior political office. Both candidates attracted attention for being outside the typical GOP candidate demographic. Fiorina was the lone female candidate in the race and Carson was the only black man. Ultimately, both candidates would enjoy brief spikes in the polls before crashing back to earth.

Fiorina was no stranger to politics. She worked in 2008 on John McCain's presidential campaign and her name was even floated at the time as a potential running mate. She was a top surrogate for the McCain-Palin ticket until she said publicly that neither McCain nor Palin had the experience to run a major corporation. She was trying to fluff up the significance of being a CEO, but the remark hurt the Republican candidates, and Fiorina soon faded out of the political media. Following the 2008 election, she became the fundraising chair for the RNC and eventually ran for the U.S. Senate in California, against incumbent Democrat Barbara Boxer.

Fiorina won a competitive Republican primary, but she went on to lose to Boxer by a steep margin, 52–42 percent. She never figured out how to answer criticism of her private sector experience, and these same attacks dogged her presidential bid. Shortly after she entered the race, left-wing politicos—and probably a fair number on the right—began circulating the opposition research from her Senate fight, most of which centered on her tenure at HP. Fiorina had pulled down a lofty salary while at the same time offshoring American jobs. Not a good look for a Republican.

As the only other female in the presidential race, Fiorina was uniquely positioned to attack the Democrat front runner. She came up with some memorable lines. In debates and various media appearances, Fiorina leveled zinger after zinger against Clinton.

"Unlike another woman in this race, I love spending time with my husband," Fiorina said during one debate. "Listen, if my husband did what Bill Clinton did, I would have left him long ago.

"Here's the deal: Hillary Clinton has been climbing the ladder to try to get power and here now she is trying for the White House. She's probably more qualified for the Big House."

The crowd loved the lines, and Fiorina would see brief jumps in the polls, but she never really caught fire with a broad swath of the electorate.

"You know everybody out there watching knows this—you cannot wait to see the debate between me and Hillary Clinton," she would say at every appearance. "You would pay to see that fight."

Unfortunately for Fiorina, voters were willing to pay more to see Trump take on Clinton, which must have been particularly painful given the often brutal exchanges between Carly and the Republican frontrunner. Like other Trump foes, Fiorina tried to link him to Clinton, to suggest that he was just the flip side of the same corrupt crony capitalism that had made the Clintons filthy rich. And Carly tried, like many Democrats, to cast Trump as a boorish misogynist. Sometimes, Trump helped with that.

In an interview with *Rolling Stone* magazine, Trump mocked Fiorina's physical appearance. By itself, that raised an interesting question: Why would he grant an interview to *Rolling Stone*, a failing magazine that had recently published a wild rape hoax and used its cover to celebrate Boston marathon bomber Dzhokhar Tsarnaev? It made no sense and still doesn't. Of course the pajama boy interviewing Trump was going to try to take him out.

But Trump did the damage himself when he pointed at Fiorina on a television screen and said, "Look at that face! Would anyone vote for that? Can you imagine that, the face of our next president? I mean, she's a woman, and I'm not supposed to say bad things, but really, folks, come on. Are we serious?"

The remark drew the predictable outrage from the predictable corners of the media world, but it also served to elevate Fiorina's candidacy. After the attack, Fiorina managed a good debate performance and saw another spike in her numbers. She was in third place for a few days.

However, she couldn't keep the momentum going, because with the added popularity came new scrutiny, both of her track record in the private sector and of her policy positions. Like ¡Jeb! and Lil Marco, Fiorina was an unabashed supporter of the Gang of Eight immigration bill. As the primary election increasingly became a referendum on illegal immigration, Fiorina faded. After lackluster performances in Iowa and New Hampshire, she dropped out of the race. But she wasn't done just yet.

Ben Carson was a world-renowned brain surgeon by the time he entered the political arena. In 1987 he performed the first successful separation of conjoined twins. He went on to expand his career into numerous corporate boards and medical associations. By 2013, he was well known in medical circles. Carson was also a devout Christian, and this combination of circumstances allowed for his first major entry into American politics: His invitation to speak at the White House Prayer Breakfast in 2013. It was a perfect moment for Carson—a captive audience with the President of the United States and broad media attention—and he took advantage.

Carson roasted the culture of political correctness that was stifling the national conversation.

"We've reached the point where people are afraid to actually talk about what they want to say because somebody might be offended," he said. "People are afraid to say 'Merry Christmas' at Christmas time." (Sound familiar?)

Carson took on the political establishment, mocking the legal background of so many of the political types in both parties who end up in what was becoming known as the swamp, as in, "Drain the Swamp!"

"I don't have anything against lawyers, but you know, here's the thing about lawyers—and I'm sorry, but I got to be truthful, okay, got to be truthful—what do lawyers learn in law school?" Short pause. "To win, by hook or by crook."

He invoked his Christian faith to take on the nation's labyrinthine tax code and the Affordable Care Act. Predictably, the White House was furious. They let their stenographers in the media know that Carson's speech was inappropriate, too political, and insulting to the president. Commentators, especially the NPR types, demanded Carson apologize and were appalled when he refused. While the elites were shocked that someone, especially a black someone, would come to Obama's White House and speak, shall we say, truth to power, Carson endeared himself to millions of conservative Americans across the country.

Thanks to the prayer breakfast, Carson entered the GOP presidential primary with a great reputation among the conservative base. He was intelligent, he was a sincere Christian, and he was a black conservative. He had kept up with his followers online since that prayer breakfast and entered the race with a baseline of support higher than most other candidates. After Bush's campaign began collapsing, Carson's support really took off.

From August 2015 until the end of the year, Carson consistently ranked second in the *Real Clear Politics* average of polls. But as time wore on Carson's weaknesses became apparent. Like Bush, he was low-energy. During debates, he had difficulty injecting himself into spirited discussions. And when he managed to get a word in edgewise, his answers were sometimes not concise. Occasionally he looked like he was drifting off to sleep on stage. He never exhibited the fire and the anger that GOP voters themselves felt. Nonetheless, Carson was tied for first with Trump in early November. Trump took notice and honed his attacks. Within a month Carson had fallen more precipitously than either Bush or Walker before him to fourth place, and he never recovered.

Sometimes Trump's barbs were tame. "Ben Carson is a very low energy person," he would say, "Actually, I think Ben Carson is even lower energy than Jeb, if you want to know the truth."

But other times the shots were wild and incendiary. Citing an anecdote Carson had told in one of his autobiographies, Trump ripped into the brain surgeon during one of his raucous campaign events.

"I'm not saying it. He actually said 'pathological temper,' and then he defined it as disease. ... If you're pathological, there's no cure for that, folks. If you're a child molester, a sick puppy, there's no cure for that."

The crowd waited for the next salvo.

"There's only one cure. We don't wanna talk about that cure."

It was a below-the-belt attack, effectively comparing Carson to a child molester. A few decades ago, it might have backfired and sent Trump's campaign into a tailspin. But now it had just the opposite effect. Carson never effectively defended himself, a fact that only reinforced his image as a phlegmatic, Jeb-like candidate whose temperament did not reflect the ire of blue-collar America.

By the time Super Tuesday arrived in March, Carson's support had evaporated. Despite having raised more than $54 million to back his campaign, the neurosurgeon failed to win a single state primary or caucus. Seeing no political path forward, Carson suspended his campaign in early March.

THE SENATE UPSTARTS

Three young U.S. Senators began as apparently credible candidates in the primaries—Sens. Ted Cruz, Rand Paul and Marco Rubio. The trio had spent their first terms in Congress trying to raise their presidential profiles. Cruz was the staunch social conservative who never backed down from a cultural battle with the left. Paul was a libertarian leader, heir to his father's unconventional pro-weed, anti-Federal Reserve political movement. Rubio was the establishment favorite whose stirring speeches sent tingles up the legs of the D.C. neoconservatives like Bill Kristol. Each of them laid claim to one ideological sector of the conservative movement. But in the end, all three would strike at Trump and live to regret it.

Rand Paul

Paul was the first of the Senate candidates to flame out. He entered the race with a natural advantage—a libertarian streak that distinguished him from the other candidates. Paul famously launched a 13-hour filibuster in 2013, holding up the confirmation of Obama's CIA Director. Paul's demand was then simple: he wanted Attorney General Eric Holder to confirm, publicly, when the federal government was authorized to launch a drone strike on a U.S. citizen on U.S. soil.

The epic filibuster attracted positive media attention from all corners, and many other senators joined his crusade. And Paul got results. The following morning, he received a letter from Holder.

"It has come to my attention," the letter began, "that you have now asked an additional question: 'Does the President have the authority to use a weaponized drone to kill an American not engaged in combat on American soil?' The answer to that question is no."

Paul's filibuster burnished his libertarian credentials, but that wasn't enough in a chaotic GOP primary fight where drone strikes on U.S. citizens were less of an immediate issue than trade, Obamacare, and immigration.

In politics, style often matters as much as substance. And Paul's feisty style in media interviews throughout the campaign did little to attract voters to his cause. CNBC's *Closing Bell* anchor Kelly Evans got a taste of Paul's prickly temperament when she asked him about corporate tax reform. At one point, Paul shushed Bell and told her to "calm down"—drawing the ire of feminist Twitter—before lambasting the anchor's political bias.

"Part of the problem," Paul lectured, "is that you end up having interviews like this where the interview is so slanted and full of distortions that you don't get useful information. I think this is what is bad about TV sometimes. So frankly, I think if we do this interview again, you need to start out with a little more objectivity going into this interview."

Did he think an interview on CNBC was going to be objective just because he asked for it? Clips of the exchange were shared broadly across social media, with amused conservatives and liberals alike shaking their heads in disbelief.

Paul's temper got the best of him again in a televised interview with Savannah Guthrie, host of NBC's *Today* show.

"Why don't we let me explain instead of talking over me, OK?" Paul told Guthrie when asked about his previous statements. But Guthrie continued pressing Paul on his foreign policy, suggesting the Kentucky senator had changed his positions on Iran, military aid for Israel, and defense spending.

"Before we go through a litany of things you say I've changed on, why don't you ask me a question, 'Have I changed my opinion?'" Paul lectured her. "That would be sort of a better way to approach an interview."

Paul also ended up arguing with an interviewer for ABC News. Somehow Paul seemed surprised that the employer of George Stephanopoulos, Martha Raddatz and Brian Ross wasn't on the level.

Like Carson, Paul is a physician by trade—an ophthalmologist. But while Carson had the traditional "bedside manner" of a Dr. Marcus Welby-type, Dr. Paul was more like the hot-headed superstar surgeon, railing against the administrators, colleagues, insurance companies, FDA, and anyone else who crosses him, in this case, female anchors.

Democrats pounced on Paul's intemperate treatment of women. And just a few days after the spat with Guthrie, Paul jumped ugly with Associated Press reporter Phillip Elliot over a question about abortion. Of course, Paul had a legitimate complaint: All of these media interviews were conducted by left-wing hacks who believed their job was to catch GOP pols in gotcha moments that would help Hillary Clinton. But still, Paul's conduct during those early interviews contributed to his image as a surly grouch.

Paul even snapped at me during an interview on my radio show. Here's a transcript of what happened after his call for cutting off U.S. support for Mideast regimes that support, either overtly or covertly, Islamic terrorism:

Rand Paul: I'm calling for it, can't make it happen, but what I can do is withhold money from these crazy countries, if they are gonna not be supportive of us, if they are indiscriminately arming crazy, radical Islam in Syria, Libya, and across the globe.

Howie Carr: Which countries would you call crazy?

RP: What I would say is …

HC: Is Jordan crazy?

RP: Jordan has been a good ally of ours, and I don't think Jordan has been fomenting or sending arms into the middle of the Syrian civil war.

HC: Saudi Arabia? Are they crazy?

RP: I wouldn't characterize it by using that word. What I would say …

HC: But that was your word.

RP: Yeah … I would say in this instance, Saudi Arabia, Qatar, and Kuwait have all sent arms indiscriminately into the Syrian civil war and many of the arms have ended up in the hands of ISIS, even American arms have landed in the hands of ISIS. And we need to let our allies in the region know this is unacceptable, and we will no longer be giving arms, selling arms, or giving money to them if they behave this way.

HC: So are Qatar and Kuwait crazy?

RP: What I would say is what I just said, Howie. Do you want me to repeat myself?

We moved on, but the reaction from my listeners was instant. My audience generally supported his position on withholding foreign aid from "crazy" Muslim nations that hate us, but none of them were charmed by his churlish demeanor. A candidate has to be held accountable for his own words—every candidate but one that is. (Hint: that candidate's initials were the same as mine, H.C.) Those were the rules of engagement in 2016.

Paul struggled with the media, but that was nothing compared to his clashes with Trump. In August 2015, Paul hit Trump with an attack ad which cited a more than decade-old interview in which Trump said, "I really believe the Republicans are just too crazy right."

Trump counter-punched: "Rand Paul is doing so poorly in the polls he has to revert to old footage of me discussing positions I no longer hold."

Then came the kill shot.

"Recently, Rand Paul called me and asked me to play golf. I easily beat him on the golf course and will even more easily beat him now, in the world of politics."

The golf line drew attention from online reporters looking for a comical click-bait headline: "Trump Trolls Rand's Golf Game." Like Trump's line about Walker presenting him with a plaque, the golf tale conjured up the image in voters' minds of a subservient politician sucking up to a hugely successful business magnate.

That wasn't the only time Trump and Paul would swap insults.

At the first Fox News debate, moderator Bret Baier presented a challenge to the gaggle of candidates on the stage: "Raise your hand if you're going to accept the results of the primary."

Trump was the only candidate who didn't put his hand up. Paul pounced:

"He buys and sells politicians of all stripes. He's already hedging his bet on the Clintons. Maybe he supports Clinton or maybe he runs as an independent. But I'd say he's hedging his bets because he's used to buying politicians."

"Well," Trump deadpanned as he stared at Paul, "I've given him plenty of money!"

At the CNN debate in September, Paul was still struggling to gain momentum and Trump was looking to finish him off for good. He came out guns blazing right from the beginning.

"First of all, Rand Paul shouldn't even be on this stage, he's got one percent in the polls."

Paul was flustered, but managed to return fire.

"Do we want someone with that kind of character?" Paul asked rhetorically. "With that kind of careless language? I think there's a sophomoric quality about Mr. Trump ... about his visceral response to attack people on their appearance, short, tall, fat ugly."

"I never attacked him or his looks," Trump shot back, "and believe me, there's plenty of subject matter right there."

Paul limped on to a feeble fifth-place finish in the Iowa caucuses, behind Cruz, Trump, Rubio and even Ben Carson. That sad performance was a harsh blow for the senator. Four years earlier, his quirky father Ron Paul, a septuagenarian Congressman from Texas, had finished a strong third. For most of his political career, supporters of Ron Paul had been quick to back his son, but the

Iowa caucus results made clear that he could no longer ride on Dad's cannabis-infused coattails.

The Iowa caucuses took place February 1. Paul's campaign must have seen the poor performance coming, because they were already looking ahead to New Hampshire. I know this because his staff had booked an interview on my show for the Wednesday after Iowa. On the day the interview was to take place, Paul dropped out of the race. His staff was caught completely off guard. Paul and his political allies had blown more than $23 million on his doomed campaign.

Marco Rubio

Marco Rubio entered the race as the darling of the neoconservatives. In his speeches, Rubio used soaring rhetoric to defend American exceptionalism, to attack the global legacy of communism, and to promote the armed forces. He was, above all, an articulate spokesman for his neocon corner of the conservative movement. That made him a prime target for the hatchet men on the left.

Trump wasn't the only candidate who chaffed against a biased press. Rubio, too, was the subject of comically over-blown "exposes" of his "lavish" lifestyle. In the summer of 2015, the *New York Times* decided to "investigate" Rubio's finances. Either that or one of Rubio's enemies handed them some opposition research. (As I always say, there's more snitchin' than sleuthin' going on these days, always has been, as a matter of fact.)

Although he had struggled financially early in his career, Rubio had scored a 2012 book deal that netted him an $800,000 advance. After paying off his student loans, Rubio made a few discretionary purchases. Here's how the *New York Times* reported his spending in a story titled, "Marco Rubio's Career Bedeviled by Financial Struggles":

"[H]e splurged on an extravagant purchase: $80,000 for a luxury speedboat, state records show. At the time, Mr. Rubio confided to a friend that it was a potentially inadvisable outlay that he could not resist."

That extravagant luxury speed boat?

It was an EdgeWater 245CC Deep-V Center Console, a/k/a a 24-foot fishing boat—the boating world's equivalent of a pick-up truck or a sensible sedan.

Given Rubio's reputation as a smooth-talker, it's ironic that public speaking failures were the catalyst to his campaign's eventual demise.

Rubio's downfall began during a debate in New Hampshire. The smooth-talking senator didn't look so smooth. He was nervous, agitated even. Perhaps he sensed that his dream of becoming a young president, a Cuban-American JFK, was slipping away. In the middle of the debate, he choked big time.

Rubio was taking a familiar course, one he had tried to follow in prior debates. His aim was to challenge President Obama, Hillary Clinton, Bernie Sanders and Democrats in the Senate. His goal was simple enough. Some voters don't like GOP infighting. So don't attack the people sharing the stage—attack the true enemy, heeding Reagan's Eleventh Commandment—a good strategy in front of Republican audiences. Unfortunately for Rubio, the rehearsed lines he'd been practicing in the mirror before the debate got crossed up in his brain and he went haywire, after which he'd spend the next few days being comically chased across the Granite State by activists dressed in robot costumes.

Christie had been campaigning extensively in New Hampshire and Rubio was a frequent target of his attacks. Rubio, Christie said, was just like Barack Obama—an untested, inexperienced first-term senator with few accomplishments. Earlier in the week, former Sen. Rick Santorum, who had just dropped out of the race and endorsed Rubio, came up empty when asked to list Rubio's accomplishments. So, at the debate in the Granite State, ABC's David Muir asked the obvious question: What are your accomplishments?

After listing off three inconsequential bills that he might have had something to do with, Rubio pivoted to attacking Obama.

"[L]et's dispel once and for all with this fiction that Barack Obama doesn't know what he's doing," Rubio spat out. "He knows exactly what he's doing. Barack Obama is undertaking a systematic effort to change this country."

It was a decent line—a crowd pleaser among conservatives who, after seven years, understood that Obama was more Machiavellian radical than liberal idealist. But it was a decent line just once. And Rubio would repeat it—over and over and over again, as Christie was there jabbing him left and right.

"Let's dispel with this fiction that Barack Obama doesn't know what he's doing." Rubio repeated. "He knows exactly what he's doing. He is trying to change this country,"

And again: "Here's the bottom line. This notion that Barack Obama doesn't know what he's doing is just not true. He knows exactly what he's doing."

Rubio was frazzled. He had lost the ball in the sun. He gulped and tried punching back, citing New Jersey's awful credit rating. But Christie was there with a devastating zinger.

"This is what Washington, D.C. does." said Christie. "The drive-by shot at the beginning with incorrect information and then the memorized 25-second speech that is exactly what his advisers gave him."

Bizarrely, Rubio returned to his talking point for yet a fourth time.

"We are not facing a president that doesn't know what he's doing," he said. "He knows what he is doing."

Christie calmly delivered the headshot: "There it is," he said. "The 25-second memorized speech."

The exchange did not help Christie much, but it was devastating for Rubio and demoralizing for his supporters. Rubio would remain in the race for several months longer, but he never fully escaped the Robot Rubio meme. His reputation as one of the most gifted political orators of his generation was destroyed that evening in New Hampshire. His campaign expired with one final death rattle when the desperate politician decided to buck his usual socially conservative public persona and fight fire with fire.

At an event in Salem, Virginia, Rubio attempted his best insult-comic routine. He acknowledged the "Lil Marco" tag Trump had stamped him with. Trump may be taller, he said, but his hands were small.

"And you know what they say about guys with small hands," he said.

The surprised crowd offered a bit of applause before Rubio added, "You can't trust 'em!"

Trump had also been making sport of Rubio's Nixon-like tendency to perspire under the klieg lights.

"I have never seen a human being sweat like this man sweats… It looked like he had just jumped into a swimming pool with his clothes on," Trump said of Rubio, before spraying a bottle of water all over the stage.

In Virginia, Rubio veered onto the subject of the water bottle, like a flailing stand-up comic working on a new routine. Yes, Rubio admitted, he does perspire, unlike Trump, whose pores, he said, are clogged with spray tan.

"Donald Trump isn't gonna make America great," Rubio said. "He's gonna make America orange."

The jokes, lame as they were, snagged Rubio some media coverage but little else. He was playing a character—a minor character, in a bit comic-relief role—and doing a poor job of it. Operation Rickles was another nail in his campaign's coffin. In a post-mortem campaign interview, Rubio later admitted to CNN's Jake Tapper that he had apologized to Trump for making jokes about him. He apologized!

"I actually told Donald—one of the debates, I forget which one—I apologized to him for that. I said, 'You know, I'm sorry that I said that. It's not who I am and I shouldn't have done it.' I didn't say it in front of the cameras, I didn't want any political benefit."

Beyond his oratorical incoherence and flailing, Rubio suffered the same fatal deficiency that crippled the campaign of his former Florida mentor Jeb Bush. Rubio was, unapologetically, for open borders and amnesty. Rubio was the pseudo-conservative face of Chuck Schumer's Gang of Eight amnesty bill.

The Gang of Eight had been a bipartisan group of senators including Rubio, Schumer, and Sens. Michael Bennet (D-Colorado), Richard Durbin (D-Illinois), Jeff Flake (R-Arizona), Lindsey Graham (R-S.C.), John McCain, and Robert Menendez (D-N.J.). The bill they crafted was the closest the Democrats ever came to passing so-called comprehensive immigration reform under Obama. It passed the Senate in the summer of 2013 by a 68-32 vote, with 14 Republicans joining every Democrat. Then-House Speaker John Boehner (R-Ohio) refused to act. Though it never got a vote in the House, this Trojan Horse of amnesty is like a zombie—it's never really dead and it's always lurking around the corner.

The Gang of Eight bill included skilled and unskilled visa handouts for the Chamber of Commerce-type Republicans eager to keep cheap labor flooding into the country. Border security was prominent in the title, but not so much in the actual bill. Building a wall was anathema to the goals of the Gang of Eight. The bill's border security provisions amounted to a promise to do something, sometime in the future—maybe. It was the same bait-and-switch Ted Kennedy had used in 1986—amnesty today for law enforcement tomorrow. And tomorrow never comes.

But the biggest problem with the bill was the "path to citizenship." The Gang of Eight senators insisted that the path to citizenship offered in their bill would only materialize once the border was secure. No one bought that. This was about giving large corporations and mega farms cheap labor. This was about supplying Democrats with thousands, even millions, more ungrateful welfare-dependent mendicants, bulking up the numbers of the underclass and the perpetually aggrieved—undocumented Democrats, in other words. Amnesty was not about helping the American people.

Republicans at the grassroots level, including listeners to my show, knew full well that the path to citizenship was the pipe dream of the left, not for humanitarian reasons but for political ones. If millions of illegal immigrants were given a "path to citizenship," including an eventual right to vote, then the Republican Party was finished. States that could always be relied on to give their support to conservatives might turn blue in less than a decade. And, if Texas flipped, then Republicans could say goodbye to winning the White House forever.

Joining the Gang of Eight was a breathtaking, if politically expedient, betrayal by Rubio of his original Tea Party base. Against all odds, they had supported Rubio, an out-of-office former state legislator, against the sitting Republican governor of Florida, Charlie Crist. In an amazing upset, Rubio not only defeated Crist, but drove him out of the GOP. And this was how Rubio repaid the ones who brought him to the dance—by embracing open borders.

The new donors backing Rubio after his "growth" only helped fuel the grassroots concerns over his sudden metamorphosis into a McCain Republican. Hedge fund billionaire Paul Singer came off the sidelines in late 2015 to back Rubio's candidacy. Singer had played a major role in the 2004 presidential contest, bankrolling the Swift Boat Veterans for Truth, whose memorable ad attacking John Kerry's Vietnam service played no small role in helping George W. Bush win reelection. Singer's support for Rubio was also a blow to ¡Jeb!, who was already struggling by that time with the donor class. But the millions the billionaire was ready to pour into Rubio's campaign came with political baggage: Singer was for open borders—openly.

"Marco Rubio's New Billionaire Backer Top Funder for Open Borders," screamed the *Breitbart* headline of a story that was shared around social media more than 35,000 times. Singer had given a generous sum to the National Immigration Forum, a George Soros-linked non-profit that advocated in favor of the Gang of Eight bill, which conservatives had taken to calling the "Rubio-Obama amnesty."

Backing the Gang of Eight bill was Rubio's original sin. It was a betrayal of his party that voters never forgot. Aligning himself with Singer signaled to political observers that, even if Rubio tried to revert to the right position on immigration to account for the new and powerful sentiment among GOP voters, he probably couldn't be trusted. Even if he hadn't short-circuited that night in New Hampshire, even if he hadn't lost a high-profile insult battle with Trump, his campaign, like Jeb!'s, was doomed from the start.

Ted Cruz

Texas Sen. Ted Cruz was the first major candidate to enter the presidential race, and he also provided the strongest challenge to Trump, winning the first caucus in Iowa and ultimately finishing second in the delegate count. And because he was the strongest challenger, Cruz was subject to some of Trump's most brutal barbs, including the most searing of all Trump's nicknames—Lyin' Ted.

Cruz himself made more than enough mistakes to cost himself the GOP nomination, but his biggest problem was that voters saw him as, for lack of a better word, creepy. It was a pejorative that surfaced time and again on my show, most often from female callers. Something about the man was off-putting to voters. He was prone to weird turns of phrases, especially when responding to Trump's more vicious attacks.

"And I would note that Mr. Stone is a man who has 50 years of dirty tricks behind him," Cruz said, referring to Trump's dodgy ally Roger Stone. "He's a man whom a term was coined for copulating with a rodent. Well let me be clear, Donald Trump may be a rat but I have no desire to copulate with him."

What? Was that Cruz's idea of a street putdown?

Copulating with rodents?

Even Cruz's prepared, rehearsed lines often fell flat or became the subject of mockery.

"If you want someone to grab a beer with, I may not be that guy," Cruz said. "But if you want someone to drive you home, I will get the job done and I will get you home."

The line appealed to Cruz's diehard supporters in the Christian right, I suppose, but the broader audience just thought it was odd, like something from a *Saturday Night Live* skit.

The struggle between Cruz and Trump was so nasty, even their wives got caught up in the crossfire. In the run-up to the Utah primary, the "Cruz Crew" was looking to swipe a few more delegates from Trump. Utah was friendly Cruz turf, given the highly religious population. Seeking to exploit the good, Mormon family values of Utah, someone affiliated with the Cruz campaign began shopping around a salacious image of Melania Trump from back in her modeling days. The implication was clear: Do you really want someone who used to pose nude in the White House?

The attack on Melania got under Trump's skin, and he retaliated in his usual manner. He brought a gun to Cruz's knife fight. Using his Twitter bazooka, Trump leveled a nasty attack on the appearance of Cruz's wife.

When all was said and done, Trump had gotten the better of Cruz once again. Trump was just responding to a dirty trick from Cruz and Cruz looked like a whimpering coward who couldn't even get angry over attacks on his spouse. A good analogy for the fight between Trump and Cruz goes something like this. Cruz thought they were playing chess. He would maneuver his queen around the board, strategically move his pawns into place, spend endless nights plotting and strategizing, always trying to outthink Trump.

And just when he thought he had Trump checkmated, Trump would flip over the chess board and punch Cruz in the mouth. Cruz was following the old Marquis of Queensbury rules of politics. He was trying to fight like a gentleman. He didn't realize, and perhaps still hasn't, that the rules had changed, that Trump was writing them, and that the first rule was: There are no rules. The Marquis of Queensbury wasn't coming down for breakfast.

Unlike Marco Rubio, Cruz did appear to be on Donald Trump's side of the immigration issue, but was that appearance deceiving? Cruz insisted throughout the debates and through all of his public pronouncements that he was not in favor of legal status for illegal aliens, that he had opposed the Gang of Eight bill. But the image of Cruz as tough on immigration came crashing down in an interview with Fox News' Bret Baier.

Baier began the interview by noting Cruz's campaign rhetoric on immigration and then playing a video of Cruz in 2013 seemingly supporting the Gang of Eight bill. In the C-SPAN clip, Cruz called on "people of good faith on both sides of the aisle" to pass a bill "that allows those that are here illegally to come in out of the shadows."

Come out of the shadows? That was Chuck Schumer talk, a euphemism for amnesty and chain migration. Any way you sliced it, that three-year-old clip showed Cruz urging passage of the Gang of Eight bill, which would have brought about legal status for illegal aliens—the very policy he now claimed he opposed. Cruz insisted that interpretation was wrong. In fact, he said, he was pushing for an amendment that would have blocked any path to citizenship.

"The fact that I introduced an amendment to remove part of the Gang of Eight bill doesn't mean I support the rest of the Gang of Eight bill." He sounded like John Kerry when he voted for the $87 billion before he voted against the $87 billion.

But Baier had more.

The Fox host confronted Cruz with a series of his own statements that he had made about the ill-fated attempt at comprehensive immigration reform. He quoted the Texas senator saying the bill was "the compromise that can pass" and saying "if my amendment were adopted, this bill would pass."

Cruz insisted his maneuvers were an attempt to attach a poison pill to the legislation, to show that Democrats were only interested in turning illegal immigrants into citizens—and voters.

But Baier raised the obvious question: "The problem, though, is that at the time you were telling people ... this was not a poison pill. You said you wanted it to pass at the time. Looking back at what you said then, and what you said now, which one should people believe?"

Cruz was unusually awkward throughout the exchange. You didn't have to be one of CNN's alleged body language experts to notice how uncomfortable he was.

That interview, more than anything, helped convince many Trump voters that Lyin' Ted wasn't telling the truth about his beliefs on immigration.

Cruz barnstormed Indiana in late April hoping to take the Midwest state from Trump. Like Kasich, Cruz had no path to the requisite 1,237 delegates at the convention in Cleveland. But his hope was to wrest enough delegates away from Trump to force the convention to a second ballot.

Indiana was seen as the final state for the "Stop Trump" movement, and it would be an uphill battle. As far back as December 2015, Trump had been nine points ahead in the Hoosier state's polls, a lead that grew consistently as winter turned into spring.

In April 2016, Cruz's desperation brought Fiorina back into the race. Cruz announced that, should he receive the GOP nomination, he would pick Fiorina as his running mate. Fiorina now holds the record for the shortest vice-presidential candidacy in modern American politics. It was probably worth a shot. Ronald Reagan had tried a similar Hail Mary pass in 1976, picking Sen. Richard Schweiker of Pennsylvania as his running mate before the GOP convention. Reagan had come very close to catching President Gerald Ford. But Cruz was no Reagan, not even close.

The Texas senator sealed his fate at a rally held just days before Indiana voters headed to the polls. He packed the Hoosier Gym Community Center in Knightstown and, in an obvious attempt to pander to the famously basketball-crazy state, Cruz tried to show off his basketball acumen. And it might have worked if Cruz had had even a passing knowledge of basketball lingo. As it happens, though, Cruz would offer his audience the most embarrassing political sports blooper since then-presidential candidate John Kerry's line about his favorite Red Sox player, "Manny Ortez."

Cruz was trying to recreate a famous scene from the movie *Hoosiers* in which Gene Hackman, in the role of the coach, measures the height of the basketball hoop to show his team should not be cowed by the enormous arena in Indianapolis. Hackman points out that the hoops in the big city are the same height as the ones in the small gymnasium his team plays in. How did any of this relate to Cruz's campaign? Who knows? But the effort backfired in hilarious fashion when Cruz called the hoop a "basketball ring."

He could have called it a hoop, a basket, a bucket, a net, a rim—but a basketball ring? No one has ever called it a basketball ring. Cruz's comment went viral and was roundly mocked across social media. Had the guy ever watched a basketball game in his life? The answer appeared to be no. It's hard for voters to relate to a guy who spends March Madness watching C-SPAN and shopping for pocket protectors. Cruz went on to lose the Indiana to Trump 53 percent to 37 percent, with Kasich pulling in 8 percent.

Cruz's dreams of a contested convention were shattered, but he was still allowed to speak at the convention. Most Republicans had long since decided that Trump was the best, if not the only, option to defeat Hillary, so they fell in line—or, at least, they didn't go out of their way to make waves. Not Cruz. He quite intentionally failed to endorse Trump in his convention speech, opting instead to tell the assembled GOP faithful to vote their conscience. What the hell did that mean? He was roundly booed out of the convention hall, all the way to Lake Erie.

Participation Trophies

The sprawling GOP field of primary candidates also included some cock-eyed optimists who had no business being in the contest. There was former Virginia Gov. Jim Gilmore, who was well known for... what exactly? Former New York Gov. George Pataki was in the race, which excited precisely zero voters. There were the perennial also-rans, the Harold Stassens of the 21st century, former Arkansas Gov. Mike Huckabee and former Pennsylvania Sen. Rick Santorum. Then there was former Texas Gov. Rick Perry, whose 2012 campaign for president expired when he was too numb on painkillers after back surgery to remember which three federal agencies he wanted to abolish. He couldn't rally support outside of Texas and was out of the race before the Iowa caucuses started. Ditto for Louisiana Gov. Bobby Jindal. And, of course, there was the confirmed bachelor of the Senate, South Carolina's Lindsey Graham, the "bro with no ho," as then-Sen. Mark Kirk of Illinois once called him (and then apologized). What the hell was Lindsey Graham doing in this race? Jim Gilmore was a more plausible candidate. Graham dropped out of the race before the primaries even started. He endorsed ¡Jeb! Bush, then Ted Cruz, then Evan McMullin.

We got a look inside Graham's operation when he tried to get on the show. One of his New Hampshire staffers sent us an email pleading for airtime. He was Graham's only staffer in the Granite State—and he was a volunteer.

Chapter Four

"Never Complain, Never Explain"

MAKE AMERICA GREAT AGAIN—IT MAY BE THE MOST POWERFUL AND effective slogan ever in an American political campaign. The simple phrase conjures visions of a better time when Americans prospered broadly, when the United States' primacy on the global stage went unchallenged, and when we had not yet been riven by identity politics and the grievance-industrial complex. Make America Great Again stood in direct contradiction to the politics of Obama, i.e. Yes We Can Bow Down to Foreign Leaders; Yes We Can Apologize For American Leadership; and Yes We Can Attack Free Enterprise.

But Make America Great Again was more than just a slogan. It wasn't just some wishful nostalgia for an era that would never return. The doctrine—call it Trumpism if you want—contained a clear and coherent policy agenda. And that agenda, as much as the candidate himself, is what inspired millions of Americans, regardless of their traditional political attachments, to invest themselves in the political process as never before.

Liberals saw Make America Great Again as just another Republican dogwhistle. What Trump really meant, they claimed, was that he wanted to bring back segregation and put women back in the kitchen. It's funny, though, that none of Democrat media personalities were upset when an earlier American politician had invoked the phrase to kick off his presidential bid.

"The country is headed in the wrong direction fast, it's falling behind, losing its way, and all we have gotten out of Washington is status quo paralysis," this politician said outside of the Arkansas State House. "Together we can make America great again."

Of course, that was Bill Clinton, in Little Rock in 1991. No one called him a racist or a xenophobe. He was a Democrat.

The Speech

It all began June 16, 2015 as Trump descended the escalator in Trump Tower, Melania at his side. He stepped up to the podium and delivered a fiery polemic that immediately upended every assumption about the 2016 presidential election.

"Our country is in serious trouble," Trump said. "We don't have victories anymore. We used to have victories, but we don't have them."

Trump listed the problems in a mostly ad-libbed tirade that indicted the smug, self-satisfied bipartisan political establishment that had failed most Americans.

"We spent $2 trillion in Iraq, $2 trillion. We lost thousands of lives, thousands in Iraq. We have wounded soldiers, who I love, I love—they're great—all over the place, thousands and thousands of wounded soldiers."

Yet the weekly casualty reports were no longer mentioned on the networks' nightly newscasts. Barack Obama was president and he had declared victory. Mission accomplished, to coin a phrase. It was an abject lie, and everybody knew it, but until now, nobody had dared speak the truth about this particular emperor's new clothes.

"Our enemies are getting stronger and stronger by the way, and we as a country are getting weaker."

Meanwhile, President Obama was cutting deals with the Taliban to bring Army Sgt. Bowe Bergdahl, who had deserted his comrades in Afghanistan, back to the U.S.

"We get Bergdahl, they get five killer terrorists… We get Bergdahl. We get a traitor. We get a no-good traitor, and they get the five people that they wanted for years, and those people are now back on the battlefield trying to kill us."

The Obama administration had negotiated, poorly, a nuclear deal that favored Iran and all but guaranteed that a medieval Muslim theocracy that called America "The Great Satan" would soon have powerful intercontinental ballistic missiles.

"Take a look at the deal he's making with Iran. He makes that deal, Israel maybe won't exist very long. It's a disaster, and we have to protect Israel."

The economy was stagnant, depressed by an entrenched, overbearing, metastasizing federal bureaucracy. The "recovery" following the 2008 financial crisis wasn't really a recovery at all. Twenty years of one-sided trade deals had hollowed out what was once the industrial heartland of the United States. Millions of American factory jobs had been lost to China, Japan and Mexico.

"Last quarter, it was just announced our gross domestic product—a sign of strength, right? But not for us. It was below zero. Whoever heard of this? It's never below zero.

"Our labor participation rate was the worst since 1978. But think of it, GDP below zero, horrible labor participation rate. And our real unemployment is anywhere from 18 to 20 percent. Don't believe the 5.6. Don't believe it. That's right. A lot of people up there can't get jobs. They can't get jobs, because there are no jobs, because China has our jobs and Mexico has our jobs. They all have jobs."

Obamacare, sold to the American people through pernicious lies, had thrown one-sixth of the American economy into chaos, created a vast new entitlement program, and was well on its way to destroying the greatest health care system the world has ever known.

"We have a disaster called the big lie: Obamacare. And it's going to get worse, because remember, Obamacare really kicks in 2016. Obama is going to be out playing golf."

From trade to health care, terrorism to foreign policy, Trump laid out a devastating critique of the governing class. It was a bipartisan mess. Trump was right about most of his criticism, but no part of his message resounded with voters more than his blunt talk on immigration.

"The U.S. had become a dumping ground for everybody else's problems. When Mexico sends its people, they're not sending their best. They're not sending you. They're not sending you. They're sending people that have lots of problems, and they're bringing those problems with them. They're bringing drugs. They're bringing crime. They're rapists."

He paused, as if he had suddenly realized how incendiary, even though undeniably true, his words were. He added quickly, "And some, I assume, are good people."

The political media were aghast. How dare he talk like that about illegal aliens? The GOP consultant types cast doubt on the strategy. You know, they would say, the only way Republicans have a future is if we pander to illegal immigrants. How's Trump going to win the Hispanic vote if he's talking like this about illegal aliens? Lost in the politically correct reaction to Trump's speech was the truth. The truth was, Trump was right. He was right about the drugs, he was right about the crime, he was right about the rapes—and the American people knew it.

In the first of his controversial throwdowns with CNN anchor Don Lemon, Trump defended his comments about illegal immigrants committing rape. Trump wasn't the first person to make this claim. Coincidentally, the first media outlet to draw attention to the sexual violence along the border was *Fusion*, a Spanish language news site owned by Univision. According to directors of migrant shelters interviewed by *Fusion*, a stunning 80 percent of Central American girls and women who illegally enter the United States were raped along the way. Trump threw the story in Lemon's face.

"Well if you look at the statistics of people coming, you look at the statistics on rape, on crime, on everything coming in illegally into this country it's mind-boggling! If you go to *Fusion*, you will see a story: About 80 percent of the women coming in, you know who owns *Fusion*? Univision! Go to *Fusion* and pick up the stories on rape. It's unbelievable when you look at what's going on. So all I'm doing is telling the truth."

Lemon pressed back, nitpicking. Those stories are about women being raped, he said, not rapists entering the country.

"Well, somebody's doing the raping, Don!" Trump said. "I mean somebody's doing it. Who's doing the raping? Who's doing the raping?"

The One-Man Show

Donald Trump never served in the military, his critics never tire of reminding us. Yet he instinctively ran his campaign on the same tactics devised by the Pentagon's premier theorists. Trump '16 was essentially a civilian version of the OODA Loop, a military concept first proposed in 1976 by Air Force Col. John Boyd. OODA stands for Observe, Orient, Decide, Act.

The theory is this: All decision making on the battlefield follows the recurring pattern of observation, orientation, decision and action. The combatant assesses the conditions, orients himself according to the environment and his opponents, makes a decision, and then carries out the action. In a military context, the OODA loop theory aims to help fighter pilots and foot soldiers understand and exploit the decision-making of the enemy. The idea is to develop a faster OODA loop than the enemy's.

The OODA loop theory also applies to politics. For example, a candidate for Congress may observe that there is widespread opposition to a certain federal policy—say, illegal immigration. So, the candidate develops some position—an orientation—with regard to that policy and subsequently makes a decision. The action then comes in the form of a vote against the policy or a political ad on the topic—say, "Build the wall!"

Rinse, wash, repeat. As with military applications, the faster, more efficient the politician can OODA, the more advantageous his position.

Trump was able to develop the fastest OODA loop in the Republican field for several reasons. He ran a campaign that was operationally unprecedented. Just compare staff size: As the establishment Republican candidates were hiring armies of staffers, communications directors, state directors, pollsters, consultants and fundraisers, Trump ran a barebones operation. For much of the primary campaign season, his staff consisted of Corey Lewandowski and Hope Hicks, the twenty-something press secretary he brought with him from the Trump Organization. There were a handful of others behind the scenes, but they were few compared to almost every other presidential campaign. There was a qualitative difference, too.

In the more traditional top-heavy campaigns, factions emerge, turf wars develop, infighting among competing cliques can grow vicious. It can happen to the best of politicians; before the New Hampshire primary in 1980, Ronald Reagan's staff was riven by dissension until he stepped in and fired his campaign manager John Sears.

Trump's original campaign manager, though, was not a Washington operative. He was a former New Hampshire environmental cop, originally from Lowell, Massachusetts, Jack Kerouac's hometown.

Lewandowksi was more like the manager of a rock band, putting together a series of one-night stands on Trump's tour across America—the Make America Great Again tour. Lewandowski's philosophy, and the eventual title of his 2017 campaign memoir, was *Let Trump be Trump* and he often compared his role to that of a jockey riding a race horse. Whereas most campaigns agonize over decision-making, using polls and focus groups to craft the perfect, risk-averse message, Trump made decisions unilaterally, often based on nothing more than instinct.

Trump's ability to instantaneously change the subject, so to speak, totally confused his opponents, who did not seem to understand the new environment, shaped as it is by social media and 24-hour news cycle. With his rambunctious rallies, his weaponized Twitter account, and his round-the-clock TV appearances, Trump could alter the political reality of the race in just seconds, leaving his challengers, and their legions of campaign consultants, struggling to respond.

Scott Walker's Beltway consultant-heavy campaign was the first to fall to Trump's guerilla style politicking. As the *Washington Post* noted in August 2015, when the Wisconsin governor's campaign was out of gas and sputtering: "Walker's backers see a campaign discombobulated by Trump's booming popularity and by his provocative language on immigration, China and other issues. They see in Walker a candidate who—in contrast to the discipline he showed in state races—continues to commit unforced errors, either out of lack of preparation or in an attempt to grab for part of the flamboyant businessman's following."

Over the next few months, this same political obituary would be written for one candidate after another, as Trump re-wrote the playbook for modern American politics.

Boycotts

Trump entered the primary campaign a world-famous billionaire with nearly universal name recognition. As a New York real estate developer, Trump had developed an empire of properties across the globe. His hotels, golf courses, and casinos were fixtures of major cities and resorts, from New Jersey and New York to Europe and China. The Trump brand was global. A big personality in New York, Trump was always in the city's tabloids. But his pathway to fame across the United States came through his NBC reality-television series, *The Apprentice*. Even if you weren't a regular viewer, you knew about the show, its celebrity host and that famous catchphrase, "You're fired!" Thanks to his successful career, Trump started the race with not only a name-recognition advantage, but a substantial cash advantage, at least when it came to his own personal wealth. Weeks after he announced a candidacy, Trump declared a net worth of more than $9 billion.

Trump's personal wealth was a major asset in his campaign. It showed that he was a successful businessman—always a plus in Republican circles. And it allowed him to self-fund his campaign. So, while the Jeb Bushes of the world were spending time sucking up to GOP fat cats, Trump was free to expend his energy on the campaign trail, flying from city to city on his private 747. Although Trump's fortune provided him with many advantages over his opponents, the sprawling business empire that generated his money also left him vulnerable to attacks, boycotts, and protests of his properties and brand. Former business partners were quick to turn on Trump once the controversies started.

Univision, the Spanish language news network, was among the first major media companies to break ties with Trump. Citing his remarks about Mexico and illegal immigration, the network announced that it would not air Trump's *Miss USA* pageant or work on any other projects with the Trump Organization. The pageant was jointly owned by Trump and NBC Universal. NBC, the media company that enjoyed such great success with Trump as their reality star, did not hesitate to cut its ties to the new candidate.

"Due to derogatory statements by Donald Trump regarding immigrants, NBC Universal is ending its business relationship with Mr. Trump," the company announced in a statement.

Trump fought back: He bought out NBC, flipped the pageant to another media company, and slapped Univision with a $500 million lawsuit.

"If NBC is so weak and so foolish to not understand the serious illegal immigration problem in the United States, coupled with the horrendous and unfair trade deals we are making with Mexico," Trump said in a statement, "then their contract-violating closure of *Miss Universe/Miss USA* will be determined in court."

Trump and Univision settled the suit in February 2016 under undisclosed terms. It was a victory for Trump, but it wouldn't be the last time he quarreled with Univision or NBC.

Macy's, a once-glittering chain of department stores, was one of the first major retail businesses to turn on Trump. Shortly after Trump came down the escalator on Fifth Avenue, Macy's caved to political correctness. The company had enjoyed a successful relationship with Trump since 2004, selling his menswear, especially his ties. But they buckled under intense pressure from the media and pulled all of his merchandise from their shelves. This was the first major test of how the businessman-turned-politician would balance his own economic interests with his political pursuits. Would he back down to protect his bank account? The answer, of course, was no.

Trump went to war.

"Clearly, NBC and Macy's support illegal immigration," Trump said, "which is totally detrimental to the fabric of our once-great country. Both Macy's and NBC totally caved at the first sight of potential difficulty with special interest groups who are nothing more than professional agitators, who are not looking out for the people they purport to represent, but only for themselves. It is people like this that are actually running our country because our leaders are weak and ineffective."

He followed with a tweet: "Those who believe in tight border security, stopping illegal immigration, [and] SMART trade deals [with] other countries should boycott Macy's."

The corporate attacks continued. NASCAR, Serta mattresses, ESPN, the Professional Golfers Association, PVH Corp (the company that manufactured Trump's clothing line), chefs at his restaurants, and even his perfume company ditched the mogul.

The decision to take on Macy's, NBC and all his disloyal former business partners was a pivotal one. It was a major financial risk for Trump's business empire, but it signaled to voters that Trump was serious about the race. More than that, it signaled that Trump was committed to Making America Great Again even if doing so came at great personal loss. The play against Macy's paid more than just political dividends. His call to boycott Macy's worked. The removal of Trump's merchandise from their stores coincided with a steep fall in the company's profits, store closures and layoffs.

As the summer wore on and Trump stared down the boycotts, it became increasingly clear that he was serious about the campaign. And as his polling numbers climbed, his rivals in the GOP were faced with a dilemma: whether to take on Trump and risk his wrath or to avoid the outsider and hope that he imploded.

Early in the race, the prospect of Trump imploding did not seem unlikely. His fast-paced one-man-show of a campaign often got him into hot water, and there were many moments when it appeared that an ill-advised remark would end his campaign.

Trump's first misstep came at the Family Leadership Summit in Ames, Iowa. The summit was typical of early election-year events. All the candidates make the pilgrimage and each gets his turn to tell some innocuous moderator, in this case an overweight Frank Luntz, why they should be elected. Such events usually pass without notice. They're bland and boring. But not this year. Trump ensured widespread coverage of the event because of the controversial bare-knuckles campaign he was running. He did not fail to deliver the sound bite the networks would replay all week long, thanks to his long-running feud with Arizona Sen. John McCain.

"He's not a war hero," Trump said. "He was a war hero because he was captured. I like people who weren't captured."

McCain, a former Navy pilot, spent five-and-a-half years in a North Vietnamese prison, the Hanoi Hilton. Despite torture and confinement, he refused to avail himself of the option to leave the prison, which would have been readily available to him because his father was an admiral. His military record was known to every voter who had followed his failed presidential bid in 2008.

"Trump might have finally crossed the line," wrote one political reporter covering the event.

Even Trump's favorite hometown tabloid, the *New York Post*, thought it might be over. The *Post* headline: DON VOYAGE. The entire Republican field denounced Trump, sensing an opportunity to end his fledging candidacy.

"After @realDonaldTrump spends 6 years in a POW camp, he can weigh in on John McCain's service," Bobby Jindal tweeted.

Scott Walker said of Trump, "I unequivocally denounce him."

"At the heart of @realDonaldTrump statement is a lack of respect for those who have served - a disqualifying characteristic to be president," tweeted Lindsey Graham.

Rick Perry joined the attacks, condemning Trump and calling on him to drop out of the race.

Every political consultant in the country would have advised Trump to walk back the statement, to apologize, to say that he "spoke inartfully," that he was sorry if anyone took offense. But that is not Trump's style. One day later, Trump went on ABC and defiantly refused to back down from his attacks on McCain. Asked whether he owed McCain an apology, Trump said: "No, not at all."

"People that fought hard and weren't captured and went through a lot, they get no credit. Nobody even talks about them. They're like forgotten," Trump said. "And I think that's a shame, if you want to know the truth."

In an interview later that day with Fox News, Trump elaborated on his criticism of McCain, pointing out the senator's failure to lead an effort to reform the Veterans Administration health care system.

"He's all talk and he's no action," said Trump.

The closest Trump ever came to acknowledging that he was wrong to attack McCain's war record was a tepid tweet in the ensuing aftermath: "Captured or not, all our soldiers are heroes!"

The episode with McCain foreshadowed how Trump would respond to political controversies. Never back down, never apologize.

I learned this lesson firsthand from Donald Trump in June 2016.

The War Whoop Heard 'Round the World—Or At Least MSNBC

The day began with a fundraiser in downtown Boston with the billionaire owner of the New York Jets, Woody Johnson, and it ended with my face and name on every nightly news program.

It was the war whoop heard 'round the world.

Donald Trump liked to be introduced by some local celebrity who could add a bit of regional color to the event. He knew I have a lot of listeners in Maine, especially the northern part, so he asked me to fly with him on Trump Force One from Logan Airport up to Bangor, home of one of my major affiliates, WVOM, the Voice of Maine, to introduce him to a weekly afternoon crowd at the Cross Insurance Center.

Behind the carefully managed staged event was a strategy driven by an understanding of the Electoral College. Maine is one of two states that can split its Electoral College votes. The Second Congressional District is much more conservative than the southern, coastal First District, where I was born and lived much of my early life. It's the northern District that is home to the voters responsible for putting conservative Gov. Paul LePage into the Blaine House in Augusta not once but twice. The Trump campaign understood that if those same voters could be brought aboard the Trump Train, they could deny Hillary Clinton at least one of the 270 votes she needed in the Electoral College. As it turned out, Trump did win the Second District in Maine, but his national

Electoral College margin was so large it didn't matter. Nonetheless, the Trump campaign's strategic focus on the Electoral College—as opposed to running up the popular vote—foreshadowed his eventual win.

On the flight up to Bangor, Trump and I talked about the campaign. He asked my thoughts, and I provided them. My biggest takeaway from flying with Trump is how obsessed he is with media coverage. Anything you read or hear in the press about that, it's not fake news. Anyway, he had a stack of policy papers sitting in his lap that his staffers had prepared for him to read. He briefly glanced over the papers, but only until one of the talking heads on the big-screen television mentioned his name. After that he was glued to the television for the rest of the flight, often speaking directly to the TV if something was said that displeased him. After enjoying a McDonald's lunch and some Vienna Finger cookies for dessert, we deplaned in Bangor and headed to the rally.

By the time I took the podium to introduce Trump, I'd decided to bring up the name of Sen. Elizabeth Warren as a way to get the crowd fired up. When she first ran for the Senate in 2012, I was among the loudest voices exposing her career-long ethnic fraud. Warren had insisted she was a Native American—a claim that helped land her coveted professorships at two Ivy League law schools, first Penn and then Harvard, where she got $350,000 a year to teach one course. And Harvard had boasted on its website that she was the first "woman of color" to hold such a position.

As we all now know, Warren's claim of Native American ancestry is total fabrication. To this day, she refuses my offer of a free DNA test. Warren is an utter fraud, but to a political party that was celebrating two other frauds, i.e. Hillary Clinton and Bernie Sanders, she was a heroine, especially when she attacked Trump. The candidate had responded in his customary fashion— ridiculing the fake Indian unmercifully, just the way I do on my radio show and in my newspaper column.

Now, Trump and I agreed on most things, but when it came to Warren we had a spot of disagreement. Whereas I prefer to call her Liawatha, Spreading Bull, or Fauxachontas, Trump settled on Pocahontas. For telling the truth, he'd been reamed by the usual talking heads who claimed to be completely ignorant of Warren's pathetic lies. And since the media had already decreed that calling out Warren's ancestral mendacity was racist, they were primed for my attack.

I stepped up to the podium and took my shot:

"I heard that Hillary Clinton and Elizabeth Warren [were] campaigning," I said. "You know Elizabeth Warren, right?"

And then I delivered my well-practiced Cherokee war cry.

I thought nothing of it at the time. It was a joke I'd used often on my radio show to remind listeners that Warren was a liar and a con artist. But now that it was connected to Trump, my B-movie war cry created another of those typical Trump media firestorms. As soon as I stepped off the stage, a Trump aide handed me his smart phone. It showed a POLITICO headline: "Boston radio host at Trump event mocks Warren with war whoop."

That was only the beginning of the coverage. CNN's Jake Tapper was shocked. MSNBC's Rachel Maddow was appalled. Mika Brzezinski was grievously offended. The *Boston Globe*, knowing full well that Warren's ethnic claims were bogus, tiptoed around the topic, saying I took a "dig" at Warren's "heritage." Montel Williams called me a crackhead. My glorious war cry was even covered in *People* magazine.

On the plane ride back to New York, the candidate loosened his tie and offered me some advice. A veteran of these kinds of controversies, he knew what was headed my way.

"Whatever you do, don't apologize," he said. "You never hear me apologize, do you? That's what killed Jimmy the Greek way back. Remember? He was doing okay 'til he said he was sorry."

I understood what he was saying. It was the same advice James Michael Curley, the four-term mayor of Boston, used to give at City Hall: "Never complain, never explain."

As the campaign unfolded, Trump would commit dozens of alleged political *faux pas* that would have doomed most politicians—but Trump was not most politicians. His refusal to apologize showed that he wasn't playing by the old political rules. Indeed, Trump was writing a new political playbook for GOP politics and his opponents were slow to catch on.

The First GOP Debate

By the time the much-anticipated GOP primary debates arrived, Trump's rivals were still struggling to come up with a way to respond successfully to the Trump insurgency. The 16 other candidates in the race had tried to make issues of Trump's support for gay marriage, his spotty track record on abortion, and his political contributions to some of the slimiest Democrats in the country—New York Democrats. Those were all non-starters.

The other candidates went on talk radio shows or Fox News and suggested that Trump was a Democrat plant, a saboteur whose candidacy was meant to help Hillary Clinton win the White House. No one bought that. Trump's rivals assailed his corporate track record, airing ads and sending out mailers in early primary states about his failed business ventures and brushes with bankruptcies. Nothing broke through.

Nine desperate candidates surrounded Trump on the stage at the first GOP debate in Cleveland. They had their own disagreements, but those took a back seat to the common objective of discrediting Trump and regaining control of the Republican Party for the establishment, i.e. themselves. The candidates, hailed by party leaders as the most promising field in a generation, had a certain smugness about themselves. The debate was, in their minds, friendly turf. Most of them had been through debates before. They had armies of consultants preparing them with poll-tested lines and researched attacks.

In contrast, Trump had never been in a political debate. For Trump's opponents, this was an opportunity to make him answer questions on their terms, to force him to conform to the old political rules. Sadly, for them, the larger-than-life personality who was drawing huge crowds at rallies across the country showed up for the debate and stole the show.

Bret Baier began the debate by asking all 10 of the candidates whether they would pledge to support the eventual GOP nominee and promise not to run as an independent. Nine candidates raised their hands and made the pledge, but not Trump. His refusal to play the game set him apart from the other candidates at the outset. Would he really have made an independent bid? No one knew, probably not even Trump himself. But the threat was now out in the open, and throughout the primaries, Trump would continue to dangle the possibility of an independent bid—his own personal political sword of Damocles.

The menace of a populist with a significant following making an independent bid had to be taken seriously—it had the potential to demolish the Republican Party. Although Trump's rivals in the race had yet to fully comprehend the phenomenon that would end up steamrolling them, they had figured out that Trump's earliest supporters were incredibly loyal to the man. The country-club Republicans doggedly maintained their belief that Trump would eventually self-destruct—the only question was which of their chosen candidates would inherit the Trump base. For this reason, Trump's refusal to make the loyalty pledge during the first debate was a brilliant opening negotiation ploy. His message to the GOP establishment was clear: You better treat me fairly or I will make you pay dearly.

Trump's not-so-veiled threat to the Republican establishment wasn't the only controversy he courted during that first debate. As many of us predicted at the time, Trump was guaranteed to face questions about the provocative and often crass statements he had made in the past, whether on *The Apprentice* or on Twitter. The debate would be the first opportunity for him to reconcile his raunchy showmanship with his new political ambitions.

Fox News' Megyn Kelly was one of the moderators, and she used her first round of questioning to attack Trump's history of leering, off-color statements. One by one, she listed his comments about women, including Rosie O'Donnell, the D-list comedienne with whom Trump had long feuded. The line of inquiry was predictable and obvious. Any other candidate would have wilted under pressure, apologized profusely, and cowered before Kelly.

Trump was undaunted.

"Mr. Trump," Kelly began, "one of the things people love about you is you speak your mind and you don't use a politician's filter. However, that is not without its downsides, in particular, when it comes to women."

Kelly had put a lot of thought into framing this question—it was supposed to be the public culmination of a broad effort to cast doubt on Trump's viability with female voters. How could he be a viable candidate against Hillary "Breaking-the-Glass-Ceiling" Clinton when he's said so many nasty things? Kelly's line of questioning was supposed to croak Trump.

She went in for the kill.

"You've called women you don't like 'fat pigs,' 'dogs,' 'slobs' and 'disgusting animals,'" she said.

"Your Twitter account is—"

Trump cut her off.

"Only Rosie O'Donnell!"

The crowd broke into laughter. Even a few of the other candidates cracked smiles. The comedic timing was perfect. The line was spontaneous, it was pure Trump. Kelly attempted to persist with her overthought question, but her moment had passed. In a matter of seconds, Trump had disarmed a potentially dangerous line of inquiry. Maybe he had made some crude remarks about women in the past, but who the hell likes Rosie O'Donnell anyway? The attacks on Trump's past use of R-rated language would never go away. But he proved that night that invoking his tabloid past wasn't going to be the silver bullet many of his foes, in politics and in the media, had thought.

Trump wasn't done with Kelly.

Following the debate, he entered the spin room—an area adjacent to the stage where candidates and their flacks go to frame subsequent media coverage in their favor. The reporters flocked to him like mosquitos to a porch light; it was a media stampede. Speaking to the throng of eager reporters, Trump continued to assail Kelly's fairness. Despite his apparent victory over Kelly in that exchange, her questions bugged him. Trump continued railing against Kelly, describing her questions as unfair. At 3:40 AM the next day, Trump lit up Twitter: "Wow, @MegynKelly really bombed tonight. People are going wild on twitter! Funny to watch."

He was still fuming that evening when he called into Don Lemon's show on CNN. That interview would kick off yet another round of premature obituaries for Trump.

"She gets out and she starts asking me all sorts of ridiculous questions," Trump said. "You could see there was blood coming out of her eyes, blood coming out of her wherever. In my opinion, she was off-base."

The reaction was immediate. All the same people who had attacked him over the McCain remark rushed back to their television studios, competing with one another to denounce Trump in the harshest tones. Erick Erickson, an Atlanta-based radio host who ran the popular conservative blogging forum *RedState. com*, withdrew Trump's invitation to speak at a major gathering of conservatives.

"His comment was inappropriate," said Erickson. "It is unfortunate to have to disinvite him. But I just don't want someone on stage who gets a hostile question from a lady and his first inclination is to imply it was hormonal."

But Trump refused, yet again, to back down or apologize or grovel before one of the traditional brokers of conservative politics.

"This is just another example of weakness through being politically correct," the Trump campaign wrote in a statement. "For all of the people who were looking forward to Mr. Trump coming, we will miss you. Blame Erick Erickson, your weak and pathetic leader. We'll now be doing another campaign stop at another location."

Trump's contentious feud with Kelly cost him a speaking opportunity at a major gathering of conservative activists. But did less politically-minded voters care that much? On August 6, the night of the debate, on average the GOP polls showed Trump with 24.3 percent support among likely Republican voters. One week later, as the media endlessly debated and analyzed the spat, Trump's numbers dropped to 22 percent. He had attacked a female anchor for asking about his past comments about women—and he only shed 2 points. By mid-September, Trump had the support of more than 30 percent of likely Republican voters. Once again the Trump policy of never apologizing in the face of withering media criticism had paid dividends.

The Establishment Schemes

None of the traditional political weapons devised by the GOP consultant class had put a dent in Trump's soaring popularity, so the establishment began conniving. One of the first attacks came from Hugh Hewitt, author of a fawning Mitt Romney hagiography and a George Will-style establishment Republican who hosts a syndicated radio show based in California. Throughout the primary race, Hewitt insisted that he was a Switzerland of conservative talkers, a neutral and honest broker of political debate. His gotcha interview with Trump proved otherwise.

"I'm looking for the next commander in chief to know who Hassan Nasrallah is, and Zawahiri, and al-Julani, and al-Baghdadi. Do you know the players without a score card yet, Donald Trump?"

The question referred to various terrorist leaders: Nasrallah, the leader of Hezbollah, Zawahiri, the leader of Al-Qaeda, al-Julani, the leader of Jabhat al-Nusra, and al-Baghdadi, the leader of the Islamic State.

Hewitt was attempting to recreate a political attack that embarrassed George W. Bush in his 1999 campaign against then-Vice President Al Gore. In an interview with a Boston TV reporter, Bush was asked to name the leaders of Chechnya, Taiwan, India and Pakistan. The Texas governor could only name the president of Taiwan. It was an embarrassing moment that let Gore mock Bush's intelligence. The Bush campaign brushed off the gaffe, saying that presidential candidates run to become the leader of the free world, not *Jeopardy* contestants.

If asking about the president of Pakistan was a game-show question, then what was Hewitt's question? He was asking Trump to draw an elaborate family tree of the entire sordid web of Islamic terrorists. Trump didn't know all of the players just yet, but his answer was nonetheless candid, cogent, and practical.

"I knew you were going to ask me things like this," Trump said, "and there's no reason, because, number one, I'll find, I will hopefully find Gen. Douglas MacArthur in the pack."

The Republican establishment feasted on Hewitt's gotcha moment.

"You gotta know who the players are," ¡Jeb! Bush said at an event that night in Laconia, N.H. "I'm sure, I'm sure he'll bone up now."

The attacks were overwrought. For starters, how many voters knew—or cared—about the names of the various Third World Islamic madmen? And why was this particular question reserved for Trump? Hewitt later asked Carly Fiorina a version of the same question, which she answered after having had the benefit of a little prep. Like all the other GOP candidates, she went out and learned the names of the terrorist bigwigs so she could pretend that Hewitt's question was legitimate and Trump was ignorant on foreign policy. To his credit, Rand Paul actually stuck up for Trump, telling Sirius XM, "I also do think that running through a list of every different Arabic name and asking somebody to respond to them is maybe a little bit of a game of 'gotcha.'"

It wouldn't be the last time the Republican establishment and its operatives would strike at Trump and fail to land a fatal blow. Ralph Waldo Emerson once said, "If you strike at a king, you must kill him." The Republicans never came close to taking Trump out, but it wasn't from lack of trying. One of the more curious attacks on Trump happened just a few weeks later at an event in Rochester, N.H.—and it reeked of dirty politics and subterfuge. Trump had just finished giving his stump speech when he decided to take some questions from the packed room. A man dressed in a Trump tee-shirt stood up, eager to ask the first question.

"We have a problem in this country," the man said. "It's called Muslims. You know our current president is one. You know he's not even an American."

Trump smelled the trap.

"We need this question?!" he joked to the audience. "This is the first question?"

"Anyway," the man continued, "we have training camps growing where they want to kill us. That's my question: When can we get rid of them?"

The man's question was outrageous on its face. It reeked of a setup to lead Trump into making an offensive racially-tinged remark. Trump, for his part, responded the way you might respond to a drunken lunatic yelling on the street corner.

"We're going to be looking at a lot of different things," Trump replied, vaguely. The looking-at-a-lot-of-things line was his characteristic reply when he wasn't yet sure where he came down on an issue. "You know, a lot of people are saying that and a lot of people are saying that bad things are happening. We're going to be looking at that and many other things."

The media pile-on was swift and furious and totally predictable. All the headlines and chyrons screamed: "TRUMP FAILS TO CORRECT CLAIM OBAMA IS MUSLIM." Clinton said she was appalled. White House Press Secretary Josh Earnest huffed from behind the podium, "Is anyone really surprised that this happened at a Donald Trump rally?" DNC Chairwoman Debbie Wasserman-Schultz screeched, "Donald Trump's racism knows no bounds." According to his critics, Trump was now to be held responsible not just for his own words, but for the words of every unhinged idiot who turned up at a rally.

Lewandowski later claimed that his candidate did not hear the entire question, which is plausible considering the environment and the fact that the man appeared to be slurring his words. That didn't matter to mainstream media. They had their video: Trump was an awful, nasty racist, just like this yahoo who showed up in Rochester.

But the question remained: Who was this guy? Given how predictable the coming news cycle would be, you would think that any reporter/gumshoe worth his salt would want to score an interview with the concerned citizen. At the very least, they'd want to identify him in their stories. But somehow, the crack scribes at the event failed to figure out who he was. New Hampshire listeners who called in to my show the next day, some of whom were at the event, had no clue who the man was. The identity of the Rochester questioner remains unknown, but I maintain that he was most likely a plant. The only mystery is whether he was sent by Clinton operatives or some right-wing dirty trickster.

The GOP establishment's attacks on Trump were just beginning. As Trump's support grew, the anti-Trump spots began dominating local TV news. Super PACs aligned with John Kasich and Jeb Bush launched six-figure ad buys in early primary states. The super PAC associated with the Club for Growth, a group of economic conservatives, openly called on donors to support its anti-Trump campaign. Beltway consultants began forming anti-Trump organizations. They did not support a specific candidate; instead, their aim was solely the destruction of the Republican frontrunner.

One notable anti-Trump effort came from Liz Mair, a former RNC communications director who had worked on Scott Walker's stillborn campaign. She formed Trump Card LLC, which she touted as a "guerilla" campaign. Formed as an LLC rather than a PAC, Mair's organization provided secrecy to wealthy insiders who wanted to fight Trump anonymously.

"The stark reality is that unless something dramatic and unconventional is done," Mair wrote in a memo, "Trump will be the Republican nominee and Hillary Clinton will become president." Rick Wilson, a Republican consultant and MSNBC contributor with ties to Marco Rubio, was also involved in the effort, cutting TV ads and web videos on the cheap.

For all the fawning press Trump Card received in places like the *Wall Street Journal*, the effort amounted to nothing. Eventually the Republican establishment resigned itself to plotting a brokered convention in Cleveland.

The Refugee Question

As the Republican primary contest unfolded, the world was on fire. The conflicts in Iraq and Afghanistan festered as ISIS and the Taliban grew in power. In

North Africa, Libya had become a failed state and an incubator for terrorism. In Syria, the bloody years-long civil war showed no signs of abating. All the chaos and turmoil produced one of the most massive migrations in recent world history. From all across the Middle East, migrants flocked by the millions into Europe.

Across the Atlantic, the progressive luminaries in control of the government were eager to take our share of the unvetted Muslims. At the time, Secretary of State John F. Kerry was advocating for huge increases in the flow of refugees into the United States. America had already welcomed 85,000 Syrians, almost all of them Muslims, into the country and the Obama administration was poised to increase that amount to 100,000 in 2016. Clinton parroted the Obama-Kerry policy, and many Beltway Republicans also shared the sentiment that the U.S. should accept high numbers of refugees.

Trump broke with prevailing U.S. political opinion when it came to the refugees pouring out of the Middle East. He was already on the record opposing the admission of Syrian refugees when a series of coordinated terrorist attacks in Europe shocked the world, once again upending the politically correct underpinnings of American politics.

Muslim terrorists under the auspices of ISIS detonated suicide vests during soccer matches in France. At the same time, Muslim gunmen carried out shooting rampages at an Eagles of Death Metal concert at the Bataclan theater in Paris. It was the deadliest attack on France since World War II, claiming the lives of 130 people, and injuring hundreds more. In the aftermath, investigators learned that the attack was planned in war-roiled Syria and carried out by a Muslim terror cell hidden in Belgium. For Americans, the horror Paris endured only underscored our own long twilight struggle against Islamic barbarism.

Trump brought up the attack the following morning at a rally in Beaumont, Texas.

"When you look at Paris—you know the toughest gun laws in the world, Paris—nobody had guns but the bad guys. Nobody had guns. Nobody. They were just shooting them one by one and then they broke in and had a big shootout and ultimately killed the terrorists.

"You can say what you want, but if they had guns, if our people had guns, if they were allowed to carry, it would've been a much, much different situation."

The gun-friendly crowd of Texans roared in approval. Who could dispute him? But he didn't stop there. The day before the attack in Paris, President Obama had bragged that ISIS was "contained." The set-up was almost too easy for Trump.

"We have leadership who doesn't know what they're doing," Trump said, before lampooning the administration's policy on Syrian refugees. "We all have hearts and we all want people taken care of, but with the problems our country has, to take in 250,000—some of whom are going to have problems, big problems—is just insane. We have to be insane. Terrible."

Trump later expounded on his refugee policy in an interview with Yahoo News. As a result of the Paris attacks, he said, the United States was going to have to change the way we approach the threat of Islamic terrorism.

"Security is going to rule," he said. He spoke fondly of the New York City Police Department's mosque surveillance program that had been ended by Mayor Bill de Blasio. Trump said he would expel any refugees admitted into the U.S. back to Syria.

"They're going to be gone. They will go back…I've said it before, in fact, and everyone hears what I say, including them, believe it or not. But if they're here, they have to go back, because we cannot take a chance. You look at the migration, it's young, strong men. We cannot take a chance that the people coming over here are going to be ISIS-affiliated."

Like so many of Trump's proposals, his call for caution on the refugee front was nothing more than plain common sense, which was obvious to voters. Why was America on the hook for hundreds of thousands of indigent refugees when nearby Saudi Arabia had taken in none of their fellow Muslim Arabs? What did it say about the sinister proclivities of the refugees that even Muslim nations weren't opening their doors? When European investigators revealed that several of the Paris terrorists had entered Europe posing as Syrian refugees, Trump's adamant opposition to the Obama administration's refugee policy became a fixture of his campaign stump speeches. He ripped Obama as an arrogant fool who was risking American lives in order to help ungrateful foreigners, who might very well turn out to be terrorists, a 21st century Trojan Horse in the heartland.

Obama bristled.

"Apparently," he sneered, "they are scared of widows and orphans coming into the United States of America."

That was another abject lie.

Every analysis conducted of the migrant population found that it skewed towards fighting-age men. In the summer of 2015, for example, the International Organization of Migration analyzed 102,753 registered arrivals in Italy and Greece. The group found that 68,085 were men, with only 13,888 women and 20,780 children. According to an analysis by *The Economist* magazine,

73 percent of Europe's asylum applicants were men, and 40 percent of those men were between the ages of 18 and 34. But we didn't need hard numbers to know that. Videos of the migrant hordes surfaced day after day, showing a seemingly endless line of surly young Muslim men marching toward the nearest welfare office in Berlin.

And when they arrived, if they arrived here, what were the odds that they would ever assimilate into American society and benefit their hosts? Obama's own statistics showed that 91 percent of Arabic-speaking "refugees" remained on welfare five years after their arrival. The Tsarnaevs were not the only Muslim terrorists who had sought "asylum" from persecution, immediately went on welfare and then returned to their Third World homelands for terror training.

The truth about the refugees didn't matter to Obama, Clinton, or their left-wing sycophants. Their bogus humanitarian interest in helping "refugees" was but a thinly disguised way to level an attack against Trump. According to a poll conducted by WPA Research, 44 percent of registered Democratic voters said they would support taking refugees from Agrabah—the fictional city from Disney's *Aladdin* movie. Nearly two-thirds of younger voters wanted to accept refugees from the imaginary nation. These were Rush Limbaugh's low-info voters, baristas living in mom's basement while majoring in womyn's studies at the local community college, taking their political cues from Facebook, semi-literate ESPN hosts and coke-addled late-night comics, all of whom agreed Trump was a nativist, whatever that was, or maybe even a xenophobe (which they couldn't spell), putting "COEXIST" bumper stickers on their Priuses as they howled about Trump's nativism.

Trump caused controversy again in November 2015 by attacking a *New York Times* reporter. At the time, the mainstream media were criticizing Trump for claiming, on a number of occasions, that American Muslims celebrated immediately following the terror attacks on 9/11. The comments came amidst Trump's push for a return to old NYPD-style surveillance of mosques and other sites where terrorist attacks could be planned. His reasoning was plain: There are Muslims here in the United States who aren't so fond of this great nation, so maybe we should keep a close eye on them. His critics called Trump's claims of Muslims celebrating the 9/11 terror attacks a scurrilous Islamophobic lie. But to support his claims, Trump referenced a 2001 article published in the *Washington Post* seven days after the terrorist attack.

"In Jersey City, within hours of two jetliners' plowing into the World Trade Center, law enforcement authorities detained and questioned a number of people who were allegedly seen celebrating the attacks and holding tailgate-style parties on rooftops while they watched the devastation on the other side of the river."

Those words were written by Serge F. Kovaleski, by now a reporter for the *New York Times*. Notice how specific the language is—tailgate-style parties on rooftops. This isn't just some reporter using artistic license; it has to have been based on some interviews with witnesses, or at least law enforcement sources. When Trump used Kovaleski's report to prove that he wasn't lying, the media turned to Kovaleski for an explanation. How could they get around the inconvenient fact that a liberal newspaper, not to mention contemporaneous local New York television newscasts, were bolstering Trump's claims—claims that could not be true because, well, because Trump was a bad man?

The tack Kovaleski took would have made Orwell shudder.

"We did a lot of shoe-leather reporting in and around Jersey City and talked to a lot of residents and officials for the broader story," Kovaleski told CNN.

"Much of that has, indeed, faded from memory. But I do not recall anyone saying there were thousands, or even hundreds, of people celebrating. That was not the case, as best as I can remember."

Imagine that! Almost 15 years after filing the story, this rumpswab was now issuing a correction. Contrary to his reports at the time, there were no reports of people celebrating on 9/11 in New Jersey. He was wrong to write of tailgate-style parties and rooftop celebrations. He had no idea where his information came from. How convenient!

No one believed Kovaleski's evolving story on the Muslim celebrations. Were there dozens of Muslims celebrating on 9/11? Hundreds? Thousands? It didn't really matter, because the thrust of Trump's claim was plainly true to his supporters: Due to permissive immigration and refugee policies, the enemy now lived among us and, for the most part, on us. No amount of revisionist history on the part of the *New York Times* and *Washington Post* could obviate that fact.

But Trump wasn't about to let Kovaleski escape unscathed. As the controversy over Trump's comments continued, he headed to South Carolina for a rally. Standing behind the podium, Trump explained how the liberal media were working overtime to discredit his claims, regardless of their original reporting on the matter, and he singled out Kovaleski, whom he called "a nice reporter," for ridicule.

"Now the poor guy, you gotta see this guy," he started, before waving his arms around in imitation. "Uhh I don't know what I said. Uhh I don't remember. He's going like 'I don't remember. Maybe that's what I said.'"

Now, Kovaleski suffers from arthrogryposis, a joint condition that is quite noticeable. Trump's enemies seized on his performance, casting his attack as a mockery of a physical disability. Reporters were in high dudgeon—one of their own had been attacked. So they set about creating yet another phony attack line against Trump: He mocks the physically disabled.

There's just one problem: Yes, Trump was mocking Kovaleski, an early practitioner of fake news, but it had nothing to do with his disability. As Ann Coulter pointed up in her campaign-season book, *In Trump We Trust: E Pluribus Awesome*, the frantic arm-waving was an antic Trump used frequently to target a whole array of individuals, including military generals and even Ted Cruz. Coulter even produced video clips of Trump engaging in such behavior. But the fact-checkers were insistent. Thus began an analysis of 20 or so seconds of footage that recalled the national fixation on the Zapruder film of JFK's assassination.

"Both impressions involve open-mouthed hand-waving, but there are obvious differences," the *Washington Post*'s Callum Borchers informed us.

"Only when Trump mocks Kovaleski does he curl his right hand and wrist in a way that mimics the effect of the reporter's condition."

Callum used to work for the *Boston Globe*—but you probably figured that out, right? In the finest tradition of Mike Barnicle, Jayson Blair, and Patricia Smith…

Like so many other events the media obsessed upon, the affray with the *New York Times* reporter did little to dampen Trump's support.

San Bernardino

Less than a month after the Paris terrorist attacks thrust the refugee question into the American presidential race, radical Islamic terrorists struck again in San Bernardino, California. Armed with semi-automatic weapons and homemade explosive devices, Syed Rizwan Farook and his wife, Tashfeen Malik, targeted the Inland Regional Center, an office park where Farook worked as a county health department employee. Farook became agitated about something and decided to fast-track plans for a murder spree that had long been in the works. He left his office Christmas party and returned with his Pakistani wife and the weapons.

The terrorist couple murdered 14 people and seriously wounded another 22. They left behind improvised explosive devices as booby traps for the first responders before fleeing the scene in a black SUV. The local SWAT team quickly hunted them down and forced their vehicle off the road. As news heli-copters captured the scene from the sky, both husband and wife were slain in the ensuing gun battle.

The San Bernardino attack once again raised uncomfortable questions about political correctness and the fight against radical Islamic terrorism. Neighbors of the terrorists admitted after the fact that they were concerned. Odd things had been happening at the Farook household. Strange bearded men came and went, sometimes at late hours. Large packages were moved in and out of the garage. It was all very unusual, the neighbors thought. They saw something, but they didn't say something. And they didn't say something because they were worried people would think that they were being... Islamophobic.

The San Bernardino terror attack also made increasingly clear that our immigration system was too permissive, especially when it came to allowing in visitors from terror-prone hotspots in the Middle East and South Asia. The terrorist bride had arrived in this country on a spousal visa. Authorities later learned that immigration officials did not inspect her social media accounts. There was no requirement to do so, but if they had, they would have found obvi-ous red flags, including open expressions of support for violent jihad.

President Obama's response to the terrorist attack was so predictable.

"We don't yet know why this terrible event occurred. We don't know why they did it. We do not know their motivations. It's possible that this was work-place-related," Obama said, recalling his administration's claim that the 2009 attack by Nidal Hassan, the Palestinian Muslim who murdered more than a dozen Americans at Fort Hood, was merely workplace violence.

After pulling the tired we-may-never-know-their-motivation routine that Americans had come to expect, Obama went right to gun control. In less than 24 hours, Obama made clear that his response to an Islamic terror attack was going to be a renewed assault on the Second Amendment. He didn't know why radical Muslims decided to murder a bunch of Americans. He didn't know how they got their guns. It didn't matter that they also had improvised explosive de-vices which could have been even deadlier than their firearms. All that mattered was using the latest Muslim atrocity to score political points.

"[W]e're going to have to, I think, search ourselves as a society," said Obama, "to make sure that we can take basic steps that would make it harder—not impossible, but harder—for individuals to get access to weapons."

Obama failed to acknowledge that, just one month earlier, all of France's gun control laws had failed to prevent a similar attack. And in the following months, investigators would learn that Farook and Tashfeen acquired the bulk of their firearms via a straw purchaser. In other words, someone else went through the background check process, bought the guns for them and handed them over. That's already illegal. What other laws did Obama think could have stopped the attack? He wasn't saying.

The other Republican candidates responded the way Republicans always respond to terror attacks, with vows to completely annihilate ISIS, Al Qaeda, the Taliban, or whatever other mob of Muslim savages was killing Americans these days. There was a lot of bellicose posturing and pounding of chests. But only Trump came forward with a solution—and it was a risky move. Standing at the podium in a speech that was carried live on every network and replayed hundreds of times afterwards, Trump proposed a shocking move in the fight against Islamic terrorism:

"Donald J. Trump is calling for complete and total shutdown on Muslims entering the country until our country's representatives can figure out what the hell is going on."

The political class was shaken to its core—again. The media couldn't believe what they had heard. How dare Trump? He wants to ban a religion from the United States. That's un-American! That is, as Barack Obama would say, *not who we are*. Except… it turns out that the majority of Americans agreed with the policy. It so happens that if Muslims keeping gunning down and blowing us up, soon enough Americans—all Americans—will get sick of it. Eventually they'll realize that they're not being murdered on the streets, at their offices, and in their cities by Buddhists or Episcopalians or Hindus. The best part of Trump's proposed freeze on immigration from the Muslim world? It was perfectly legal because of the Immigration and Nationality Act of 1952, which was passed by a Democrat-controlled Congress.

Trump's proposed limits on immigration from the Islamic world demonstrated his ability to control the media narrative and to put his GOP opponents on the defensive with fast, agile decision-making. As the other candidates sought to fine-tune their own messages, they were instead forced to respond to Trump's politically incorrect proposal. Think of the pickle they were in: They could admit that Trump's idea was a prudent response to the lurking threat of Islamic terrorism, but then they would be perceived as followers who didn't have the courage to make the original pronouncement themselves. Or, they could rebuke Trump and be seen as PC quislings, afraid to speak the truth about Islamic terror.

Jeb Bush was the first to take the bait.

"I hope you reconsider this because this is a policy that makes it impossible to build a policy that takes out ISIS. Sending that makes it impossible for us to be serious about taking out ISIS and restoring democracy in Syria," he said. "I hope you'll reconsider."

Trump did not waver.

"I want security for this country," he said. "I'm tired of seeing what's going on."

We all were.

Chapter Five

Hillary vs. Bernie

THE RACE BETWEEN HILLARY CLINTON AND BERNIE SANDERS WAS ALMOST as interesting as the showdown happening on the Republican side. On the one hand, the Democrats had a septuagenarian socialist from Vermont who'd never worked a day in his life. On the other hand, they had one of the most corrupt human beings to ever seek the White House. It recalled the old joke about the Iran-Iraq War—why can't they both lose? Despite his age, his crankiness, and his crackpot policies, Sanders would rise in 2016 from Senate back-bencher to become a powerful force within the Democrat Party and a formidable foe for Clinton.

For her part, Hillary Clinton made the inevitable announcement on April 12, 2015, via a sterile internet video. Perhaps she was already worried about her ability to attract a crowd.

The video was typical progressive mush. Actors and actresses, chosen for their skin color, smiled at the camera.

"Everyday Americans need a champion," the 67-year-old grandmother said, the first of many poll-tested, focus-grouped lines that she would repeat for more than 18 months. That Clinton would run was obvious to anyone who observed her following her loss to Barack Obama in 2008, or her political posturing in Foggy Bottom as Secretary of State. Clinton believed Obama had stolen that election from her. Now, more than ever, it was *her time*, and it was up to "everyday Americans" to accept the inevitable, unless they wanted to be sneered at as "deplorables," which they would be, in due time.

Hillary's sense of entitlement was legendary. The woman hadn't driven a car in more than two decades, and she'd been protected by the U.S. Secret Service for just as long. As First Lady of the United States, she had lived high on the hog. Bill Clinton's pollster Dick Morris once said that in order to live Bill and Hillary's lifestyle outside of the White House, you would need an income of least $50 million a year. The Clintons turned the White House into a political sewer: Whitewater, the disappearance of Hillary's Rose Law Firm records, the use of extensive FBI files to blackmail enemies, Waco, Webb Hubbell, Chinagate, just to name a few. The most consequential, of course, was Bill Clinton's affair with a young White House intern named Monica Lewinsky—and Hillary's subsequent involvement in the cover-up and intimidation campaign that involved perjury, obstruction of justice and ultimately Bill Clinton's disbarment and impeachment.

Clinton had done little to improve her public reputation after leaving the White House. She relocated to New York and successfully ran for Senate—a stepping stone for her inevitable presidential bid. Her time in the Senate was unremarkable—legislative accomplishments were not her strong suit. From 2001 to 2009, Sen. Clinton managed to get just three pieces of legislation passed. In 2004, she secured unanimous support for the pivotal Kate Mullany National Historic Site Act. But she wasn't ready to rest on her laurels just yet. In 2006, she returned with a resolution to name a post office after Major George Quamo, a Vietnam War POW. In 2008 she got a New York highway named for Tim Russert, the late host of *Meet the Press*. Unfortunately for Clinton, this stellar track record was not enough to overcome the wave of Hope and Change and white guilt that swept Barack Obama into the presidency in 2008.

Sen. Clinton had to settle for becoming Secretary of State Clinton, and she took her same Senatorial work ethic to Foggy Bottom. On the surface, Clinton was busy jet-setting around the globe, glad-handing foreign dignitaries and working to prop up Obama's feckless foreign policy. As we learned from the release of some of the State Department emails she didn't get around to destroying, Clinton's real mission as Secretary of State was racking up frequent-flier miles and evolving her politics to suit the ever-shifting progressive winds. In a sense, Secretary Clinton's job had less to do with managing American diplomacy than with preparing for her future return to presidential politics.

Clinton was in the White House when her husband signed the Defense of Marriage Act, a law that advocates of gay marriage loathed. Throughout her time in the Senate, she had been vocal about the sanctity of marriage and the complementary nature of men and women. That had to change. Under Obama, the national mood had shifted and left-wing advocates had scored numerous victories, usually in courtrooms, almost never at the ballot box. Even Obama, who was for same-sex marriage before he was against same-sex marriage, returned to the pro-gay marriage position he had held as an unknown Illinois state senator. In 2013, Clinton published a choreographed video on the official State Department channel in which she fully recanted her entire history of support for traditional marriage. One year later, in an interview with NPR's Terry Gross, Clinton would awkwardly deny having changed her position at all.

Hillary also needed to update her environmental policy. In 2010, she said she was inclined to support the controversial Keystone XL Pipeline. The pipeline, which would transport crude oil from Canada to refineries in the U.S., later became a *cause célèbre* in the environmentalist left's war against fossil fuels. She flip-flopped when it became apparent that the pipeline would become something of a litmus test for liberals who believed every word of Al Gore's "documentary," *An Inconvenient Truth.*

Clinton's only real accomplishment, if you can call it that, came in North Africa, where the Secretary masterminded regime change in Libya. According to Clinton's State Department emails, she was the chief advocate in Obama's cabinet for an aggressive push to oust Libyan dictator Muammar Gaddafi. Her advisors, especially her off-the-books dirty trickster Sydney Blumenthal, insisted that bringing peace and democracy to Libya would be a powerful accomplishment to tout in the next presidential campaign. As we all now know, things didn't go quite the way Hillary and Sid Vicious had planned. That lone "accomplishment" would come back to haunt Clinton before she even departed the Obama administration.

Despite this paltry record of accomplishment, Clinton entered the Democrat primary as the prohibitive front-runner. The Democrats had a thin bench. Any Democrats with a slight inclination to seek higher office were afraid of challenging the Clinton Machine. She would have money—gobs of it—and she would have the support of a powerful alliance of liberals she and her husband had built up over the years. To face her and fail would mean ignominy and banishment from polite liberal circles. Vice President Joe Biden was perhaps the only Democrat who could have mounted a successful, mainstream challenge. But the untimely death of his son Joseph "Beau" Biden III had sapped his zeal for politics.

Some Democrats stepped up. Former Maryland Gov. Martin O'Malley threw his hat in the race. He enjoyed unlikely, early support from the Drudge Report, which posted images of O'Malley playing his guitar shirtless, an attempt, no doubt, to highlight Clinton's age. Former Rhode Island Gov. Lincoln Chaffee jumped in with a rousing call to get America on the metric system. Jim Webb, a former U.S. Senator from Virginia, who served as Secretary of the Navy under President Ronald Reagan, entered the race. But Webb, with his patriotism, his war record, and his unabashed love of country, was a non-starter in the modern Democrat Party. The stage looked clear for Clinton to waltz with ease to the Democrat nomination, but Vermont Sen. Bernie Sanders didn't get the memo that it was *her time.*

Clinton's struggle against Sanders would open gaping fissures in the left wing, exposing her vulnerabilities as a candidate. In some ways, I sympathized with the fight Clinton had on her hands against Sanders. In many respects, it was the same fight that conservatives had fought against the Democrat Party since at least Franklin Delano Roosevelt's New Deal and the concept of economic rights. In his 1944 State of the Union Address, FDR proposed a Second Bill of Rights.

Unlike the natural, inalienable rights Thomas Jefferson had articulated in the Declaration of Independence—life, liberty, and the pursuit of happiness—FDR's new economic rights flowed not from God but from government. It was the first time a president had proposed that the federal government be responsible for employment, housing, medical care, and retirement. Now, in addition to life, liberty, and the pursuit of happiness, the Democrats would add a fourth "inalienable right" for Americans—the right to free stuff, at somebody else's expense. Republicans quickly learned a hard lesson: You can't beat Santa Claus.

The progressive transformation of the federal government began with Roosevelt, but it metastasized with Lyndon B. Johnson's Great Society welfare programs. The Democrat Party had taken the political theories of socialism and attempted to bring into being a palatable America variety. It wasn't socialism, they said, it was social welfare, a safety net. But these policies of wealth redistribution, aimed nominally at helping the poor, also gave rise to a new political dynamic: welfare voters, i.e. low-income Americans who would vote according to which political party offered them the biggest slice of the tax-dollar pie. Democrats were rarely open and honest about this strategy, but it was nonetheless very effective at allowing the party to capture the votes of a large swath of the electorate. These were the "47 percent" that Mitt Romney had mentioned during the 2012 campaign—his numbers, which included Social Security recipients, were a little high, but not by much.

Most Democrats wisely remained mum about this strategy of buying off poor voters with welfare and handouts, but Sanders was a by-the-books socialist—not that he'd read very many—and he shamelessly embraced the give-away-free-stuff approach to politics. Subsidized student loans were not enough—all college would be free in Bernie Land. Health care? That's going to be free, too. Housing? Why should anyone have to pay for their own housing? He didn't want to reform entitlement programs, he wanted to expand them and create new ones. And he wanted to increase discretionary spending across the board, except for the military, of course.

And how would Bernie pay for his veritable cornucopia of free stuff?

By taxing the "millionaires and billionaires"—the oft-maligned boogeymen of Sanders' political rhetoric. Who cares if the math doesn't work? The platform of democratic socialism resonated with ignorant millennials who can't pay for their own health care because they'd rather spend their parents' money on marijuana and avocado toast.

Sanders was not some aberration. He was merely the culmination of what the Democrat Party has come to stand for: wealth redistribution, confiscatory taxes, government intervention in the economy, and cradle-to-grave subsidies. So, when Clinton stood up to Sanders and challenged the plausibility of his Santa Claus platform, she was challenging the very essence of the modern Democrat Party. Clinton was forced to make reality-based arguments to legions of Obamaphone-wielding voters who had been conditioned to deny reality.

Few could have predicted the way Sanders would electrify young American voters. His age alone made him an unlikely choice for the 18–34 year-old cohort that the Democrats relied on for activism, especially on college campuses. Beyond support for his free-stuff platform, Sanders the man became a viral social phenomenon. On Twitter, Sanders had 6.5 million followers. His supporters formed a Facebook group to create and share memes about him, posting pictures of the candidate with often comical captions. That group attracted 420,000 members. There was an online dating service established for Sanders supporters—Bernie Singles. The Sanders for President forum on *Reddit.com* reached 200,000 subscribers.

Sanders ran a campaign that was almost Trump-like. He toured progressive cities and gave speeches to packed rallies. He drew the kind of crowds that Hillary could only dream of: 3,000 in Minneapolis; 5,000 in Denver; 5,000 more in New York City; 10,000 in Madison, Wisc.; and 11,000 in Phoenix. In Portland, Ore., 28,000 of his supporters turned out and the following day in Los Angeles, 27,000 more showed up. Sanders' crowds were so big you could almost see the clouds of pot smoke rising above the arenas for miles.

But Sanders proved to have weak political instincts. At times, he gave Hillary gifts. For example, at the first Democratic debate, hosted by CNN in Las Vegas, Sanders exonerated Hillary for using the private e-mail server to conceal official government business from journalists and watchdog groups.

"Let me say something that may not be great politics," Sanders said. "The American people are sick and tired of hearing about your damn emails!"

Clinton smiled, laughed and nodded. She knew she could count on her supporters and former employees at every TV network to make sure that that clip would play thousands of times. Lincoln Chaffee, a former Republican, was the only candidate on the Democrat side foolish enough to raise the ethics issue, and even he was restrained.

"I think we need to have someone who has the best in ethical standards," the metric man said.

While Sanders was trying to take the high road, refusing to hit Clinton where it could have hurt her, Clinton and her allies were busy trying to shank the old codger. Take for example the emergence of an odd essay Sanders penned in 1972 for a hippie paper called *The Vermont Freeman*. The paper no longer exists, but somehow Sanders' article found its way into the hands of mainstream media reporters, forcing the socialist to answer some awkward questions.

"A woman enjoys intercourse with her man—as she fantasizes being raped by 3 men simultaneously," Sanders had opined. In another passage, he wrote, somewhat incoherently: "Do you know why the newspaper with the articles like, 'Girl, 12, raped by 14 men' sell so well? To what in us are they appealing?"

Sanders recanted his reminiscence on the topic of child gang rape.

The DNC, replete with Clintonistas and "Friends of Bill," also worked against Sanders in subtle, structural ways. The debate schedule was manipulated to ensure the smallest audiences possible. Four of the ten debates happened on Saturday or Sunday nights. Some debates were even scheduled against NFL games. Compared to the rollicking primetime debates happening on the Republican side, barely anyone was watching Sanders take on Clinton—and that worked to Clinton's advantage. She knew she just had to run out the clock and not make the kind of unforced errors that so often occur in debates.

As we learned later from the Podesta emails, Democrat agents within CNN, including Donna Brazile, then vice chair of the DNC, leaked questions before a debate to the Clinton campaign. If there's any doubt that Clinton was scared of the debates, just consider the last one on the schedule. It was scheduled just before the massive California primary, and Clinton bailed at the last minute. And it wasn't just the debates that were tilted in favor of Clinton. As we learned from the vast leaks of Democrat emails, the entire party apparatus was rigged against Sanders.

The first leaked emails to shake up the Democrat contest came from the website *DC Leaks*. Created in June 2016, the site was run by anonymous individuals and provided access to select journalists. *DC Leaks* revealed what Clinton's rivals had long suspected, that the Clinton campaign and the DNC were one and the same, working in concert to nominate Clinton while simultaneously sandbagging the Sanders campaign. This riled the left wing and eventually led to an unsuccessful lawsuit brought by Sanders supporters who had given money to the DNC.

DC Leaks revealed that the Clinton campaign and the DNC were spying on delegates loyal to Sanders. In a leaked email from May 2016, Marlon Marshall, a Hillary staffer, circulated two documents with several other campaign dirty tricksters. One was a spreadsheet with detailed information about several Sanders supporters and delegates, including physical addresses, email addresses, phone numbers, and histories of political giving pulled from the FEC.

The documents were titled, "Unity Check." How Orwellian…and it got creepier. The depth of research the campaign had conducted suggested that the campaign devoted a great deal of time to investigating the social media accounts of Sanders' supporters. Hillary's people even graded their fellow Democrats according to how likely they would be to defect from Hillary.

"Denise Groves is critical of Hillary Clinton for being a war hawk and she hopes for a contested convention," wrote the researchers. "All of her Facebook posts are strong pro-Bernie."

More than 700 of Sanders delegates were subjected to the Unity Check.

In another email exchange from May 2016, top DNC staffers appeared to be conducting opposition research on Sanders and theorizing on how it might be used against him. The most notorious involved Sanders' religion—or lack thereof. The DNC's chief financial officer, Brad Marshall, was the author of that smoking-gun email. He wrote to several colleagues at 1:31 AM suggesting that southern voters might be put off by Sanders' atheism.

"It might make no difference," Marshall wrote, "but for KY and WVA can we get someone to ask his belief. Does he believe in a God? He had skated on saying he has a Jewish heritage. I think I read he is an atheist. This could make several points difference with my peeps. My Southern Baptist peeps would draw a big difference between a Jew and an atheist."

"It's the Jesus thing," Marshall added in a separate email minutes later, to which the DNC's Chief Executive Officer Amy K. Dacey replied, "AMEN".

DNC chair Debbie Wasserman Schultz was also caught up in the leaks. The Nevada state Democratic convention had been a raucous affair, with Sanders supporters alleging shenanigans by pro-Hillary party officials. Sanders' campaign chair had made the media rounds stoking the allegations, and the Florida congresswoman wasn't pleased.

"Damned liar," she wrote, "Particularly scummy that he barely acknowledges the violent and threatening behavior that occurred."

That wasn't Wasserman Schultz's only controversial quip to make it into the public domain. Responding to a POLITICO story in which Sanders said the Democrat Party wasn't treating him fairly, Wasserman Schultz wrote, "Spoken like someone who has never been a member of the Democratic Party and has no understanding of what we do."

Wasserman Schultz wasn't feeling the Bern.

On the eve of the Democrat primary in New York, Sanders again lashed out at Clinton and the DNC, raising questions about fair treatment. This time, Sanders alleged that Clinton had violated campaign finance laws via a joint fundraising committee set up the previous year with the national party organization. The flap never materialized into any serious campaign finance investigation, but it did prompt Clinton campaign lawyer Mark Elias to pen some advice for the DNC, further evidencing unethical, potentially illegal, coordination between the groups.

"My suggestion is that the DNC put out a statement saying that the accusations the Sanders campaign [is making] are not true," wrote Elias. "Just as the RNC pushes back directly on Trump over 'rigged system', the DNC should push back DIRECTLY at Sanders and say that what he is saying is false and harmful to the the the [sic] Democratic Party."

In other words, Clinton's top campaign lawyer was instructing the DNC to call Sanders a liar, publicly and directly, even though his accusations of unfair play were entirely merited.

All of the DNC leaks reinforced the Sanders supporters' claims that the DNC was rigging the process in favor of Clinton. And Trump was there, ready to crystallize the narrative for voters.

"Leaked e-mails of DNC show plans to destroy Bernie Sanders. Mock his heritage and much more. On-line from *Wikileaks*, really vicious. RIGGED," he tweeted.

The DNC leaks were embarrassing to the party apparatus. They showed that this allegedly neutral arbiter of Democrat Party politics was corrupt; they were proof that the system was rigged to protect connected insiders and destroy those who questioned the party elite. However, by the time the DNC leaks started flowing, Clinton was already a sure bet to win the nomination.

Failing to take the gloves off with Clinton wasn't Sanders' only mistake. Some were simple gaffes, but others pointed to the candidate's fundamental ignorance of the policy areas he talked about the most, often in hilarious fashion. Take student debt. The promise to wipe out every college student's loans was one of Sanders' biggest talking points. Polling consistently showed that young voters with student loan debt were inclined to support him. But did he really understand the financial side of the student loan industry, or lending in general?

"You have families out there paying 6, 8, 10 percent on student debt but you can refinance your homes at 3 percent. What sense is that?" Sanders tweeted in December. That tweet led to widespread mockery of Bernie on social media. Collateral, how does it work? Of course, students have no collateral, so they pay higher rates than people who have homes that can be foreclosed upon. The *Weekly Standard*'s Bill Kristol summed up the reaction, calling it the "most economically illiterate tweet ever."

That wasn't the only time Sanders revealed his basic economic ignorance.

In an interview with CNBC's John Harwood, Sanders lamented the over-abundance of choice in American supermarkets, especially when it came to deodorant.

"You can't just continue growth for the sake of growth" he said, "in a world in which we are struggling with climate change and all kinds of environmental problems. Alright? You don't necessarily need a choice of 23 underarm spray deodorants or of 18 different pairs of sneakers when children are hungry in this country."

Sanders, like many other Democrats, was opposed to *Citizens United* and wanted new laws that would prevent wealthy organizations and individuals from participating in the political process. But his vision for getting money out of politics was often incoherent.

"Let's ask why it is that we pay by far the highest prices in the world for prescription drugs and your medicine can be doubled tomorrow and there's nothing the government can do to stop it." he said in a February speech. "You think it has anything to do with the huge amounts of campaign contributions and lobbying from the fossil fuel industry?"

Huh?

On foreign policy, Sanders often revealed that he was a lightweight, pre-ferring instead to stay safely within the bounds of a social welfare policy. For example, in a debate following the ISIS terrorist attacks in Paris, the modera-tors asked Sanders to respond. He said he was "shocked" and "disgusted," but then he immediately pivoted back to domestic policy, i.e., free stuff.

Sanders also struggled to comprehend the emerging force in leftist politics that was the Black Lives Matter movement. On the trail, he provoked the ire of young black activists by talking about poor blacks living in "ghettos." And the activists confronted him in person on more than a few occasions.

"We're shutting this event down—now," shouted an activist who had leapt on stage and stolen Sanders' microphone. Sanders stood meekly to the side while the young leftist raved. After a four-and-half minute "moment" of silence for Michael Brown, the young black thug who was killed in Ferguson, MO, after trying to steal a police officer's service weapon, Sanders ended the event.

For all his flaws, and there were many, Sanders understood better than Clinton—and better than many Republicans—what the Trump phenomenon was all about. In an interview on *Face the Nation*, Sanders said "[m]any of Trump's supporters are working-class people and they're angry, they're angry because their jobs have left this country and gone to China or other low-wage countries, they're angry because they can't afford to send their kids to college so they can't retire with dignity."

Sanders' Trumpian position on trade, specifically the Trans-Pacific Partnership (TPP), put Clinton in an uncomfortable bind. The TPP was a sweeping trade agreement that included the U.S., Australia, Canada, Japan, Mexico, Singapore, Vietnam, and a handful of other Pacific nations. The agreement covered virtually every aspect of the economy, from manufacturing and intellectual property to pharmaceuticals and beef.

During the Obama administration, U.S. trade representatives and multinational corporations designed the document out of public view. But as the public learned more about the pact and its potential influence on America's already struggling manufacturing sector, the once inevitable agreement was jeopardized. Thanks to the twin populist movements emerging with Sanders on the left and with Trump on the right, the American people were souring on massive, secretive trade deals. The TPP became a symbol in the battle of the populists versus the elites, and this was a big problem for Clinton, because her fingerprints were all over it. Clinton only aggravated her TPP problem by doing what a Clinton always does: lying.

Clinton's involvement with and support of the TPP was a matter of extensive public record. In 2011, she told a committee in Congress that even though the State Department was not directly in charge of negotiating the trade pact, her office worked closely with the trade representatives who were. Diplomatic cables obtained by *Wikileaks* showed that Clinton's top staffers discussed the TPP with various heads of state. In 2012, Clinton told an Australian audience that the TPP would "lower trade barriers, raise labor and environmental standards, and drive growth across the region."

According to one tally, Clinton openly expressed support for the trade deal at least 45 times during her tenure as Secretary of State.

"We've used trade negotiations over the Trans-Pacific Partnership to find common ground with a former adversary in Vietnam," she said in her 2013 remarks to the Council on Foreign Relations.

A year before that she called the TPP the "gold standard" in free trade agreements.

Clinton's support of the TPP was extensive, but somehow she thought she could turn a 180 and convince voters that she truly, in her heart of hearts, opposed the very trade deal she had helped negotiate and once called the gold standard.

"I did not work on TPP," Clinton told reporters in July 2015.

By October, her transformation was complete. "As of today, I am not in favor of what I have learned about it," she told PBS's Judy Woodruff. "I don't believe it's going to meet the high bar I have set."

Conservative media joined Sanders in mocking Clinton's transparent flip-flop.

No one believed Clinton. By the time she was nominated, her closest allies were openly confirming that her flip-flop was fraudulent, a cynical ploy for Sanders' voters. After his convention address in Philadelphia, Virginia Gov. Terry McAuliffe, a longtime personal friend of the Clintons, told POLITICO that Clinton would get back on the globalist-trade train after the election.

"Once the election's over," he said, "and we sit down on trade, people understand a couple things we want to fix on it but going forward we got to build a global economy."

Pressed on whether Clinton would reverse her reversal after she became president, McAuliffe for once was honest: "Yes. Listen, she was in support of it. There were specific things in it she wants fixed."

This was a classic Kinsley Gaffe—the longtime Friend of Bill was telling the truth, but it was a little too early for Clinton. She still had to overcome a Republican candidate whose antipathy for the TPP surpassed even Sanders'. And so Hillary's campaign manager Podesta endeavored to correct the record: "Love Gov. McAuliffe, but he got this one flat wrong," he tweeted. "Hillary opposes TPP BEFORE and AFTER the election. Period. Full stop."

Sanders pie-in-the-sky political platform was bonkers, but at a human level he understood why people were attracted to Trump, and he understood the economic anxieties that left millions of Americans feeling like they were no longer in control of their own destinies. He was tuned into the broadly shared sense that the elite powerbrokers in Washington, D.C. and on Wall Street were running roughshod over the American working class. Hillary, on the other hand, had drunk deeply of the left-wing identity politics Kool-Aid. The only reason she could possibly imagine that working-class people would support Trump is because they were all a bunch of irredeemable, bitter-clinging racists.

Sanders never stood a chance against the powerful Clinton machine and he probably knew that. But he was interested in dragging the Democrat Party even further left. Because of his popularity, Sanders was able both to skew the policies of the party in his favor and seriously damage Clinton's credibility with a large swath of liberal voters.

By the time Clinton arrived at the Democrat convention to accept the nomination, she had won just 55.2 percent of the popular vote, with Sanders taking 43.1 percent. Clinton won 34 states, while Sanders won 23, including Michigan and Wisconsin—two states that would later become pivotal for Trump. Sanders' challenge was serious, but due to the structure of the Democrat Party's nomination rules, it was never more than an annoyance. Clinton ended with 2,842 delegates to Sanders' 1,865, thanks to the Super Delegates—politically connected party insiders who can always be counted on to be loyal to the power and money centers of the party.

The fallout from the bitter primary was severe, and it was greatly exacerbated by not only the DNC leaks, but by additional leaks that would emerge late in the general election campaign. What was once a small group of Sanders supporters who said they would refuse to vote for Clinton began to grow. Inflamed by the treachery of the Democrat establishment, a new movement formed: Bernie or Bust. It was basically the left-wing version of the Never Trump movement. At the DNC convention in Philadelphia, the Bernie Bros came ready to make it clear that they would not fall in line. Sanders took the podium to speak and the crowd of liberals loved it. They cheered all of his usual stump speech lines. They even cheered when he called for the defeat of the GOP nominee.

But when he said, "We have got to elect Hillary Clinton," the crowd booed.

Chapter Six
Everything But the Kitchen Sink

DONALD TRUMP KICKED OFF 2016 WITH A BANG. WITH THE FIRST PRESIDENTIAL primary just weeks away, Trump enjoyed a striking lead in the polls. As the New Year began, more than one-third of GOP primary voters were backing the real estate mogul, and his GOP rivals were floundering. His closest competitor was Ted Cruz, who was struggling to break 20 percent in the polls. Trump had even begun making television ad buys in the early primary and caucus states, a rare event for a candidate who was already a ubiquitous presence on American television screens.

In early January, campaign manager Corey Lewandowski made the call to bring the GOP front-runner to his hometown of Lowell, Mass., about five miles south of the New Hampshire border. It turned out to be one of the larger rallies of his campaign. The campaign had ambitiously booked the 8000-seat Tsongas Arena, named after the late Sen. Paul Tsongas. Afterwards local officials said the rally was probably over capacity. The line to get into the event stretched several blocks, with thousands of die-hard Trump fans from New Hampshire and Massachusetts waiting hours in the 29-degree weather for a chance to see Trump perform. Lewandowski knew his old neighbors, and how much they loved his new boss.

In Lowell, Trump rattled off his usual lines for the audience and introduced some new material as well. He didn't want to run for office, he said, but there were too many stupid things going on for him not to offer his unique skill set to the nation.

The crowd cheered.

On the Iran deal: John Kerry has no idea what he's doing. Again, the crowd roared in agreement.

On Jeb Bush: He's spent $59 million and he's at the bottom of the barrel. Laughter.

Trump even invoked his friend and golf partner, New England Patriots quarterback Tom Brady.

"He's a winner," said Trump. "Even injured, he's better than anyone else."

At the time, the so-called experts were still proclaiming that crowd size had no connection to election support. But it was difficult for me to believe that anybody willing—actually eager—to stand in line outside in the frigid New England dusk to see Trump speak wouldn't pull a lever for him. Trump himself was well aware of his supporters' loyalty. In Sioux City, Iowa, he told a gaggle of reporters that he "could stand in the middle of Fifth Avenue and shoot somebody and I wouldn't lose voters."

Trump's GOP opponents were likewise uncomfortably aware that his voters were more loyal than any they'd encountered in their previous campaigns. The struggle to win over Trump supporters led the opposing campaigns to make some tone-deaf mistakes that mushroomed into significant blunders. Take, for example, the reaction of Cruz's campaign after 2008 Vice Presidential candidate Sarah Palin decided to endorse Trump.

In mid-January, rumors were swirling about Palin's endorsement. Although her star had faded more than somewhat after she prematurely resigned as governor of Alaska, she still retained a following among conservatives, especially the kind of Christian conservatives and Tea Partiers who were sure to be involved in the Iowa caucuses. The more conservative candidates had been lobbying behind the scenes to earn her endorsement. By Cruz's own admission, Palin's help had been critical to his 2012 Senate victory in Texas, an upset over the GOPe candidate, the state's lieutenant governor. So Cruz was naturally eager to recreate that winning formula. But when Cruz staffers started to realize that Palin was going to endorse a New York billionaire over their candidate, whom they considered more ideologically (and theologically) compatible to Palin, things got nasty.

Bristol Palin, the former governor's daughter, quickly turned the simmering cold war hot in a Facebook post.

"Is my mom going to endorse Donald Trump for president of the United States?" Bristol Palin wrote. "That's the rumor, and I've been too busy with diapers to delve too much into politics these days. But the rumors were enough to cause staffers from Ted Cruz's office to slam my mom."

She quoted remarks by Rick Tyler, Cruz's campaign spokesman, during a CNN hit, effectively threatening to label Palin a Christian hypocrite if she failed to back Cruz.

"I think it [would] be a blow to Sarah Palin," he said, "because Sarah Palin has been a champion for the conservative cause, and if she was going to endorse Donald Trump, sadly, she would be endorsing someone who's held progressive views all his life on the sanctity of life, on marriage, on partial-birth abortion."

Bristol went on: "Hearing what Cruz is now saying about my mom, in a negative knee-jerk reaction, makes me hope my mom does endorse Trump. Cruz's flip-flop, turning against my mom who's done nothing but support and help him when others sure didn't, shows he's a typical politician. How rude that he's setting up a false narrative about her!"

The younger Palin's comment raced across the internet, fueling speculation and fostering the type of obsessive media coverage that Trump had mastered. Trump and Palin further stoked the flames. She tweeted out a link to her daughter's rant about Cruz, saying, "Is THIS Why People Don't like Cruz?" And Trump tweeted out a warning that he would be joined at his Ames, Iowa rally that evening by a special, mystery guest. (Spoiler alert: It was Palin.)

Cruz's most memorable attack on Trump happened on my radio show, and it's safe to say it backfired.

Trump had been raising questions about the senator's eligibility to run for president, claiming that the Canadian-born Cruz would face lawsuits from the Democrat Party if he won the nomination. Trump had even adopted Bruce Springsteen's "Born in the U.S.A" as the theme song of his rallies. So of course I had to give Cruz the needle when he came on my show. I played a few bars of the song and asked Cruz to respond. He was prepared.

"I think he may shift in his new rallies to playing 'New York, New York,' because, you know, Donald comes from New York and he embodies New York values."

If you're keeping score at home, that's four mentions of the Big Apple in his first sentence of the interview. That's what Comrade Chris Matthews calls a dog whistle. What Cruz meant was that, among other things, Trump did not hold traditional Republican positions on gay marriage, his stance on abortion had "evolved," and he had run casinos.

But Cruz couldn't just come out and say that. Instead, he wrote off an entire state—the Empire State, as it used to be called—and irritated everyone with even remote ties to New York City. I'm sure the line poll-tested well in Kansas and Colorado, but it was yet another display of Cruz's passive-aggressive smarminess—a style of campaigning that put off many voters. When NBC and ABC started calling the studio asking for audio of the exchange, I knew that Cruz's jab was going to make the nightly news.

By the time the New York primary rolled around, Cruz was probably wishing he could have gotten that line back.

Skipping the Debate

Trump's campaign, to that point, had been a series of bold, unprecedented moves that no campaign consultant in his right mind would have recommended. He had sparred head-on with a Vietnam war hero and survived. He had taken on a popular Fox News anchor and prevailed. He had mocked, ridiculed, and jabbed his way to the top of the most competitive GOP field in generations. And, as the non-politician in the race, he had easily won every early GOP primary debate. When it came to the last debate before the Iowa caucuses in January, Trump again triumphed—and without showing up.

Trump understood better than anyone in the modern post-mass media era how to exploit the 24-hour news cycle. With a simple tweet, Trump could set the news narrative for the day and ensure himself universal coverage on both broadcast and cable TV networks. He was outrageous and over-the-top—in other words, he was great TV.

Conservative networks like Fox, Newsmax and some emerging online networks covered him 24/7 because the conservative audience loved the spectacle. They couldn't get enough of Trump trashing the idols of the progressive left and the establishment GOP.

The liberal networks like MSNBC and CNN covered him non-stop, too, but for a different reason. They kept the cameras rolling because they had a deep, abiding faith that if they aired Trump being Trump long enough, he would eventually commit some singularly devastating gaffe that would end his political career. Trump courted controversy, and he was rewarded with billions of dollars worth of earned media, which is to say, free coverage.

Bombastic remarks on anything—immigrants, food stamps, trade, Rand Paul's hair, Marco Rubio's boots, anything!—helped Trump keep the media focused on himself. But he also skillfully managed feuds with the media themselves to keep himself in the headlines. He was living in their heads rent-free, as they say. And the last debate in Iowa was no exception. In the runup to that spectacle, Trump renewed his grudge match with Fox anchor Megyn Kelly. Ever since the "blood" remark, the pair's relationship had been icy. So, Trump laid down a marker: He'd only do the Fox debate, he said, if Kelly were replaced as a moderator. Fox didn't budge; neither did Trump.

Cruz responded to Trump's debate threats by throwing down a gauntlet of his own. The Princeton-trained master debater challenged Trump to a one-on-one showdown in Iowa. He reserved a venue and matched Trump's pledge to give a seven-figure sum to charity. The canny Canadian thought he'd boxed Trump in, that the front-runner would shy away. But Trump responded in an unorthodox manner that would leave Cruz reeling to explain how someone who was born in Canada could become the U.S. President.

Trump's reply to Cruz was simple: After we know you're constitutionally eligible to be president, Senator, then we'll debate.

"Once you've gotten that ruling from the federal judge and you're the last man standing in this presidential contest next to Donald Trump," Corey

Lewandowski said, "we'll be happy to have a debate with you one on one, anywhere you want, because that's the way the system works. But, as it stands right now, we don't even know if Ted Cruz is legally eligible to run for president of the United States. And the bottom line is, you know, what we've said to Ted Cruz: go into court, seek a declaratory judgment to find out if you're even legally eligible to run for president of the United States."

Cruz dropped his publicity stunt. And so, for the first time in modern presidential history, the front-runner of a major party skipped a nationally televised debate.

Blowing off the debate seemed an extraordinary risk. At the time, the lesser candidates were elbowing one another to break out, each hoping to become the last man standing against Trump. Without the front-runner on the stage, his competitors would be more comfortable—one less wild card to deal with. Trump would also not be able to defend himself against the inevitable attacks lobbed his way. That's precisely how the debate started out.

"I'm a maniac, and everyone on this stage is stupid, fat and ugly," Cruz said, an attempt, as he put it, to get "the Donald Trump portion" of the program over with.

Which, of course, just reminded everyone of Donald Trump yet again. And Trump, like the TV pro that he was, was engaged in what the networks call counterprogramming against the debate.

As the other candidates pulled out their white papers and droned on about top marginal tax rates, the GOP front-runner held a boisterous competing event in a nearby hall. He billed it as a fundraiser for veterans. By the end of the night, Trump's effort had raised, according to the candidate, $6 million for various veterans' groups. But the real purpose of the telethon was to show, once again, that Trump would not be bound by the norms and shibboleths of the GOP establishment.

Even Fox News, the most powerful force in conservative media, couldn't contain him. Trump told reporters that he had received several calls from Fox representatives and even then-CEO Roger Ailes imploring him to change his mind about boycotting the Iowa debate. Trump challenged the network: Give $5 million to veterans' charities and I'll consider gracing your event with my presence. Fox balked.

In a statement from his campaign after the event, Trump let Fox know they were still more than welcome to join his effort by making a charitable contribution. The message to Fox was clear: You need me more than I need you. Judging by social media that night, he was right: Trump dominated the various online platforms despite his absence from the stage. Thirty-six percent of all Twitter traffic mentioned Trump. He was the most-searched-for candidate, according to Google.

Two days later, Iowa held its first caucuses—the first time in his life that Trump would officially be on a ballot. As the first official contest of the primary season, Iowa is important. Its outcome can elevate candidates who have been struggling, as Trump's opponents had been. In 2012, for example, Rick Santorum's surprise win in Iowa briefly gave new life to a lackluster candidate's campaign. The last thing Trump needed was a Santorum-type, say, Ben Carson, beginning a surge in the Hawkeye State.

Expectations were not high for Trump. In the final days, his polling edge was well within the margin of error. And there was some question as to whether the Iowa GOP's mostly evangelical Christian voting base would turn out for a candidate whose life had been, shall we say, less than Biblical. Plus, Iowa was a caucus state, not a primary state.

That caucus system heavily favored traditional Republican candidates and hindered insurgent candidates who might attract independent voters—the type of people who were unlikely to find themselves at an hours-long caucus on a snowy Midwestern evening. Moreover, Trump's thin campaign organization stood in stark contrast to the establishment candidates. Cruz, Rubio, Bush, Paul—they all had seasoned operatives on board who could probably name every county in Iowa, and had been working most of them for four months.

When the night was over, Cruz had edged Trump, grabbing 27.6 percent of the vote to Trump's 24.3 percent. Rubio came in third with 23.1 percent, and Carson finished a distant fourth. In terms of delegates, it was not a huge loss for Trump; he walked away with seven to Cruz's eight.

Cruz touted his victory as a sign that, despite all the unconventional bluster of the campaign season, Republican voters still favored traditional, socially conservative politicians. But accusations of dirty tricks marred his narrow victory. Carson, who was competing with Cruz for the evangelical vote, pointed the finger at Cruz for spreading rumors throughout caucus sites that Carson had dropped out of the race. A vote for Carson, the Cruz operatives whispered, would be wasted. The accusation that Cruz, that self-proclaimed paragon of moral virtue, would stoop to dirty tricks sucked much of the air out of his victory.

"Ted Cruz didn't win Iowa," Trump tweeted, "He stole it. That is why all of the polls were so wrong and why he got far more votes than anticipated. Bad!"

Donald Trump didn't dwell on his loss in Iowa. He flew east in his 747 to New Hampshire, coming on my radio show the day after the caucuses. I was broadcasting live from Milford, N.H., the site of Trump's first post-Iowa campaign rally. Scott Brown, the former US senator from Massachusetts who had unsuccessfully run in New Hampshire against Sen. Jeanne Shaheen in 2014, was on hand to deliver Trump his first big Granite State endorsement. (Brown is now the US ambassador to New Zealand.)

"Were you expecting to win last night in Iowa?" I asked Trump.

"Well, I didn't know," he said. The tone of his voice suggested he was expecting a victory. "I didn't spend overly there. I started thinking that I maybe could have, but I came in second, and you know, frankly, I'm very happy with it. I guess I got almost the same number of delegates."

Winning almost as many delegates was small consolation for Trump. I could tell he was more interested in winning outright—keeping his juggernaut going. When I brought up the amount of money his opposition had spent in Iowa, Trump remarked on the efficiency of his campaign. "I did the best job per dollar spent," he said. But then, for the first time in his campaign, he began to suggest that his pledge to self-fund his campaign might not be worth it.

"You know," he mused, "nobody goes around into the voting booth and goes, 'Oh, Trump's self-funding his campaign so I'm going to vote for him.' And, you know, I could have hundreds of millions of dollars put in, you know, because I know all the rich people. They would contribute in two seconds if I asked them to. I would make Jeb Bush's fund, where he had $128 million, I'd make it look like small potatoes."

He paused to consider the possibilities.

"I could have had a fund, $300-400 million, I think," he finally said.

I asked him about Cruz's dirty tricks against Carson.

"I think it's disgusting," he said. "It turned out to be a totally disgusting, bogus lie."

Was he going to go after Cruz? I asked.

"I didn't think it was nice what he did to Ben Carson," Trump said.

I let him know that Bush had been in New Hampshire attacking him.

"You know," he said, "it's sad what's going on with Jeb."

We turned to Hillary. The Democratic caucus in Iowa had been a nail biter. It wound up coming down to coin tosses in several counties. Remarkably, Clinton won six consecutive coin tosses.

"Howie, I want to see the coin!" he said, "I want that coin!"

He brought up Clinton's email server, so I asked: Do you think she should be indicted?

"Well it looks to me like it was a criminal act," he said. "I think personally she's going to be protected by the Democrats, if you ask me."

That turned out to be prescient, to say the least.

"She's guilty," he added. "It's not like 'oh, gee, let's study it.'"

The New Hampshire Debate

The first-in-the-nation Primary is always a critical moment in the presidential elections cycle. Although Iowa comes first, it's a caucus state, and Hawkeye voters are notoriously quirky and not necessarily reflective of the broader American electorate. New Hampshire, by comparison, is an open primary election with high turnout and a somewhat more mainstream voting base. The establishment GOP candidates once again pumped massive sums of money into advertisements, mailers, and ground game. Donald Trump, in contrast, spent very little on paid advertising, relying instead on spirited rallies and interviews on my radio show, which is broadcast on eight stations throughout New Hampshire.

What turned out to be New Hampshire's most consequential primary debate happened in Goffstown, just three days before Granite State voters headed to the polls. Several lesser candidates had dropped out of the race before the Iowa caucuses and the field was beginning to thin. More voters were turning into free agents as their preferred candidates suspended their campaigns.

On the night of the debate, Trump was a clear leader in the current public opinion surveys, but Marco Rubio was coming on. On Feb. 3, Trump led the field of candidates with 33 percent support from Republican voters. But three days later, his support had fallen to 30 percent. Marco Rubio climbed from 10 percent to 17 percent, after a stronger-than-expected third place finish in Iowa. Trump's support appeared to be wavering, while Rubio's was growing. Comparisons were being made to another famous Saturday-night debate in New Hampshire—the 1980 faceoff in Nashua, when Ronald Reagan schooled both George H. W. Bush and the debate moderator, yelling "I paid for this microphone, Mr. Green!" (His name was actually Breen, not Green.) That evening, Rubio was dreaming of using his Saturday-night debate to become the next Reagan. But it was not to be.

As we all know now, Rubio gave one of the worst debate performances of his entire career, and it had next to nothing to do with Trump. The sweaty Floridian had taken his consultants' advice to pivot away from primary spats and press his argument against the Obama administration and Hillary Clinton.

Rather than attack his GOP competitors, he would focus his barbs on Democrats. But the typically well-spoken Senator was nervous and unfocused, and his campaign train derailed that night in Goffstown.

Amid an exchange with Chris Christie, Rubio leveled the same canned anti-Obama line not once or twice, but four times. He might have gotten away with it, but Christie was there to mock and belittle the Florida senator for acting like a typical politician, and doing it so poorly. It was an odd moment in politics, and no one really knew what happened.

"Rubio Repeats Himself 4x In Epic Debate Fiasco," read one headline.

Three days after Rubio's self-immolation, New Hampshire voters headed to the polls and voted overwhelmingly for Trump. The New Yorker earned 100,735 votes, more than 35 percent of the total. Kasich finished second with 15.7 percent, followed by Cruz with 11.6 percent. Rubio finished a dismal fifth—behind even low-energy Jeb Bush. Christie, having played a key role in destroying Rubio's short-lived post-Iowa momentum, finished last in the primary and dropped out of the race shortly after. It was a triumphant moment for Trump—his first major electoral victory. And the win only added more vigor and enthusiasm to a movement that continued gathering steam.

One other fact must be noted about the New Hampshire primary—it proved how little newspaper endorsements now mean. Thanks in large measure first to television and then to the internet, newspapers had been declining in power for decades. As recently as the 1990s, newspaper endorsements were highly coveted by both Republicans and Democrats. Local voters had strong, loyal relationships with their dailies. There was trust. And if the editors of the paper you read every morning said Candidate Smith was the right choice for whatever office he was seeking, that meant something. Even well into the 2000s, candidates would still make the obligatory pilgrimage to a newspaper for an audition in front of the editorial board, pleading for support.

Trump's striking victory in New Hampshire rendered newspaper endorsements meaningless.

The right-leaning *Union Leader* endorsed Christie, as did my paper, the *Boston Herald*, which has strong circulation in the southern part of the state. The *Conway Daily Sun* backed Bush. The *Portsmouth Herald*, *Foster's Daily Democrat*, and the *Nashua Telegraph* all threw their support behind Kasich. Not a single New Hampshire paper backed Trump, making his victory a complete rebuke of the Granite State's establishment media.

The so-called newspaper primary even spilled over into the national media after Trump went to war with *Union Leader* publisher Joe McQuaid. He had succeeded legendary New Hampshire kingmaker William Loeb, but Joe Mc-Quaid was no William Loeb. McQuaid, however, demanded respect for the power he and his newspaper had long since ceded to the new media.

Of all the daily newspapers in New Hampshire, the *Union Leader* was historically the most important, mostly because the paper had resisted the almost-total liberalization of print media. The paper held fast to its right-of-center editorial bent, which gave its endorsements extra weight in the GOP primary. Under McQuaid's leadership, the *Union Leader* endorsed Chris Christie in November 2015. And following that decision, McQuaid routinely used the pages of his paper to level blistering, Loeb-style broadsides against Trump.

In December 2015, in a front-page editorial, McQuaid compared Trump to "Biff," the buffoonish villain from *Back to the Future*.

At a rally in New Hampshire, Trump returned the favor.

"You know, I don't know how you feel about this, but I have to do it," he said. "So, you have a newspaper up here, the *Union Leader*."

He paused to savor the scattered boos from the crowd.

"Do you know about this newspaper? This guy's a bad guy. His name is Joe McQuaid," he said. "He's a bad person, and he uses his weight, pushes his weight around, thinks he's hot stuff."

Trump predicted the imminent demise of the paper, insisting McQuaid had run it into the ground. He even suggested that McQuaid's anger with Trump stemmed from his decision not to purchase ads in the paper.

The next day, in another front-page editorial headlined "Con man Trump," McQuaid accused the New York businessman of insulting voters and laughing at them behind their backs. The publisher mocked Trump's reputation as a straight talker, saying he was as "slick and oily a pol as any we have seen." McQuaid described Trump as a "school-yard rich-kid bully who thinks he can push around networks, newspapers and opponents while conning voters at the same time."

McQuaid continued: "We have seen that con before and we don't think New Hampshire voters are going to fall for it."

Trump's convincing triumph in the New Hampshire primary showed that the *Union Leader*'s glory days as a political powerhouse were long gone. But McQuaid's humiliation was not yet complete. After Christie, the preferred candidate of the *Union Leader*, suspended his campaign, the New Jersey governor threw his support behind Trump. In an unprecedented and utterly pointless move, the scorned McQuaid then retracted his endorsement of Christie.

Who could blame McQuaid for his frustration? The writing was on the wall. In a time of shrinking circulation, plummeting advertising revenue, and overall irrelevance for the *Union Leader*, Trump's easy victory over the traditional brokers of political power in New Hampshire media indicated a sea change. Would future candidates come crawling to the Joe McQuaids of the world to plead on bended knee for endorsements? I doubt it. Ed Muskie famously began weeping in front of the *Union Leader* building back during the 1972 Democrat primary after the paper ran a devastating story about his wife. William Loeb had reduced the Democrat frontrunner to tears. Loeb's successor 44 years later reduced the Republican frontrunner to tears … of laughter and derision.

The defenestration of newspaper editors was just one change among many to American politics brought about by the historical candidacy of Donald Trump.

War with The Pope

Before New Hampshire town clerks had even finished counting the ballots, the controversy that would dominate the news going into the South Carolina primary was already building. Just one day earlier, Pope Francis had delivered passive-aggressive remarks aimed at Donald Trump and his central campaign plank, building a wall on the southern border. The Argentine-born leader of the Roman Catholic Church backhanded Trump, saying that building a border wall "is not Christian."

The pontiff no doubt intended his statement to serve as a call to American Catholics to reject Trump's politics and support a different, less "divisive" candidate. But like so many other powerful institutions, the Vatican had yet to realize that Trump was rewriting the political rule book. The Pope unknowingly handed Trump a major gift that would ensure his continued dominance of the headlines.

"I don't think he understands the danger of the open border we have with Mexico," Trump said on Fox Business. "And I think Mexico got him to do it because Mexico wants to keep the border just the way it is, because they're making a fortune and we're losing."

The Vatican initially insisted that Francis was speaking about migration generally, not trying to inject himself into U.S. politics. But that non-denial denial didn't stand up. On his flight back to the Vatican from the U.S.-Mexico border, the Pope again took aim at Trump—this time directly.

"A person who thinks only about building walls—wherever they may be—and not building bridges, is not Christian," the Pope pronounced. "This is not in the Gospel."

The Pope was asked if he was planning to endorse anyone else.

"As far as what you said about whether I would advise to vote or not to vote, I am not going to get involved in that," he said. "I say only that this man is not Christian if he said things like that. We must see if he said things in that way and in this I give the benefit of the doubt."

Trump fired back in a written statement: "For a religious leader to question a person's faith is disgraceful. I am proud to be a Christian and as President I will not allow Christianity to be consistently attacked and weakened, unlike what is happening now, with our current President."

In other words, the Pope's statement was Papal bull.

Trump's Papal spat was covered wall-to-wall for nearly two weeks. The back-and-forth dominated the media's election coverage. Nothing the other candidates did mattered. Who wanted to cover an endorsement for Rubio or a policy paper from Jeb Bush when a New York billionaire was openly feuding with the Holy See?

As the remaining GOP candidates headed into South Carolina for a pivotal debate, Ted Cruz had to be wishing the Pope had put the blast on him.

The Never Trump Movement

The Never Trump movement had been building all winter. As more and more GOP candidates fell by the wayside, disgruntled former staffers and supporters were bitter. The dreams of following their candidate into the White House had been dashed, so they were angry at Trump. Like Joe McQuaid before them, pundits, columnists, and media personalities who fancied themselves opinion leaders were dismayed that no one cared any longer about their opinions. In February, the Never Trump movement launched its salvo via an entire issue of *National Review* magazine dedicated to bashing Trump.

All the good anti-Trump conservatives took turns bashing the GOP frontrunner.

Recovering drug addict-turned-Mormon Glenn Beck attacked Trump for supporting the bailout of General Motors and Obama's stimulus program. David Boaz, president of the libertarian Cato Institute, compared Trump to George Wallace and called him an American Mussolini. Brent Bozell, the head of the Media Research Center, criticized Trump for not reading *National Review* enough. *Weekly Standard* Editor Bill Kristol took aim at Trump's commercial proclivities, calling him the epitome of vulgarity. Radio host Michael Medved told us that there was nothing conservative about building a wall or deporting illegal immigrants. Atlanta-based talker Erick Erickson signed on, but he at least acknowledged that Trump would be preferable to Clinton.

As it became more than likely, mathematically speaking, that Trump would secure the GOP nomination, all the talk of pledges and promises to support the GOP nominee suddenly ceased. The same pundits who were aghast that Trump wouldn't promise to fall in line should he lose the nomination were now refusing to support the GOP front-runner.

The special anti-Trump issue of the *National Review* was just the first salvo of a movement with the potential to destroy the GOP's populist prairie fire. In retrospect, it was but the death rattle of conservative Beltway elitists who saw their once-solid grasp on the American right slipping away.

That issue of *National Review* amused me, because a year earlier, I had attended a fundraiser for the magazine in Palm Beach—at Mar-a-Lago. I still wonder if Rich Lowry et al. paid full price for the room, the hors d'oeuvres, the open bar with the top shelf booze, etc. But if Trump did give them a discount before he started running, well, I guess the old axiom holds true—no good deed goes unpunished.

South Carolina Brawl

The ninth Republican primary debate took place in Greenville, South Carolina, on February 13. Organized by CBS, the debate was moderated by Obama bum-kisser John Dickerson, with CBS' Major Garrett and the *Wall Street Journal*'s Kim Strassel chipping in occasional questions. The new, slimmed-down field of candidates included Trump, Bush, Cruz, Kasich, and Rubio, with Carson just barely making the cut. Cruz was looking to regain his momentum after a lopsided, though predictable, beatdown in New Hampshire. Meanwhile, the increasingly desperate establishment candidates were eager to put some points up on the board. With the smaller cast of characters, Trump's rivals thought they would have more time to expose his policy weaknesses and, conversely, that Trump would have more time to self-destruct. Once again, they were wrong.

The South Carolina debate was blood sport and ¡Jeb! would not survive.

The debate began amicably enough, with all the players agreeing that Obama should not be the president to name the late Antonin Scalia's replacement to the Supreme Court. But it quickly took a nasty turn as Bush summoned the courage to attack the frontrunner on foreign policy, including the U.S. relationship with Russia and the fight against ISIS. Trump, Bush said, was too accommodating to the Kremlin's interests in the Middle East.

"Jeb is so wrong," Trump said. The Bush-friendly country-club crowd booed Trump, but he pressed on. "Just so you understand—that's Jeb's special interests and lobbyists talking."

Low-energy Jeb returned fire: "This comes from a guy who gets his foreign policies from the shows."

It was a fair enough shot. Trump had earlier told a TV interviewer that he relies on the morning news programs to inform his foreign policy. Jeb wasn't done taking potshots, and Trump wasn't about to let Jeb get away with them. Still bitter over Trump's factually accurate assessment that 9/11 occurred when his brother was president, Jeb revisited the subject in hopes of currying favor with South Carolina voters, whom his polling had suggested were fond of W.

"While Donald Trump was building a reality TV show," Bush said, "my brother was building a security apparatus to keep us safe."

Trump retorted: "The World Trade Center came down during your brother's reign. Remember that?"

As the crowd again booed Trump, Jeb pressed on. He reminded the crowd how Trump had earlier mocked him for bringing his 90-year-old mother Barbara out on the campaign trail with him, whining, "You had the gall to go after my mother."

"She should be running," Trump said with a shrug.

The *contretemps* over foreign policy and the Bush era was a wash. Both Bush and Trump landed some body blows, but neither had delivered the knockout punch. Then the conversation turned to Bush's greatest weakness, his political preexisting condition: immigration.

"The weakest person on this stage by far on illegal immigration is Jeb Bush." Then he used Bush's own words against him.

"'They come out of an act of love,'" said Trump, paraphrasing what had become a punchline on the campaign trail. "He is so weak on illegal immigration it's laughable, and everybody knows it."

Bush attempted a comeback: "This is the standard operating procedure, to disparage me. That's fine—"

"Spend a little more money on the commercials," Trump airily told him.

Having fended off Bush's feeble thrusts, Trump set about quarreling with Cruz. The Texas senator, in his characteristic style, began with one of his snide, college-debate style digs. But as so often happened, what Cruz thought was smooth was in fact slimy—and Trump made him pay.

"I like Donald, he is an amazing entertainer," Cruz snickered. "But for most of his life his policies have been very, very liberal. For most of his life, he has described himself as very pro-choice and as a supporter of partial birth abortion. Right now, today as a candidate, he supports federal taxpayer funding for Planned Parenthood. I disagree with him on that."

Trump cut Cruz off.

"You probably are worse than Jeb Bush," Trump shot back. "You are the single biggest liar. This guy's lied—let me just tell you, this guy lied about Ben Carson when he took votes away from Ben Carson in Iowa and he just continues. Today, we had robo-calls saying, 'Donald Trump is not going to run in South Carolina'—where I'm leading by a lot."

Cutaway of Cruz, looking just as Trump was describing him—shifty, shady.

"This guy will say anything, nasty guy," Trump said, "Now I know why he doesn't have one endorsement from any of his colleagues."

Trump survived the debate and managed to score some points against Bush and Cruz, but it wasn't like the clear-cut victories he'd enjoyed in the past. Heading into the debate, Trump was the prohibitive front-runner in the South Carolina primary with nearly 40 percent in the polls. But when Palmetto State Republicans finally went to cast their ballots, the latest polls were showing Trump just over 30 percent, as both Kasich and Rubio gained support. By the end of the night, it appeared that Trump's slide in the polls was real, as was Rubio's surge. Trump netted 32.5 percent of the vote, while Rubio hauled in 22.5 percent, with Cruz just behind him at 22.3 percent. Jeb! finished a lame fourth, with just 7.8 percent.

At 8:40 pm EST that night, a sullen Bush held a press conference.

"The people of Iowa and New Hampshire and South Carolina have spoken," he said. "And I really respect their decision, so tonight I am suspending my campaign."

Just like that, the Bush political dynasty, three generations old, was over, finished, kaput and legions of failed Beltway consultants headed to their local taprooms to contemplate their futures.

Sessions Endorses Trump

"Now I know why he doesn't have one endorsement from any of his colleagues."

That was the humiliating jab Trump had leveled against Cruz in the South Carolina debate just days before the real estate developer won all 50 delegates at stake in the primary election. Trump would now torment Cruz even more by accomplishing what the Texan could not—earning the support of a U.S. Senator.

Two days before the delegate-heavy slate of primaries known as Super Tuesday, Trump landed the much-sought-after endorsement of Alabama Sen. Jeff Sessions. Sessions, a close ally of Cruz's in the Senate, had previously appeared at rallies with Trump, even donning a MAGA hat at one point in his hometown of Mobile in the summer of 2015. But he always stopped short of making the official endorsement, owing, in part, to his close relationship with Cruz.

Sessions was the first and only senator to endorse Trump, but his support was, in many ways, more important than that of any other senator. A senator since 1997, Sessions had fought for Trumpian policies on immigration well before Trump started pushing them on the campaign trail. My listeners knew him well. He was a frequent guest on the show, calling out not just illegal immigration, but also systemic abuses of the H1-B visa program. In a Republican party dominated by the Chambers of Commerce and big business—whose profit margins often relied on cheap foreign labor—Sessions stood defiantly in favor of the interests of the American worker.

Sessions' early support for Trump was repaid after the election with his nomination to serve as attorney general.

"Do You Disavow?"

Donald Trump's joy over winning in New Hampshire and South Carolina was quickly ended by a failed racist agitator from Louisiana. David Duke, the former Louisiana state rep, was a perennial candidate in both the Republican and Democrat parties, but he was known mostly as a former Grand Wizard of the Ku Klux Klan. Duke had always been a political nuisance for Republicans. In saner times, the barroom-style ravings of some pasty redneck would have been dismissed outright. But not with Trump. In the Trump era, when anyone could watch his ranting videos online, Duke became a political cudgel the Democrats could use to bludgeon Republicans as racists. Except on the internet, Duke was a nobody. But Duke's fulminations suited the needs of the mainstream media desperate to draw blood from the Republican frontrunner. In late February, Duke endorsed Trump in a Facebook post.

"I think he deserves a close look by those who believe the era of political correctness needs to come to an end," Duke wrote, before veering off into the wild, conspiratorial racism and anti-Semitism that characterized most of his public statements. Instantly both the media and Trump's opponents began trying to turn Duke into a weapon against Trump.

The attempt to pin Duke's sordid career on Trump was all the more ridiculous given that Trump had already repudiated the former Klansman's support and clearly knew nothing of the man. In a 2015 interview with Bloomberg, John Heilemann had pressed him on the subject.

"I don't need his endorsement," Trump said. "I certainly don't want his endorsement."

"Would you repudiate David Duke?" Heilemann asked.

"Sure, I would do that, if it made you feel better," Trump said. "I don't know anything about him."

Fast-forward to February and the media were collectively hyperventilating, as if the exchange with Heilemann on Bloomberg had never occurred.

Trump was pressed at a Feb. 26 news conference: "How do you feel about the recent endorsement from David Duke?"

"David Duke endorsed me? Okay, all right, I disavow, okay?"

With any other candidate, that would have been the end of it. But with Trump, the liberal media set a new standard for double standards. Trump, unlike any candidate before him, was to be held personally and perpetually responsible for every single reprobate with a Facebook account who supported him. Unfortunately, Trump missed his opportunity to put a dagger through the heart of the David Duke controversy when he stumbled in an interview with CNN's Jake Tapper, a former employee of Chelsea Clinton's mother-in-law.

Tapper: I want to ask you about the Anti-Defamation League, which this week called on you to publicly condemn unequivocally the racism of former KKK grand wizard David Duke, who recently said that voting against you at this point would be "treason to your heritage." Will you unequivocally condemn David Duke and say that you don't want his vote or that of other white supremacists in this election?

Trump: Well, just so you understand, I don't know anything about David Duke. Okay? I don't know anything about what you're even talking about with white supremacy or white supremacists. So, I don't know. I don't know, did he endorse me or what's going on, because, you know, I know nothing about David Duke. I know nothing about white supremacists. And so you're asking me a question that I'm supposed to be talking about people that I know nothing about.

Tapper: But I guess the question from the Anti-Defamation League is, even if you don't know about their endorsement, there are these groups and individuals endorsing you. Would you just say unequivocally you condemn them and you don't want their support?

Trump: Well, I have to look at the group. I mean, I don't know what group you're talking about. You wouldn't want me to condemn a group that I know nothing about. I would have to look. If you would send me a list of the groups, I will do research on them. And, certainly, I would disavow if I thought there was something wrong.

Tapper: The Ku Klux Klan?

Trump: But you may have groups in there that are totally fine, and it would be very unfair. So, give me a list of the groups, and I will let you know.

Tapper: Okay. I mean, I'm just talking about David Duke and the Ku Klux Klan here, but…

Trump: I don't know any—honestly, I don't know David Duke. I don't believe I have ever met him. I'm pretty sure I didn't meet him. And I just don't know anything about him.

Trump had already disavowed and repudiated Duke in at least two media appearances as well as on his Twitter account, but that didn't matter. His enemies had video of him claiming ignorance of Duke's odious career. The interview was a disaster for Trump. At best, he appeared neutral or at least uninterested on the question of the KKK. Anti-Trump social media users ensured the clip would go viral, and his remaining rivals seized on the opportunity to cast Trump as a Klan fellow traveler.

"Really sad," tweeted Cruz. "@realDonaldTrump you're better than this. We should all agree, racism is wrong, KKK is abhorrent."

"I don't know what's in his head," John Kasich said in a CNN interview. "All I know is that white supremacist groups have no place in our society and clearly not in the Republican Party."

"America's first black president cannot and will not be succeeded by a hatemonger who refuses to condemn the KKK," chimed in Bernie Sanders.

The David Duke controversy was exasperating on several levels. For starters, why the hell does anyone care about Duke? That's a rhetorical question, of course, but it's important nonetheless. The same liberal talking heads who insisted that Trump was an evil racist for failing to meet their entirely made-up standards of disavowal did more to elevate an actual evil racist than Trump. Duke's notoriety stems entirely from the mainstream media's attempt to use him as a weapon against Republican candidates. Without the left-wing news networks, and their casts of paid Democrat operatives like Tapper et al., few Americans outside of Louisiana would even know who Duke is. As Ann Coulter has said, "If David Duke did not exist, the Democrats would have to invent him."

But the baseless charges of racism and anti-Semitism Trump faced throughout the campaign were especially ludicrous, considering Trump's career prior to the start of his presidential campaign. During his rise to prominence in New York, Trump was good friends with the Rev. Jesse Jackson, the black civil rights activist and former Democrat presidential candidate. There are hundreds of images in the public domain of the two men together at galas and making small talk at parties. Ditto for another flamboyant black civil rights activist, the Rev. Al Sharpton. In the 1990s, back when Sharpton was fat, he and Trump often appeared together at charity events and other New York celeb-fests. If Trump was secretly a Klan-supporting racist all along, he had a weird way of showing it.

The Return of Willard

Trump ruled Super Tuesday.

The hectic March 1 primary day, dubbed the SEC (Southeastern Conference) Primary by media pundits, included primary elections or caucuses in Alabama, Arkansas, Colorado, Georgia, Massachusetts, Minnesota, Oklahoma, Tennessee, Texas, Vermont, Virginia, and North Dakota. Trump won eight states as Cruz took Texas, Oklahoma, and Alaska, and Rubio was victorious in Minnesota. Trump ended the day with 256 more delegates. You didn't have to be a handicapper in Las Vegas to see that, barring some extraordinary event, Trump would now win the GOP nomination four months hence. Behind closed doors, the Beltway class was conspiring against him more furiously than ever, and one of the elder statesman of the party was ready to lead the attack.

Two days later, speaking to a friendly audience at the University of Utah in Salt Lake City, former GOP Presidential nominee Willard Mitt Romney issued a resounding call to the Never Trumpers, the Cruz lovers, and the Rubio fanatics. He assailed Trump's character and his success as a businessman. He called Trump a "fraud," his promises "worthless." He predicted that nominating Trump would hand the election to Hillary Clinton. For 45 minutes, reading off a teleprompter, he laid out the best case the establishment GOP could muster.

Romney's diatribe sent a tingle up the legs of Trump's rivals, the Never Trumpers, as well as the left-wing commentariat. Cruz, Kasich and Rubio were still clinging to dreams of increasingly unlikely paths to the nomination. The Never Trumpers, of course, were entertaining a fantasy whereby a brokered convention would turn to Romney to lead the GOP to… something. At least the anti-Trumpers were consistent in their delusions. The liberal celebration of Romney's speech, however, was a classic example of liberal hypocrisy.

The same Democrat operatives who had mercilessly pilloried Romney in 2012 as a callous vulture capitalist who wanted the poor to suffer now hailed him as a hero. The same liberal activists who cast the former Massachusetts governor as a racist, misogynist, dog-abusing Hitlerian figure when he was running against Obama now revered him as a shining example of decency. It was enough to make you want to throw up on TV, as Dapper O'Neil used to say.

But the biggest hypocrite in the whole affray was Romney.

The 2012 election should have been an open-and-shut case. After four years, Obama had revealed himself to be not the centrist he campaigned as, but a left-wing radical bent on transforming America, by whatever means necessary, into a European-style social democracy. He had succeeded with Obamacare—the statist takeover of the health care system—and he was advancing his agenda unilaterally through the executive branch with the pen and phone that he endlessly bragged about using to subvert the Constitution. At the same time, the economy was "recovering" more slowly than ever. Two years earlier, in 2010, Republicans had won a wave election thanks to the rise of the Tea Party phenomenon. The stage was set for Romney to put an end to our long national nightmare.

Willard choked. He got a bone in his throat.

Romney ran the traditional feckless Republican campaign. He spoke in lofty terms, but folded under pressure. He apologized, he was meek, he was timid. Even when the Obama administration engaged in an obvious cover-up of the Muslim terrorist attack in Benghazi, Romney couldn't capitalize. He wilted under pressure, he turned the other cheek, he fumbled at the goal line, he went into a fetal position, just as he had 18 years earlier in Massachusetts, running against Ted Kennedy for the Senate. He had a political glass jaw. Dudley Do-Right couldn't take a punch. And now, after handing Obama another four years to bring to fruition his progressive nightmare for America, after being scared out of the 2016 race by Jeb's donors, Romney had the stones to tell Republicans to abandon their last best hope at putting an end to the dynastic liberal politics of Obama and Clinton.

But Romney's utter futility four years earlier wasn't the only reason his new assault on Trump was hypocritical.

In 2012, questions over Romney's wealth and taxes bedeviled his campaign against Obama. Then-Senate Minority Leader Harry Reid (D-Nev.), one of the most odious figures in modern American politics, backstabbed his fellow Mormon with the suggestion that an anonymous source had called his Senate office to inform him that Romney was a tax evader.

"The word's out that he hasn't paid any taxes for 10 years," Reid stated on the floor of the U.S. Senate. He told the *Huffington Post* that an investor in Romney's firm, Bain Capital, had given him this information. Then he later told reporters in Nevada that "I have had a number of people tell me that."

As Fusion GPS would five years later, Reid refused to reveal his alleged "sources."

"I don't think the burden should be on me," he said. "The burden should be on him. He's the one I've alleged has not paid any taxes."

In an interview a few years later, Reid was asked about his mendacious attack: "They can call it whatever they want. Romney didn't win, did he?"

Romney never fully recovered from Reid's despicable charges, which makes it even more appalling that Romney would use the same shameful tactics in his anti-Trump fusillade.

"We will only really know if he is the real deal or a phony if he releases his tax returns," Romney said. "I predict that there are more bombshells in his tax returns."

Despite his best efforts, Romney's Reid-like tactics did little to alter the trajectory of the race. As the pace of the primaries picked up, Trump's winning streak continued. In the days following Romney's polemic, Trump won Kentucky, Louisiana, Hawaii, Michigan, and Mississippi, while Cruz took Kansas, Maine, and Idaho. Rubio got two consolation prizes that perfectly summed up the limitations of his appeal to the GOP's primary electorate— Puerto Rico and Washington, D.C. Running his 10,000-calorie-a-day, all-u-can-eat campaign, Kasich inexplicably remained in the race despite having not won a single state.

Trump's winning streak created a political reality that required his competitors to reinvent their nomination strategies. Town halls, TV ad buys, mailers—none of them counted anymore. All that mattered was math. Specifically, delegate math. The only question for Cruz, Kasich and Rubio was how to stop Trump from reaching the delegate total necessary to capture the GOP nomination. So they turned to the strategic voting strategy Romney had laid out during his speech in Utah.

"If the other candidates can find some common ground," Romney had said, "I believe we can nominate a person who can win the general election and who will represent the values and policies of conservatism. Given the current delegate selection process, that means that I'd vote for Marco Rubio in Florida and for John Kasich in Ohio and for Ted Cruz or whichever one of the other two contenders has the best chance of beating Mr. Trump in a given state."

It wasn't about ensuring any one candidate won the nomination; it was about ensuring Trump did not. Rubio, with his roots in Florida, would focus on the Sunshine State. Meanwhile, Kasich, the governor of Ohio, would concentrate on the Buckeye State. Cruz would work the other states whose voters would cast ballots on March 15.

With the exception of Ohio, Romney's call for strategic voting failed. In Florida, Trump humiliated Rubio, pulling in 46 percent of the total vote. Rubio, the former Speaker of the House in the Florida legislature, won just 27 percent of the vote, while Cruz got 17 percent. That means that even if every single Cruz voter had instead voted for Rubio, the Florida wonder boy would still have fallen short. Trump carried every county except Rubio's home, Miami/Dade.

Trump rounded out the day with wins in Illinois, Missouri, North Carolina, and the North Mariana Islands, winning a total of 228 delegates. Only the Buckeye State eluded Trump—and not by much. Kasich won with 47 percent—his first and only victory of the season.

Following his embarrassing defeat in Florida, Rubio "suspended" his campaign and quickly announced he would now run for reelection to the Senate, an embarrassing fallback plan he had haughtily dismissed weeks earlier. Kasich would remain in the race until the bitter end, turning his tired act into a bizarre farewell tour. But as March turned into April, the race became a contest between Cruz and Trump.

"Violent" Rallies

Trump wasn't just facing opposition from the GOP establishment and the Never Trumpers. He was now also the target of a dirty-tricks campaign orchestrated by Democrat operatives who targeted the candidate's trademark rallies. Trump's boisterous events attracted tens of thousands of his supporters, but they also brought in liberal activists. Outside agitators, as George Wallace used to call them. If these moonbats thought they were spoiling the party, they were wrong. Indeed, Trump fed off the energy the few protesters provided. Everyone in public life needs a good foil, especially if getting a few laughs is part of your repertoire.

At a November 2015 rally in Worcester, some fat guy stood up and started screaming about something or another. At that point, Trump was railing about welfare and the food stamp program. As the protester was being dragged out, Trump made the obvious crack, saying what everyone had been thinking: "I mention food stamps and that guy, who's seriously overweight, goes crazy!"

The crowd loved the Don Rickles insult comic act.

Usually, though, Trump responded to hecklers by calmly pausing and bellowing, "Get 'em out! Get 'em out of here!" And the crowd would drown out whatever vapid message the protesters were trying to deliver with chants of *U.S.A., U.S.A., U.S.A.*

Trump's pitched rallies often involved hot tempers and fisticuffs. On more than one occasion, a protester got socked in the face by a Trump voter, which allowed the media to tout one of their favorite narratives—that Trump, the budding authoritarian, was giving license to his supports to assault dissenters. But weeks before the election, investigative journalists working with James O'Keefe's *Project Veritas* uncovered indisputable evidence that much of the violence at the rallies was the result of liberal subterfuge, financed by the DNC.

In the undercover videos, two long-time Democrat operatives bragged to a *Project Veritas* journalist about the scheme to incite violence at Trump rallies. O'Keefe's marks were Robert Creamer, founder of Democracy Advocates and husband of Rep. Jan Schakowsky (D-Ill.), and Scott Foval, the national field director for something called Americans United for Change.

The videos show Foval and Creamer, who pleaded guilty in 2005 to charges of bank fraud and tax violations, explaining how they hired agitators, including union thugs, the mentally ill and even homeless people to disrupt Trump rallies. The protesters were coached on how to provoke Trump supporters by wearing Planned Parenthood t-shirts.

"I mean, honestly, it's not hard to get some of these assholes to pop off," Mr. Foval said. "It's a matter of showing up, to want to get into the rally, in a Planned Parenthood T-shirt. Or, 'Trump is a Nazi,' you know. You can message to draw them out and draw them to punch you."

Both Foval and Creamer were the recipients of open-ended contracts from the DNC—one of the organizations most responsible for spreading the canard that Trump's rallies were violent because of Trump.

Cruz vs. Trump

Early in the GOP primary, Ted Cruz stood apart from the other Republican candidates in his approach to handling the outsider candidacy of Donald Trump. Perhaps, like so many other political observers, he thought that Trump's campaign would self-destruct when he finally crossed some heretofore unknown line. Or maybe he figured that Trump's run was a publicity stunt, that he would pull out when the timing was optimal for his business interests. Either way,

Cruz pointedly refused to criticize Trump and even appeared to buddy up to the New Yorker. Trump had teased Cruz over his Canadian birth and Cruz in turn needled Trump for being a New Yorker. But this was child's play compared to the scorched-earth exchanges Trump had with other Republicans.

As the race narrowed down to just Cruz and Trump, however, the contest turned into an unrestrained Texas death match, with both men using every weapon at their disposal to bludgeon one another.

Arizona was something of a foregone conclusion. The border state had seen more than its fair share of unbridled illegal immigration. It was on the front line of the drug-cartel wars and Arizonans had experienced all the illegal-alien crime Trump pointed to in his first campaign speech. Predictably, Trump won 46 percent of the vote, with the other candidates lagging far behind. In Utah, however, Cruz's allies saw an opportunity to win some delegates from a predominately Mormon electorate that had always been skeptical of the brash East Coast businessman.

To ensure a victory in Utah, Cruz's allies sought to capitalize on the Mormon majority's concerns about Trump's morality. Anonymous operatives began circulating an image of Melania Trump, scantily clad and posing evocatively. Is this what you want in a first lady, the meme asked?

Trump responded with his brutal attacks on Cruz's wife—and her sanity—via his Twitter account. Those tweets earned Trump any number of media appearances in which he always pointed the finger back at Cruz, the man who had cast the first stone in the War of the Wives. Utah always was a longshot for Trump, given that it was a caucus state and especially after the withering attacks by Romney, a favorite son of sorts since he had saved the 2002 Winter Olympics in Salt Lake City from becoming a total disaster. When the dust settled in Utah, Cruz had walked away with a 55 point margin over Trump.

One day after Utah, on March 23, the *National Enquirer* teased a front-page scorcher: "CRUZ'S 5 SECRET MISTRESSES."

"Private detectives are digging into at least five affairs Ted Cruz supposedly had," claimed a Washington insider, according to the Trump-friendly tabloid. "The leaked details are an attempt to destroy what's left of his White House campaign!"

The scandalous but thinly-sourced accusations created a media firestorm. Internet sleuths raced to identify the anonymous women named in the story. Social media users began drawing connections between Cruz and the notorious DC Madam, whose list of johns had never been made public due to a judge's order. Politicos speculated as to who was behind the attack. Some asserted with certainty that Trump, who was friendly with the *Enquirer*'s publisher David J. Pecker, had orchestrated the blast. Others suggested that Rubio's dirty tricksters had been shopping around the extramarital rumors for weeks. Many people looked at Cruz and thought, "Yeah, that makes sense."

As I always say on my show, it's the ones who preach the loudest about Christian morality that you have to keep an eye on. Regardless of who was behind the hit, Cruz's campaign had to expend precious time and energy telling reporters that Cruz was not a serial philanderer.

It wouldn't be the last time the *National Enquirer* caused Cruz headaches.

As Trump and Cruz slugged it out in the final weeks of the primary campaign, the establishment GOP found itself in a an untenable position. The powerbrokers in the Republican Party loathed Cruz, the one-time George W. Bush establishment Republican who had become Tea Party firebrand. He refused to be a team player and he was a show boater. But Washington, D.C.'s hatred for Trump ran even deeper. In late March and early April, several well-known GOPers began swallowing their pride to stand behind Cruz. Romney had already endorsed Cruz just prior to the Utah caucuses. Bush and Walker followed suit heading into the Wisconsin primary. Outside groups, such as the Club for Growth, dropped massive ad buys in the state, as local anti-Trump talk-radio hosts pressed the case for Cruz. With the boost from the establishment, Cruz won Wisconsin with 48 percent to Trump's 35 percent.

Cruz followed up his Wisconsin win by sweeping Colorado, but his joy was short-lived. The so-called Acela Primary came on April 26 and Trump cruised to five overwhelming victories on the Eastern seaboard—his backyard as it were. Trump won Connecticut with 58 percent of the vote, Delaware with 61 percent, Maryland with 54 percent, Rhode Island with 63 percent, and Pennsylvania with 57 percent of the vote. Trump's blowout win in the Acela Primary officially placed the crucial delegate total of 1,237 out of reach for both Cruz and Kasich. Neither of them had a path to the nomination, but they still had a chance to force a brokered convention. Desperate, they returned to the Mitt Romney strategy. Kasich would focus his energy on Oregon and New Mexico while Cruz would challenge Trump in Indiana.

The anti-Trump forces wanted Indiana to be their Little Round Top—the last key position held to the end, preventing utter defeat. But it wound up being their Battle of Little Big Horn, a massacre by the hostiles.

The May 3 Indiana primary was a winner-take-all event with 57 delegates up for grabs. Heading into the contest, Cruz announced that he would nominate former candidate Carly Fiorina to be his running mate, and he secured the endorsement of Indiana Gov. Mike Pence. Cruz's campaign was further bolstered by a huge spending advantage over Trump. But one exchange Cruz had on the campaign trail led me to believe that he had lost the state even before Trump's tally reached 53 percent—and I'm not talking about Cruz's "basketball ring" gaffe.

On the morning of the Indiana primary election, Cruz was outside of the Wagon Wheel restaurant in Bloomington, pressing the flesh and trying to get out the vote. Cruz told one woman, a teacher, that he wanted to abolish the Department of Education and end Common Core—two standard promises he had made throughout the campaign. The woman's husband then asked a pretty obvious question: "Can you get it done?"

"Um, it depends," Cruz tepidly replied. "We can get some of it done."

Cruz followed that exchange by insulting Ohioans in an attempt to curry favor with the neighboring Hoosiers. But the best exchange occurred outside of the restaurant when Cruz was confronted with mockery from Trump voters.

"Go home Ted!" shouted one guy with a thick, Larry Bird-like Midwestern twang. "Raphael! Why do you hate Latinos? Do you have to make yourself whiter?"

Cruz replied like the student-council candidate with a pocket protector that he had once been.

"Sir, you seem to have real problems with anger. I would advise decaffeinating brands, they work just as well."

Another Hoosier approached Cruz looking for a friendly handshake. When Cruz extended his arm, the voter yanked his hand away and drawled: "Too slow, Joe!"

"God bless you, sir," said Cruz, to which the man replied, "You look like a fish monster!

"You're a terrible person!" the heckler added, unnecessarily.

Cleveland

Donald Trump arrived at the 2016 RNC convention in Cleveland with 1,725 delegates—488 more than he needed, squashing the dreams of the Never Trumpers. The strategic schemes of the Cruz and Kasich campaigns had all been for naught. Cruz's desperate ploy to make Fiorina his running mate had likewise failed, just as Ronald Reagan had failed to derail Gerald Ford in 1976 when he picked Sen. Richard Schweiker as his pre-convention vice presidential candidate. So many of the Republicans had tried to recreate Reagan's winning ways, but

The speech heard 'round the world: Trump announces his candidacy, New York, June 2015. (AP Photo/Richard Drew)

Trump supporter's "Build the Wall" body painting, April 2016. (AP Photo/Elise Amendola)

GOP debate in Milwaukee: Trump w, l-r, "Lil Marco" Rubio, "pathological" Dr. Ben Carson and "Lyin' Ted" Cruz, November 2015. (AP Photo/Morry Gash)

Jorge Ramos of Univision, just before he was ejected from Trump press conference in Dubuque IA, August 2015. (AP Photo/Charlie Neibergall)

Sen. Jeff Sessions of Alabama, Trump's first supporter in the US
Senate, December 2016. (AP Photo/Brynn Anderson)

"Please clap": Ex-Florida Gov. Jeb Bush considers some of the
"really cool things" he could have been doing instead of becoming
a national laughingstock. (AP Photo/Andrew Harnik)

Fat guy ejected from rally at DCU Center in Worcester MA as Trump points out to the crowd that the heckler had been silent until Trump mentioned cutting food stamps, November 2015. (AP Photo/Steven Senne)

Ohio Gov. John Kasich ate his way across the USA, April 2016. (AP Photo/Andres Kudacki)

On Trump One flying back to New York after the war-whoop rally in Bangor ME, June 2016.

At a Cape Cod fundraiser with then 2016 Republican Presidential Nominee Donald J. Trump, August 2016.

In the Oval Office with POTUS, July 2017.

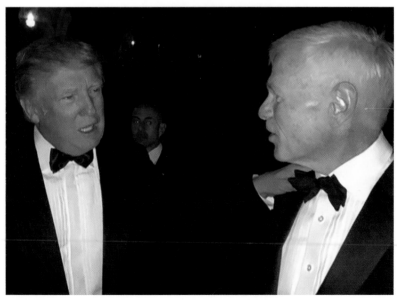

At Mar-a-Lago in Palm Beach, New Year's Eve, 2016.

Trump with first campaign manager Corey Lewandowski, May 2016. (AP Photo/Gerald Herbert)

Howie Carr, seated at table, moderating town hall meeting, Sandown NH, October 2016. (AP Photo/Robert F. Bukaty)

Trump listening to Juanita Broaddrick, who accused Bill Clinton of raping her in 1978, at press conference in St. Louis, October 2016. (AP Photo/Evan Vucci)

With Hillary at the town-hall style debate in St. Louis, October 2016. (AP Photo/Rick T. Wilking)

New Jersey Gov. Chris Christie offers congratulations to the president-elect early on the morning of November 9, 2016. (AP Photo/Dennis Van Tine/STAR MAX/IPx)

The Trumps at an inaugural ball in Washington, January 2017. (AP Photo/Patrick Semansky)

POTUS with Ivanka and Melania in Oval Office, February 2017.
(AP Photo/Evan Vucci)

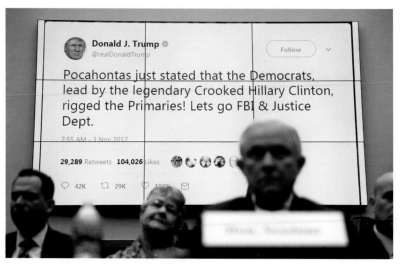

Attorney General Sessions testifies on Capitol Hill in front of a
blow-up of a POTUS tweet re: Sen. Elizabeth "Pocahontas" Warren.
(AP Photo/Carolyn Kaster)

only one seemed to be channeling the magic of the man Rush Limbaugh called Ronaldus Magnus.

Trump was headed for general election showdown with Hillary Clinton. The only question was whether the malcontents in the Republican Party would set aside their grievances and egos to support him in this final winner-take-all struggle.

Early indications suggested Trump's defeated foes would not fall in line. The convention was in John Kasich's home state, so his absence was nothing less than a conspicuous middle finger to Trump and his supporters. Of the former candidates, only Chris Christie and Ted Cruz gave speeches. Christie, who had long ago made clear his commitment to backing Trump, gave a rousing anti-Clinton speech. Cruz's convention speech, in the other hand, was all about Ted Cruz.

That speech began with some awkward political pandering. Fresh off his "basketball ring" gaffe, the Texan referenced the Cleveland Cavaliers' recent NBA championship with a shout-out to LeBron James. But after rehashing his "I'm-the-most-conservative-conservative" routine, Cruz pointedly refused to endorse Trump.

"If you love our country, and love your children as much as I know that you do," Cruz exhorted, "stand and speak and vote your conscience, vote for candidates up and down the ticket who you trust to defend our freedom and to be faithful to the Constitution."

The convention center thundered with boos. Cruz's "vote your conscience" line was nothing less than a rebuke of the GOP nominee and a call for conservatives to abandon the only real alternative to Hillary Clinton. Trump had allowed the Calgary Comet into his convention in the hopes of broadcasting Republican unity to the country. But Cruz was too petty, his ego too large, to rise to the occasion. He may well hold all the most conservative beliefs, but on that night in Cleveland, Cruz showed that his personal ambitions were more important than defeating Clinton.

"I appreciate the enthusiasm of the New York delegation," Cruz retorted to the booing masses. Then he walked off the stage alone, as the booing escalated.

I was in a luxury box at the convention that night, and as the chorus of catcalls continued, I noticed that standing a few feet away from me was Woody Johnson, the billionaire owner of the New York Jets, a quintessential Republican megadonor who is now Trump's ambassador to the Court of St. James.

Johnson had started out with ¡Jeb!, had even cohosted a fundraiser for him the previous Christmas in Palm Beach with Miami Dolphins owner Steve Ross.

"Woody's a friend of mine from New York," Trump told me later. "He'd have been with me from the start, but he didn't think I was really running."

There'd been a lot of that going around, that's for sure.

Now I was watching Johnson's reaction to Cruz's Et-tu-Brute speech. I was pretty sure Cruz saw himself as laying the groundwork that night for his 2020 I-told-you-so campaign for president. He would need a lot of money to run again—Woody Johnson-type money.

But Johnson was staring at Cruz as he walked off the stage, and he was frowning. His jaw was set, his arms were crossed, he was shaking his head. Like most of the other Republicans in the hall, Woody Johnson was pissed.

I made a mental note to myself: Ted Cruz's 2020 campaign for president was getting off to a poor start.

Pulse Night Club

Even before the primaries began, Muslim terrorist attacks were already driving the presidential campaign, first with the ISIS attacks by "refugees" in France and again with the attack on a Christmas party in San Bernardino. And the scourge of Muslim terrorism returned once again in June 2016 when a 29-year-old savage carried out a murderous rampage at a gay night club in Orlando, Florida.

Omar Mateen, the son of Afghan immigrants, murdered 49 people and wounded 58 others. As is always the case when a member of a protected class carries out a heinous act, the feds and the media tried desperately to avoid telling the truth to the American people.

But the usual PC "We-may-never-know-the-motive" routine fell apart instantly. Once Mateen was identified as the gunman, all the obvious Religion-of-Peace red flags were uncovered. Mateen was notoriously short-tempered. He had once threatened to kill some of his classmates at a cookout after his hamburger touched some pork on the grill. A former co-worker said he had talked about killing people and that he hated blacks, Jews and women. He'd been reported to federal authorities several times and even interviewed by the FBI which of course dropped the ball, just as the G-men had done with the Tsarnaev immigrant terrorists in Boston three years earlier. If that wasn't enough, the 911 calls Mateen placed during his murder spree were explicit about his motive.

Orlando Police Dispatcher: Emergency 911, this is being recorded.

Omar Mateen: In the name of God the Merciful, the beneficent [said in Arabic].

OPD: What?

OM: Praise be to God, and prayers as well as peace be upon the prophet of God [said in Arabic]. I wanna let you know, I'm in Orlando and I did the shootings.

OPD: What's your name?

OM: My name is I pledge allegiance to Abu Bakr al-Baghdadi of the Islamic State.

OPD: Okay, what's your name?

OM: I pledge allegiance to Abu Bakr al-Baghdadi may God protect him [said in Arabic], on behalf of the Islamic State.

OPD: Alright, where are you at?

OM: In Orlando.

Mateen made several more 911 calls repeating the same message: He said he was a soldier of ISIS and he had visited this terror upon the Pulse nightclub as part of the holy jihad.

The body count from the night was still being revised—upward, of course—as the candidates began responding. Although Mateen was himself a natural-born U.S. citizen, he was the son of an Afghan immigrant, which only bolstered Trump's immigration proposals, including his desired ban on immigration from certain Muslim-majority terror hotspots across the globe.

"The only reason the killer was in America in the first place was because we allowed his family to come here," Trump pointed out.

Clinton took the opposite tack, insisting the progressive policy of inclusivity was the proper remedy.

"Our open, diverse society is an asset in the struggle against terrorism, not a liability," she said.

Trump even positioned himself as the better friend and ally of the LGBT community.

"Ask yourself: Who is really the friend of women and the LGBT community?" Trump said. "Donald Trump with actions, or Hillary Clinton with her words? Clinton wants to allow radical Islamic terrorists to pour into our country—they enslave women, and they murder gays."

Clinton, for her part, deflected to the Democrat play book. The attack was not about terrorism, but about guns and the Second Amendment.

"If the FBI is watching you for suspected terrorist links, you shouldn't be able to just go buy a gun with no questions asked," Clinton said. "You shouldn't be able to exploit loopholes and evade criminal background checks by buying online or at a gun show."

In other words, Clinton's response to the terrorist attack in Orlando was a policy of denying law-abiding citizens their constitutional right to bear arms without due process or trial.

A woman who, as a former First Lady would enjoy a lifetime of Secret Service protection, did not believe that her fellow citizens should be allowed to defend themselves from the "refugees" that she dreamed of flooding the red states with.

We would later learn from one of Mateen's fellow mosque-goers that he was a Clinton supporter who had voted for Hillary in the Florida primary. What's more, his father Seddique Mateen was a Democrat donor who would soon be appearing behind Clinton at political rallies.

Celebrate diversity!

Chapter Seven
The Server

JUDICIAL WATCH, A NON-PROFIT GROUP THAT FIGHTS FOR TRANSPARENCY in the federal government, did more good work during the Obama administration than just about anybody else in what was the real resistance. They battled Attorney General Eric Holder during the Fast and Furious gun-running scandal. They revealed secrecy and unethical behavior at the Environmental Protection Agency. And they were on the front lines of the fight to hold the Internal Revenue Service responsible for the targeting and intimidation of hundreds of conservative Tea Party organizations.

But Judicial Watch's greatest victory may have come via a Freedom of Information Act (FOIA) lawsuit the group filed to obtain emails sent and received by Hillary Clinton and her State Department team during her tenure in Foggy Bottom.

That lawsuit, along with the efforts of the House committee investigating the 2012 Muslim terrorist attack on the American consulate in Benghazi, Libya, led to one of the greatest revelations of the presidential election. Clinton used a private server to conduct official State Department business.

Despite what Bernie Sanders would later claim during a Democratic debate, the American people did in fact care about Hillary Clinton's emails. They cared greatly, which is one of the major reasons Donald Trump is now president, and she is on an endless book tour.

The ramifications of her private server were profound and, for her, dire. Her campaign never really recovered from the revelation. But it wasn't just about emails, any more than Richard Nixon's Watergate scandal was about a third-rate burglary. The American people cared about the email scandal because of what it told them about a controversial figure who already had a reputation for congenital lying, self-serving secrecy and corruption.

Although Clinton insisted that the private server arrangement was for convenience, even a Luddite like me knew that creating and maintaining your own email server is more complicated than letting the government's IT pros handle it. It was obvious that Clinton took extraordinary measures to ensure that her communications, private or otherwise, would not be vulnerable to the prying eyes of journalists and government watchdogs—and cops. And that prompted the question that would haunt Clinton throughout the campaign and continues do this day:

What was she hiding?

In addition to Clinton's coordinated effort to keep her dirty laundry out of the public eye, the private server had implications for national security. As Secretary of State, Clinton was privy to some of the nation's most closely guarded secrets—intelligence about terrorists in the Middle East, high-level diplomatic cables from U.S. ambassadors, internal deliberations of the executive branch. They were all about national security, which is why the federal government spends billions of dollars to protect them from prying foreign eyes. But by using her own private email server, Clinton had placed all of that information—some of it classified at the highest levels—in jeopardy.

As FBI Director James Comey later noted in his Congressional testimony regarding the server, Clinton's emails would have been more secure on Gmail. Members of the U.S. intelligence community noted at the time that it would amount to malpractice if the intelligence agencies of Russia, Iran, China, and North Korea hadn't been trying to hack into Clinton's server. Several cyber-security experts have claimed that it was highly likely that they had succeeded in doing just that.

We eventually learned from reading emails exchanged among Clinton's IT staff that the server was subject to several cyber attacks, which they claimed were unsuccessful. Before the criminal case against Hillary was broomed, the FBI had concluded that it was "reasonably likely that hostile actors" gained access to the server. If foreign governments did infiltrate Clinton's server, that meant America's enemies were potentially reading the U.S. Secretary of State's emails in real time.

According to the FBI, Clinton's server contained 110 emails that were "classified," 65 emails that were "Secret," and 22 that were deemed "Top Secret." The mishandling of such information, in addition to being a criminal act, also cast doubt on Clinton's credentials to be president. Getting sloppy with national secrets can get U.S. military members killed. How could Clinton command the armed services when her carelessness and disregard for the law, not to mention common sense, put American lives at risk?

From a political perspective, the mishandling of classified information was just the tip of the email iceberg. The broader liability was what the email scandal revealed about Clinton. She cared nothing about breaking the law, was deeply paranoid and opposed to transparency, and she fervently believed that her actions, whatever they might be, must never ever be exposed to the prying eyes of journalists or citizens or... prosecutors. Her 33,000-plus deleted emails became a *tabula rasa*—a blank slate—that let voters project onto them whatever nefarious schemes they could imagine. She could claim all she wanted that the emails were not work-related or were mundane, but that excuse was laughable.

Given what we knew about the Clintons' many years in "public service," no suggestion as to what was deleted seemed too far-fetched. And as with most Clinton scandals, the information trickled out month after month, and each new revelation brought an evolution of Clinton's forked-tongue excuses for her behavior. Her response was more damaging to her candidacy than anything that was in the emails.

The old axiom held true: The cover-up is worse than the crime.

Clinton's attempt at damage control began at, of all places, the United Nations. After some meaningless conference, she arranged a press conference to spin the scandal in her favor and take a few questions from carefully selected reporters from the Andrea Mitchell school. Her performance on Turtle Bay would quickly become an oft-cited benchmark against which to compare Clinton's ever-changing rationale for using the secret server.

"I know there have been questions about my email," said Clinton. "So I want to address that directly."

Then she began dissembling.

"First," she said, "when I got to work as Secretary of State, I opted for convenience to use my personal email account, which was allowed by the State Department, because I thought it would be easier to carry just one device for my work and for my personal emails instead of two."

Right out of the gate, she was lying. We would later learn that establishing her favored system was not more convenient, but was in fact quite involved and complicated. We would also discover that she carried multiple devices that could access her email and that those emails passed over multiple servers. This lie wasn't even that hard to prove. As Secretary of State, Clinton was photographed by journalists—a lot—and a casual search through images available on the Internet yielded dozens of pictures of Clinton using all her different devices. Also, State Department rules expressly forbid what Clinton had done. These regulations too were easily accessible to the most casual observer. To sum up, every aspect of her first attempt to address the email scandal was a lie, and it only got worse.

"Second," she said, "the vast majority of my work emails went to government employees at their government addresses, which meant they were captured and preserved immediately on the system at the State Department."

While it might have been true that Clinton's emails to State Department staff were preserved according to the standards of the federal government,

Clinton's statement avoided the obvious. The American people were not interested in the humdrum missives she sent to the entire State Department, or to bureaucratic underlings whom she wouldn't even recognize in an elevator. Clinton quite obviously knew at the time that those emails would be preserved, and would therefore be subject to FOIA requests. Keenly aware of that vulnerability, she would have been careful. What the American people were interested in were the emails that were not sent to State Department employees—and there were plenty of those, as we would soon find out.

Then Clinton dropped some of the biggest whoppers on us.

"I responded right away and provided all my emails that could possibly be work-related, which totaled roughly 55,000 printed pages," she said. "We went through a thorough process to identify all of my work-related emails and deliver them to the State Department. At the end, I chose not to keep my private personal emails."

There is a kernel of truth to this line. In an era of unsurpassed technological capabilities—at a time when sharing information digitally has never been easier—Clinton and her lawyers provided *paper copies* of the emails to the State Department. Could this have been anything less than a deliberate attempt to delay the ultimate release of these emails to the public? Some miserable federal employees would eventually have to spend countless hours re-digitizing the emails so that they could be made available on the State Department's website.

That being said, does anyone really think that Clinton provided "all" of her "work-related" emails? Of course not. The proposition was ludicrous on its face. Most of us wanted to know: Why the hell does Hillary get to decide what is and is not a public record? That would be like the DEA showing up to a suspected drug dealer's house with a search warrant and then letting the drug dealer turn over only the evidence he deemed important. The FBI would later discover that Clinton's legal team did not review the emails one-by-one, but instead used keyword searches to retrieve emails that they were willing to turn over. And when, by the way, was the last time you just willy-nilly deleted any of your personal emails, let alone more than 30,000?

None of Clinton's excuses came anywhere near to passing the smell test. And she added insult to injury by suggesting that the deleted files contained nothing but, as she put it, "emails about planning Chelsea's wedding or my mother's funeral arrangements, condolence notes to friends as well as yoga routines, family vacations, the other things you typically find in inboxes."

After news broke that Clinton's emails had not just been deleted but had been purged from the server using a program called BleachBit, Clinton again faced new questions over her secretive behavior. Asked by a reporter whether she had "wiped" the server clean, Clinton responded: "What, like with a cloth?"

"I don't know how it works digitally at all," she said. Another lie.

Months after Trump was sworn into office, two national political reporters published a book on Hillary's campaign, *Shattered: Inside Hillary Clinton's Doomed Campaign.* Authors Jonathan Allen and Amie Parnes revealed that Clinton had her aides download all of the emails from her campaign staff following the 2008 election. She wanted to personally review all of their communications. She wanted to know who was talking to whom and who was leaking to the press. She wanted to understand what went wrong. That Clinton had the wherewithal to download all of these emails and scour them for clues shows she was acutely aware of how emails and servers work—and why secrecy is important, especially if you're doing something that's not, shall we say, on the level.

Luckily, the extreme steps Clinton took to conceal her dark activities from the American people failed. Clinton was forced to turn over the emails on her private server, and a federal judge ruled that the emails, at least the ones that were not deleted, would be released on the State Department's website on a rolling basis, once a month. That set up an interesting dynamic in the political media. Every month at the same time, we waited with bated breath, refreshing the website to see whether a new batch had become available. And when they did, the race was on to find the headline grabbing missives Clinton had exchanged. And boy were there some headlines.

The Emails

Clinton had sought to portray herself as pivotal to almost every decision made in the Obama White House. The idea was to burnish her policy credentials and inflate her resume. She never missed an opportunity to let us know that when SEAL Team Six took down Osama bin Laden in 2011, she was "monitoring" the operation from the situation room. However, the emails told a different story. The emails told the story of a Secretary of State who was often frozen out of the White House and only marginally aware of the executive branch's activities.

In June 2009, at the beginning of her tenure, Clinton was riding around Washington, D.C., listening to the all-news radio station WTOP when she learned about some official business. "I heard on the radio that there is a Cabinet mtg this am," she wrote in an email to her staffers, including Huma Abedin. "Is there? Can I go?"

On other occasions, the White House had stood Clinton up. "I arrived for the 10:15 mtg and was told there was no mtg," she wrote, also in June. "This is the second time this has happened. What's up??"

Clinton's lack of access to Obama bugged her. In December 2009, she told her smarmy communications hand Phillipe Reines that she was jealous of the access Henry Kissinger had had to President Richard Nixon.

"I see POTUS at least once a week while K saw Nixon every day," she wrote. "Do you see this as a problem?"

Obama wasn't the only Democrat president that Clinton sometimes had trouble communicating with. Following the 2010 earthquake in Haiti, former President Bill Clinton, referred to in the Clinton emails as "WJC," accepted a United Nations appointment as special envoy. He did so without consulting, or informing, his wife.

"WJC said he was going to call HRC," Doug Band, an adviser to Bill, told Clinton's staff, "but (he) hasn't had time."

Then there was this surreal get-well message from Maryland Democrat Sen. Barbara Mikulski:

"Am so glad to hear frm you//// knew this was painful combined with logistics of being a woman—know. How streddful this must be——the other night the. Senate. Women had dinner anyway—all sent good words. And encouragement. To a woman theyb all said. Oh my imagine just getting dressed and the. Hair thing. Get your therapy. Get better. The senate is slogging along—health care is starting to sag.—some days it feels like we are doing the public option off backof envelope. Call when you can. X."

Uh, Senator, want to take another crack at that?

Other Clinton emails painted a picture of Hillary as a relic of an earlier age who could barely manage basic technology, such as a fax machine. A few days before Christmas 2009, Clinton and Abedin spent almost an hour just trying to send out a fax.

Clinton: I thought it was supposed to be off hook to work?

Abedin: Yes but hang up one more time. So they can reestablish the line.

Clinton: I did.

Abedin: Just pick up phone and hang it up. And leave it hung up.

Clinton: I've done it twice now.

Clinton relied on her staff not just for faxing, but also for getting her food. "Pls call Sarah and ask her if she can get me some iced tea," she wrote in an email to her underlings.

Clinton even needed her staffers' help to engage in basic human interaction. Prior to a party in Los Angeles in October 2011, Clinton had her team write talking points in case she ran into Ellen DeGeneres. Talking points—for a party! "I'm very excited about the possibility of using your incredible platform to help us raise awareness about eliminating HIV/AIDS," the talking points read. Clinton couldn't have come up with that on her own?

The emails showed Clinton was highly concerned with her public image, monitoring even the reaction to her clothing when she took foreign trips.

"Your arrival in Kabul landed the front page picture in the NYT and sparked an online poll in *Huff Post* about your coat," a staffer told her. "Its favorability was 77 percent."

Clinton's State Department emails portrayed her as a self-serving, out-of-touch liberal with a habit of sleeping in late and going to bed early. In a 2013 email exchange, for example, Huma Abedin asked Clinton staffer Monica R. Hanley if she had reviewed the schedule of phone calls Clinton would need to make the following morning.

"She was in bed for a nap by the time I heard that she had an 8am call," Hanley replied, at 4:59 pm.

Abedin instructed Hanley on the importance of going over the call schedule with the Secretary of State.

"Very imp to do that," she wrote. "She's often confused."

Hillary's struggle to get enough sleep, her confusion over technology, her awkward interactions with other employees—this all made for entertaining chat on my radio show. However, these were the least consequential emails Clinton turned over to the State Department.

Sid Vicious

Sidney Stone Blumenthal served under President Bill Clinton as a senior adviser. On the surface, Blumenthal's job was advising the White House on policy and communications. But like anyone who has served long enough in the employ of the Clintons, Blumenthal developed a reputation as a dirty trickster and a spinmeister.

In 1998, for example, during the Monica Lewinsky scandal, Blumenthal was accused of attempting to discredit the investigation of Special Counsel Kenneth Starr by sharing dirt on Starr and his aides with the media. Blumenthal's loyalty to the Clintons was the stuff of Democrat legend in Washington, D.C. and it continued long after Clinton left office.

Blumenthal was a top adviser to Hillary's first failed run for the presidency. The arduous nature of campaign life must have taken a toll on Blumenthal, as he was arrested on Jan. 7, 2008 in Nashua, New Hampshire, for driving while intoxicated. (He pleaded down to misdemeanor DWI.) During that campaign, Blumenthal used his "talents" to spread opposition research about Obama, including stories about his birthplace and his upbringing. So sordid was Blumenthal's reputation, even among his fellow Democrats, that the Obama administration prohibited him from serving under Clinton.

Imagine that—Blumenthal was too crooked for Obama!

(Blumenthal at one time lived in Boston, and in the 1970's worked for one of the hippie "alternative" weekly newspapers, *The Real Paper*, I believe. I recall one morning in probably 1980, speaking to him on the phone from my kitchen in Somerville about a subject I no longer recall. For some reason, he made me vaguely uneasy; I didn't trust him. At the end of our conversation he said, "Let's keep in touch," and I thought to myself, "I don't think so." That was the first and last time I ever spoke to Sid Vicious.)

Never one to be cowed by rules, Clinton persisted in retaining Blumenthal's services despite strict orders from Obama's Chief of Staff Rahm Emanuel. She couldn't offer him an official job at State, so instead she made him something of an outside adviser and arranged for him to receive $10,000 per month from the Clinton Foundation.

Blumenthal was *persona non grata* in Obama's Washington, and the Clinton team knew it. According to a June 2009 email, Clinton's staff took pains to ensure Blumenthal's occasional visit to Foggy Bottom went unnoticed. "FYI, we have heard from an AP reporter that Sidney outed himself about coming to the Department, mentioning it without realizing he was talking to someone who actually covers our building," a State staffer wrote in an email to Cheryl Mills, Clinton's attorney. There's no indication whether action was taken to put out that fire or prevent future visits.

Among Hillary's State Department emails were hundreds of missives back and forth with Blumenthal. He would send Hillary encouraging notes, forward her pieces from his rabidly anti-Semitic son, Max Blumenthal, and inform her when he had placed a story in the alt-left media on her behalf. How odd it was to see her pull the full Sgt. Schultz routine and pretend that Blumenthal was just some casual acquaintance who sent her occasional emails that she rarely read. But that's exactly what she did.

In May 2016, Clinton was on a campaign stop when a reporter asked her about Blumenthal. The entire Clinton email archive was not yet available to the public, so no one outside of her inner circle knew the full scope of the relationship between the two. But already there was enough there to pique at least one reporter's interest. Pressed on her ties to Blumenthal, Clinton prevaricated:

"He's been a friend of mine for a long time," Clinton said, "and he sent me **unsolicited** emails, which I passed on in some instances." (Emphasis added.)

In the following months, that statement too would prove to be totally false. As later batches of emails were released by the State Department, more and more exchanges with Blumenthal were exposed. Additionally, Congress compelled Blumenthal to hand over his copies of the emails, which included several that Clinton herself had failed to produce.

"Greetings from Kabul!" Clinton cheerily wrote to Blumenthal in July of 2012, a response to his memo regarding the recent Libya election. "And thanks for keeping this stuff coming!"

That sure sounds like solicitation to me.

In another instance, Clinton responds to an August 2011 Libya memo from Blumenthal with the following: "I'm going to Paris tomorrow night and will meet [with National Transitional Council] leaders so this and additional info useful."

In yet another exchange, Clinton clearly requests additional emails from the man who was collecting a handsome paycheck from the Clinton Foundation.

"I shared your emails w Bill who thought they were 'brilliant'!" she wrote. "Keep 'em coming when you can."

Far from being a mere friend who sent unsolicited emails to Clinton, Blumenthal was one of her most trusted advisors. A review of her State Department emails shows that she corresponded with Sid more than anyone else outside of the State Department. So why did she think she could get away with the lie? That's a rhetorical question. She's a Clinton, after all.

Perhaps Clinton wanted to distance herself from Blumenthal because the adviser was directly involved in some of her worst decisions as Secretary of State—namely, Libya. Nearly one-third of all the emails Clinton received on the deteriorating political situation in Libya came from Blumenthal. Many were written in what would now be called Fusion GPS style—in other words, to look like official intelligence-agency documents. Blumenthal prepared these memos with the help of his business partner, former CIA operative Tyler Drumheller. Blumenthal and Drumheller were partners in a company called Osprey, which hoped to profit from plush government contracts from the Libyan transitional government. In other words, Blumenthal had encouraged Clinton to enforce a policy of regime change in Libya while positioning himself to profit handsomely if his own advice was followed.

Did I mention that any contracts Osprey would have acquired would have been sent up for approval by the Clinton State Department?

On August 22, 2011, it appeared that Blumenthal had gotten his wish. Qaddafi's government fell. In a celebratory note, Sid Vicious heralded this historic moment in the career of Hillary Rodham Clinton:

First, brava! This is a historic moment and you will be credited for realizing it.

When Qaddafi himself is finally removed, you should of course make a public statement before the cameras wherever you are, even in the driveway of your vacation house. You must establish yourself in the historical record at this moment.

The most important phrase is: "successful strategy." ...

This is a very big moment historically and for you. History will tell your part in it. You are vindicated.

Unfortunately for Hillary, history, rather than Sid Blumenthal, would tell of Hillary's role in Libya. Indeed, if you want to know what *really* happened in the 2016 election, we must examine the shining jewel in Hillary Clinton's foreign policy crown: Benghazi.

Benghazi

At 9:40 pm on September 11, 2012, armed Islamic militants from Ansar al-Sharia launched a coordinated terrorist attack on an American diplomatic outpost in Benghazi, Libya. The night of violence would end with the deaths of four Americans—CIA contractors Tyrone S. Woods and Glen Doherty, U.S. Foreign Services Information Management Officer Sean Smith, and U.S. Ambassador to Libya J. Christopher Stevens.

How could this have happened? How could Americans in hostile territory have been caught off guard? Who did this to us? These were the questions most Americans were asking.

But President Barack Obama and Secretary of State Hillary Clinton had other concerns. Obama was in the middle of his campaign for re-election against Mitt Romney. Osama Bin Laden is dead, GM's alive, and Al-Qaeda is on the run—that was the incumbent's refrain. The Benghazi attack, however, proved the utter fatuity of this narrative. So the Obama spin machine needed a new story line, and Clinton, always cognizant of her own political future, was willing to play ball.

In the days following the attack, Obama and Clinton would work together to foist an utter falsehood on the American people: that the Benghazi attack wasn't a coordinated terrorist attack by Islamic militants. It was instead a spontaneous reaction to a YouTube video.

In other words, the problem here wasn't clueless foreign policy or an unwillingness to confront the Islamic terror threat. The problem wasn't a reckless Secretary of State who disastrously advocated regime change in Libya, then in the wake of her folly failed to even provide adequate security for the State Department staffers, American citizens, all of whom were trying to manage the wreckage of the failed state that Libya had become.

Rather than tell the American people the unvarnished truth about Libya before the election, Hillary and Obama instead blamed the bloodshed in Benghazi on an insensitive filmmaker who offended Muslims, a Christian filmmaker, wouldn't you know it?

"Some have sought to justify this vicious behavior as a response to inflammatory material posted on the Internet," Clinton said in a State Department statement on the night of the attack. "The United States deplores any intentional effort to denigrate the religious beliefs of others."

Forty minutes after she issued her first statement, Clinton emailed her daughter's pseudonymous email handle, "Diane Reynolds," and told her the truth: "Two of our officers were killed in Benghazi by an Al Qaeda-like group," wrote Clinton. "The Ambassador, whom I handpicked and a young communications officer on temporary duty w a wife and two young children. Very hard day and I fear more of the same tomorrow.'"

Right after emailing Chelsea, Clinton contacted Libyan president Mohammed Magariaf with the same message: "There is a gun battle ongoing, which I understand Ansar [al] Sharia is claiming responsibility for."

The following day, Clinton continued to spin some politically expedient fiction about the inflammatory material.

"We are working to determine the precise motivations and methods of those who carried out this assault," Clinton told the American people in a speech at the State Department. "Some have sought to justify this vicious behavior, along with the protest that took place at our Embassy in Cairo yesterday, as a response to inflammatory material posted on the internet."

After lying to the public, Clinton reverted to the truth in a conversation with Hisham Qandil, the Egyptian prime minister: "We know the attack in Libya had nothing to do with the film. It was a planned attack—not a protest. Based on the information we saw today, we believe that the group that claimed responsibility for this was affiliated with al-Qaeda."

The truth was good enough for her daughter, the president of Libya and the prime minister of Egypt, but it wasn't good enough for the American people.

Two days after the attack, Clinton lied even more outrageously. She was at Andrews Air Force Base for the arrival of the flag-draped coffins of the four murdered Americans. Publicly, Clinton again said, "We've seen rage and violence directed at American embassies over an awful internet video that we had nothing to do with."

According to Tyrone Woods' father Charles, Hillary told him privately: "We'll make sure that the person who made that film is arrested and prosecuted."

Clinton would later assert that Woods was lying about the exchange, but this was one promise Clinton kept. Nakoula Basseley Nakoula, the Egyptian-born Coptic Christian who produced the YouTube video in question, was thrown in jail on some trumped-up charges. The Obama campaign was so committed to supporting the Benghazi lies that the U.S. Embassy in Pakistan, at Clinton's direction, spent $70,000 to produce and air a commercial on Pakistani television repeating her bogus internet-video claims.

In October 2015, when Clinton was called to testify before the House Committee investigating the Benghazi attack, she continued her brazen lies, blaming the intelligence community and the "fog of war" for her serial prevarications about the YouTube video. She even claimed to be heartbroken over the loss of American life.

"I would imagine I've thought more about what happened than all of you put together," she said. "I've lost more sleep than all of you put together."

She cared deeply about Chris Stevens. Just ask her! But subsequent testimony revealed that Stevens did not have Clinton's private email address. The ambassador she cared for so much had no way of contacting her, but Sid Blumenthal did.

Pressed by Rep. Jim Jordan (R-Ohio) on the discrepancies between her public statements following the attack and her private messages to her daughter and foreign leaders, Clinton offered bland denials and suggested that any criticism along those lines was political.

"You tell the American people one thing," Jordan said. "You tell your family an entirely different story."

"If you look at my statement as opposed to what I was saying to the Egyptian prime minister, I did state clearly, and I said it again in more detail the next morning," Clinton said incoherently. "I'm sorry that it doesn't fit your narrative, Congressman. I can only tell you what the facts were. And the facts, as the Democratic members have pointed out in their most recent collection of them, support this process that was going on, where the intelligence community was pulling together information."

Clinton even persisted in the widely debunked claim that the Nakoula video contributed to the attack: "Congressman," she said, "I believe to this day the video played a role."

Conservatives had long suspected that Obama and Hillary were lying to cover up the true nature of the attack. The administration, however, working in concert with the useful idiots of the mainstream media, was able to dismiss questions about Benghazi as conspiracy theories long enough for Obama to win re-election. But thanks to the investigative work of the House Benghazi committee and outside watchdog groups, the truth about that terrorist attack—and Clinton's lies throughout—was eventually exposed.

Most politicians would slink off into the shadows after such a disaster. But not Hillary. And who could blame her? The Clintons had gotten away with more potentially career-ending scandals than any couple in modern American politics. Why stop now? They knew, of course, that they could always count on the alt-left media to ignore her corruption. And that's precisely what they did. Clinton's 11 hours of testimony before the Congressional committee became a courageous accomplishment. Just ask Andrea Mitchell.

Tarmac Meeting

A pivotal moment of the campaign came on June 27 at an airport in Phoenix as Bill Clinton and Attorney General Loretta Lynch met on the tarmac to discuss...golf and grandchildren. Or so they said later. It was one month before Clinton would officially be nominated in Philadelphia as the Democratic nominee for president.

The Clintons needed to talk to the attorney general, a Clintonista from way back. Bill had appointed her U.S. Attorney in Brooklyn in 1999. From 2002 to 2010, she was a partner at the Washington-based law firm that handled the Clintons' tax returns. The two Democrats had more than a passing acquaintance with one another when Bill Clinton ambled onto her government jet that sunny afternoon in Phoenix.

As attorney general, Lynch was responsible for the criminal investigation into Hillary Clinton's use of a private email server. That she would meet privately with the husband of the subject, if not target, of an investigation was a major breach of ethics. Obviously, she never thought the public would learn about the meeting. The only reason we did is because of a local reporter, Christopher Sign of KNXV-TV in Phoenix. The Washington political press corps knew nothing of the secret meeting, although even if they had known, most likely they would not have reported on it—unless of course it could have somehow been spun into an anti-Trump story.

According to local reporter Sign, the FBI instructed everyone in the vicinity of the tarmac meeting that pictures and videos would not be allowed—an interesting measure to take considering the purely social, completely innocent, not-at-all-suspect nature of the get-together.

The day after she was busted, Lynch insisted the conversation did not stray into the ongoing criminal investigation of Bill's wife by the Department of Justice. "I did see President Clinton at the Phoenix airport as he was leaving and (he) spoke to myself and my husband on the plane," Lynch said. "Our conversation was a great deal about grandchildren, it was primarily social about our travels and he mentioned golf he played in Phoenix."

That excuse did not hold up. Sources told Sign that Clinton did not play golf when he was in Phoenix. As for Lynch—she doesn't have any grandchildren.

Of course Sign's scoop was not the kind of story that the *New York Times* or CNN were interested in following up. Indeed, after the election, FOIA requests from outside watchdog groups revealed emails from reporters belatedly assigned to the story. Turns out, the alt-left media were reluctant to even cover the story, and some seemed more than eager to spin on behalf of Lynch and the Clintons.

In one email, a DOJ staffer writes to a superior using the subject line "FBI just called."

"Jack Date from ABC called [the FBI] about this report from their Phoenix affiliate that the FBI was instructing people not to take pictures. [REDACTED] at FBI received the call and is looking for guidance and to know if we will provide any comment on this," wrote Patrick Rodenbush.

The DOJ team was apparently working overtime to explain away the tarmac meeting and the suspicious orders from the FBI.

Although the local station and its parent company were interested in fleshing out this major story, other mainstream outlets were less enthusiastic, to say the least.

"I've been pressed into service to write about the questions being raised by the Attorney General's meeting with Bill Clinton," *New York Times* reporter Mark Lander complained to Melanie Newman, then-director of the Justice Department's Public Affairs Office.

Washington Post reporter Matt Zapotsky seemed eager to help Clinton and Lynch concoct a plausible alibi for their chicanery.

"My editors are still pretty interested in it," he wrote in an email, "and I'm hoping I can put it to rest by answering just a few more questions about how the meeting came about—who approached who, and how did they realize they were in the same place?"

The tarmac meeting provided Trump, who was already telling his voters that the investigation into Crooked Hillary was not on the level, with even more ammo. And it set in motion a series of unusual decisions from the Justice Department. As criticism of the tarmac meeting intensified, Lynch told an audience in Colorado that it was reasonable to ask questions about the encounter. She added that she would be accepting whatever recommendation FBI director Comey delivered on whether to prosecute Clinton.

"I will be accepting their recommendations and their plans for going forward." Lynch said. "It's important to make it clear that that meeting with President Clinton does not have a bearing on how this matter is going to be reviewed, resolved and accepted by me."

The tarmac meeting, combined with Lynch's non-recusal recusal, set the stage for one of the most controversial press conferences ever held by an FBI director.

On July 5, Comey summoned the political media to the Justice Department headquarters in Washington. For 15 minutes, Comey laid out the evidence against Clinton that had been revealed in the course of the investigation. It appeared to be an open-and-shut criminal case against Clinton.

Yes, Clinton had sent and received classified information through the server, despite her myriad denials.

"Although we did not find clear evidence," he said, "that Secretary Clinton or her colleagues intended to violate laws governing the handling of classified information, there is evidence that they were extremely careless in their handling of very sensitive, highly classified information."

The reference to extreme carelessness was an important one, as legal analysts at the time were suggesting that such "gross negligence," as it is described in the statute, might be all that a prosecutor would need to make the case against Clinton.

No, the lawyers did not read all of her emails, as she claimed. Instead, they relied on keyword searches which meant, in Comey's estimation, some work-related emails might not have been turned over.

"It is also likely that there are other work-related e-mails," he said, "that they did not produce to State and that we did not find elsewhere, and that are now gone because they deleted all e-mails they did not return to State, and the lawyers cleaned their devices in such a way as to preclude complete forensic recovery."

As for Hillary's convenience excuse? Comey demolished that as well. The FBI, he said, found that multiple servers, multiple devices, and multiple staffers and administrators were involved in the creation and management of Clinton's clandestine email arrangement.

And despite the denials by Clinton and her campaign that her server had been compromised, Comey said Clinton may have indeed been hacked because she used email extensively on foreign trips, where sophisticated adversaries operated with impunity. Further, individuals with whom she corresponded had been hacked.

The press conference was shocking. I remember watching it from my radio studio. I know the Famous But Incompetent agency far too well to have ever expected the G-men to bring Clinton to justice, but as I watched the FBI Director lay out the evidence, I dared to dream that he was building toward a surprising conclusion. How could he let her skate after revealing evidence that she broke the law?

As we all now know, Comey stunned the nation by exonerating her.

"Although there is evidence of potential violations of the statutes regarding the handling of classified information," Comey said, "our judgment is that no reasonable prosecutor would bring such a case."

Comey even seemed to admit that Hillary Clinton was being held to her own separate standard—or lack of standard. More than ever she seemed to be above the law—or perhaps below it.

"To be clear," Comey said, "this is not to suggest that in similar circumstances, a person who engaged in this activity would face no consequences."

Two hours later Clinton boarded Air Force One with President Obama, bound for a campaign rally in Charlotte.

Chapter Eight

Immigration

THE MAKE AMERICA GREAT AGAIN AGENDA WAS A COMPREHENSIVE platform spanning all areas of policy and philosophy. But the foundation of the MAGA agenda, from the very beginning, was immigration.

In his opening speech Trump clearly (and defiantly) threw down the gauntlet to the establishment of both parties. Illegal immigration would be the centerpiece of his campaign—political correctness be damned. The Democrat Party and the mainstream media worked tirelessly to demonize Trump for talking about the scourge of sexual violence occurring on the U.S.-Mexico border. But their attacks failed to resonate. Far from hurting Trump, the relentless focus on his immigration rhetoric elevated his candidacy like no other issue, creating a media phenomenon that his primary opponents could never overcome.

Liberals insist that illegal immigrants do not commit more crimes than U.S. citizens or legal immigrants. That's a lie. For reasons of political correctness, the true statistics about illegal immigrant crime are swept under the rug.

Often, research on the subject will conflate illegal immigrants and legal immigrants, which is hardly helpful if you're looking for an honest assessment of the crimes committed by illegal aliens. Groups like the Center for Immigration Studies, a conservative non-profit that researches immigration, have struggled for years just to pry facts and data out of the federal government. For their trouble, they are branded a "hate group" by the likes of the Southern Poverty Law Center. But although we don't have perfect information about the scale of the illegal alien crime problem, we see it every day with our own eyes.

Illegal immigrants committing crimes and getting off with light sentences had become, sadly, a fact of life for Americans. Democrat politicians, like former Mass. Gov. Deval Patrick, insist that stories of illegal immigrant crime are mere "anecdotes." But if you've been paying attention, the anecdotes are really starting to pile up.

Matthew Denise was a 23-year-old Milford man. In 2011, he had just graduated from Framingham State University. He had his entire life ahead of him. Then, one Saturday while he was riding his motorcycle, a drunken illegal alien from Ecuador struck him with his pick-up truck. Denise became entangled in the wheel well of the vehicle. The oblivious Ecuadorian drove on for another quarter mile, dragging Denise to his death.

Nicolas Guaman, the illegal immigrant driving the truck, had a dozen or so empty beer cans at his feet and his toddler anchor-baby son next to him in the passenger seat. In 2013, he was ruled incompetent to stand trial. Judge Janet Kinton-Walker said Guaman's "unique cultural background" and language barrier meant that he could not understand the legal process or consult properly with his public defender.

What's more, the defense insisted that Guaman's native language was not Spanish but one of 47 different dialects of a rare central American language. Translation? John Q. Taxpayer was going to spend a lot of money for a Quechua translator before justice could be served.

The excuse was bogus, of course. Guaman had had previous run-ins with the law and had used a Spanish translator or no translator at all. But the facts didn't matter. Guaman was a member of a protected class, and no effort was to be spared to keep him from facing the consequences of his deadly actions.

Guaman's taxpayer-funded public defenders even created an entire new excuse for Central American illegal aliens who get busted for DUI. With the help of a court-ordered psychologist, the defense insisted that Guaman could not be held responsible for his drunken criminality because he lacked the enzyme to metabolize alcohol.

"Nearly half of indigenous South Americans from Mongoloid descent are deficient in an enzyme required to break down and metabolize alcohol," the psychologist told the judge.

You see how this works? If Joe Six Pack gets caught driving under the influence, he's going to have the book thrown at him and Mothers Against Drunk Driving will picket the courthouse. But if you're an illegal immigrant, you get a slide. And the Politically Correct crowd won't even flinch.

If you're an illegal, you don't lose your job, or your license because you have neither. You won't do time, because that might get you deported and you wouldn't be able to vote Democrat in the next election. On the other hand, a tax-paying citizen is lucky if he can scratch together $10,000 of his own money to hire a connected lawyer who judge-shops to get him a continued-without-a-finding, but the citizen still loses his license for six months and get slapped with years of insurance surcharges.

Guaman was charged with second-degree murder, but his public defender got him acquitted of that charge. That was an egregious affront to justice. Is there any doubt that a U.S. citizen would have been convicted of, at the very least, vehicular homicide or manslaughter? But when you're an illegal immigrant, you get your own set of rules—and did I mention a taxpayer-funded attorney? Guaman was, however, convicted of reckless endangerment of a child, leaving the scene of an accident which caused personal injury or death, failing to stop for police, and driving without a license. He was sentenced to 12 to 14 years in prison. He will be out of jail around the time Denise would have been in his mid-thirties, building a life for himself and chasing the American dream.

That was just one "anecdote," as former Massachusetts Gov. Deval Patrick would say. Illegal immigrant crime was happening all over the country.

In Texas in 2010, Laura Wilkerson reported her 18-year-old son Joshua missing, a week before Thanksgiving. Her worst fears were confirmed when police found Joshua, hands bound, beaten to death and burned in a field. Hermilo Vildo Moralez, a 19-year-old illegal alien from Belize, later admitted to murdering Wilkerson. He tied him up, bludgeoned him with a wooden rod, and then set him on fire.

Moralez was a so-called DREAMer, brought here by his parents when he was a child, and he grinned for his mug shot.

One evening in the spring of 2008, Jamiel Shaw heard gun shots ring out as he sat in his home in Arlington Heights, a neighborhood of Los Angeles. His son, Jamiel Shaw II, was walking home from a community center and had just gotten off his cell phone with his dad. Young Jamiel was only three blocks away from home when Pedro Espinoza, a Mexican member of the 18th Street Gang who was in the U.S. illegally, murdered him in cold blood as part of a gang initiation.

Like so many illegal alien criminals, Espinoza had previous brushes with law enforcement. But the permissive laws of a liberal city in a liberal state meant he was never deported nor imprisoned. Instead, he remained free to continue his barbaric crime spree against American taxpayers. I met the elder Mr. Shaw in person once. He's become an advocate for fair immigration laws— laws that might have saved his son's life. He's a good and honest man, and there's not an ounce of malice in his heart. But the pain in his eyes—it's the agony of a man who wakes every morning and falls asleep every night tortured by unfathomable loss.

Sgt. Brandon Mendoza was a 13-year veteran of the Mesa, Arizona police department. He was headed home after a long shift in 2014 when a vehicle travelling the wrong-way crashed head-on into his. The driver of that vehicle was Raul Silva-Corona. He did not have a driver's license and his blood alcohol content was 0.24. He drove over 35 miles the wrong way down the Interstate before killing Mendoza.

During his 20 years living illegally in the U.S., the enzyme-deficient Mexican racked up a criminal record. According to Colorado court records, he pleaded guilty to criminal conspiracy charges as part of a deal in which prosecutors dismissed more serious charges, including leaving the scene of an accident. Silva-Mendoza, like many other criminal illegal aliens, would have been granted permanent legal status under the Gang of Eight immigration bill before he killed Mendoza.

Kathryn "Kate" Steinle was a 32-year-old from Pleasanton, California. She was shot to death by an illegal alien wielding a stolen firearm on Pier 14 in the Embarcadero district of San Francisco. Steinle's killer was Jose Ines Garcia Zarate, a Mexican national, and the path he took to that tourist-destination pier would enrage a nation.

Garcia Zarate had been deported from the United States a total of five times, most recently in 2009, and was on probation in Texas at the time of the shooting. He had seven felony convictions. No one knew how old he was.

He had drifted into the U.S. sometime after 1991, the year he was first charged with a drug offense in Arizona. In 1993, he was convicted in Washington state on charges of heroin possession. He served another jail sentence in Oregon before he was deported in 1994, but he promptly returned to the U.S. and was convicted again of heroin possession.

In 1997, he was deported a second time. In 1998, he was caught near the border attempting to illegally enter the country and deported for a third time. Border Patrol caught him trying to sneak back in just six days later. He was deported in 2003 and again in 2009 after serving federal prison sentences.

Just three months after Garcia Zarate's fifth and final deportation, the Mexican national was caught attempting to cross the border in Eagle Pass, Texas. He pleaded guilty to felony re-entry, and a federal court sent him to a federal medical facility.

In 2015, the San Francisco Sheriff's Department asked the U.S. Bureau of Prisons to turn him over to local authorities who held a drug warrant. ICE issued a detainer that would have allowed immigration authorities to detain and deport him, but San Francisco is a sanctuary city. They refused to comply.

What makes illegal-alien crime so infuriating is the preventable nature of each and every one of them. If the United States had secured our southern border any time between when Garcia Zarate first snuck into the country in 1991 and 2009, then Kate Steinle would still be alive. And how many others just like her?

(In December 2017, Garcia Zarate was shockingly acquitted of the murder charge against him by a San Francisco jury. He was convicted of one felony count and sentenced to time served. The illegal alien faces new charges and remains in custody, but at his latest hearing in January 2018, he was smiling and shaking hands with his public defenders, who had denounced President Trump after their client's acquittal.)

These were the kinds of frustrations Trump tapped into, as millions of Americans read new reports daily of more American victims of violent illegal-alien crime. In a free society, things are going to get sloppy. There will always be crime. But when an individual who should not even be in the country is the offender, the government that failed to control its borders must bear responsibility for the senseless carnage.

While the elite political class ignored these victims and their surviving family members, Trump reached out to them, heard their pleas, and promised that he would do everything in his power to stop American families from being torn apart by illegal-immigrant crime.

Dominic Durden was a dispatcher for the Riverside County sheriff in Moreno Valley, California. In 2012, he died after the motorcycle he was driving was struck by a pickup truck. The driver, Juan Zacarias Tzun, was an illegal alien from Guatemala. He had no driver's license, but had two prior drunken-driving convictions.

Tzun was sentenced to just 90 days in jail and 180 days on a work-release program. He was deported in 2014. At his deportation proceedings, he blamed God for the car crash.

Dominic's mother, Sabine Durden, was one of the Angel Moms to whom Trump reached out. Durden, a legal immigrant from Germany, spoke in favor of Trump's candidacy at the Republican convention in Cleveland.

"I have been talking about illegal immigration since 2012, since he got killed, and no one listened until Donald Trump," she said. "Donald Trump is not only my hero, he's my lifesaver."

Through his campaign, Trump drew attention to these families, whom he dubbed the "forgotten" men and women of the country. He introduced many Americans to Angel Moms, the surviving parents of victims of illegal immigrant crime.

For the liberal commentators, bringing the parents of murder victims on stage during his rallies was a cynical ploy to stoke feelings of nativism, xenophobia, racism, you name it. In fact, Trump was offering them hope—hope that the federal government might one day hear their pleas and take common-sense measures to save the country from the tidal wave of Third World crime. The illegal immigrants had armies of non-profit lawyers and public defenders and media sob sisters assisting them, but the Angel Moms had no one speaking on their behalf, until Trump came along.

Trump's solution to illegal immigration was simple: Build the Wall! That three-word call to action became the battle cry of his campaign. Trump wasn't well versed in the intricacies of the State Department's visa policies, but the real estate developer understood construction and knew what it would take to build a big, beautiful wall on the southern border.

Advised by former Jeff Sessions adviser Stephen Miller, Trump knew that you did not have to be an Angel Mom to be a victim of America's permissive immigration system. Indeed, millions of Americans had suffered as the result of unskilled foreigners competing in the work force. And even if they hadn't yet lost a job, anyone who'd ever visited a hospital emergency room on a week-end, or a district court on a Monday morning, could view with his own eyes the catastrophic effects of unlimited Third World immigration on the fabric of civilized American society.

Trump's immigration plan was the most comprehensive policy document his campaign ever produced. It was based on three principles: 1) a nation with-out borders is not a nation; 2) a nation without laws is not a nation; and 3) a nation that does not serve its own citizens is not a nation. The truth of those principles was self-evident for most of us.

Trump's liberal critics couldn't fathom why someone would want to build a wall on the southern border. They insisted that it was insane, a waste of money, and that it would not work because the illegal immigrants would simply buy ladders or dig tunnels. But one can make a good argument that building the wall would actually save U.S. taxpayers money in the long run. There is broad agree-ment among researchers that illegal immigrants to the United States have, at best, a modest level of education and command lower wages relative to U.S. citizens and legal immigrants. This means the contribution they pay in taxes, when they do pay taxes, is far less than the cost of welfare they enjoy by living in America.

Using data gathered by the National Academies of Science, Engineering, and Medicine (NAS), the Center for Immigration Studies has calculated that a wall on the southern border would pay for itself over the next decade—even if it only stopped just 9 to 12 percent of attempted border crossings. From the CIS report:

"Based on the NAS data, illegal border-crossers create an average fiscal burden of approximately $74,722 during their lifetimes, excluding any costs

for their U.S.-born children. If a border wall stopped between 160,000 and 200,000 illegal crossers—9 to 12 percent of those expected to successfully cross in the next decade—the fiscal savings would equal the $12 to $15 billion cost of the wall."

Trump always insisted that Mexico would be called upon to pay for the wall. That claim was mostly an applause line, but it's not such a stretch. Remittances back to Mexico from the U.S. still account for a major share of Mexico's economy, and it would not be impractical to place a fee or tax on foreign wire transfers. Ironically enough, it is one of the few taxes Democrats oppose, because it would be mainly imposed, not on "deplorables," but on illegal-alien criminals, i.e., future Democrat voters.

Trump's plan also suggested paying for the wall by increasing visa charges for Mexican CEOs and increasing fees for Mexican border crossing permits.

In their attacks on Trump's plan to build a wall, his critics on both the left and the right displayed a striking complacency. According to their understanding of border security, America was helpless to stem the hordes of violent Third World criminal gangs and drug traffickers pouring into the country. Letting the carnage continue was the price we had to pay to be an inclusive society. Or so they said.

The anti-wall posturing from liberals was particularly obnoxious considering that top Democrats, including then-Sen. Hillary Clinton, had voted in 2006 for the Secure Fence Act, which allocated funds for the construction of a physical barrier on the southern border. Until the Democrats realized the political advantages of Barack Obama's "fundamental transformation" of America, the notion that the U.S. needed to secure the southern border and crack down on illegal immigration was a subject of broad bipartisan agreement.

In 1996, when Bill Clinton was running for reelection as president, his speeches on the topic were eerily similar to the words Trump used 20 years later.

In 1993, before his rise in leadership, Sen. Harry Reid was likewise clear about where he stood on illegal immigration. In newspaper op-eds and in his floor speeches, Reid espoused polices that he would later describe as racist when they were proposed by the Republican presidential nominee.

"If you break our laws by entering this country without permission and give birth to a child, we reward that child with citizenship and guarantee a full access to all public and social services this country provides," Reid said on the Senate floor in September 1993. "That's a lot of services. Is it any wonder that two-thirds of babies born at taxpayer [inaudible] county hospitals in Los Angeles are born to illegal alien mothers?"

Reid even introduced legislation that would limit birthright citizenship, ending the so-called "anchor baby" phenomenon.

The 1996 national platform of the Democrat Party was even more explicit in its opposition to illegal immigration and various amnesty proposals. Which is why I handed Trump a copy of the ur-Trumpian document in August 2015, at his rally on Ernie Boch Jr.'s estate in Norwood.

"Today's Democratic Party also believes we must remain a nation of laws," the platform read. "We cannot tolerate illegal immigration and we must stop it. For years before Bill Clinton became President, Washington talked tough but failed to act. In 1992, our borders might as well not have existed. The border was under-patrolled, and what patrols there were, were under-equipped. Drugs flowed freely. Illegal immigration was rampant. Criminal immigrants, deported after committing crimes in America, returned the very next day to commit crimes again."

Twenty years earlier, pre-Trump, the top Democrats had even opposed welfare benefits for illegal immigrants.

"We continue to firmly oppose welfare benefits for illegal immigrants," the platform stated. "We believe family members who sponsor immigrants into this country should take financial responsibility for them, and be held legally responsible for supporting them."

What a striking transformation the Democrat Party had undergone in just two decades! Far from the reasonable positions on immigration upheld by Bill Clinton, today's Democrat Party is opposed to the enforcement of the law and stridently defends a separate, weaker system of criminal justice for illegal aliens. Twenty years ago, Democrat leaders were honest enough to admit that illegal aliens were taking advantage of America's generous welfare state. Today's Democrats pretend that foreign nationals are never eligible for such benefits as food stamps, Temporary Assistance to Needy Families (TANF), Section 8, and Obama Care.

How out of control was the welfare system? Well before her death, the president's own Aunt Zeituni, an illegal alien from Kenya, was openly living in a public housing project in South Boston, giving television interviews in which she admitted that she was collecting welfare. Auntie Zeituni was totally unapologetic. She said it was God's will. Millions of other illegals obviously agreed with the President's beloved aunt.

Bill Clinton wasn't the only top Democrat who forcefully opposed illegal immigration until it was no longer politically expedient. His wife did, too. In 2003, Sen. Clinton was on the record as "adamantly against illegal immigrants."

But she shifted, too, as the political winds changed, backing a full "pathway to citizenship" for illegal aliens in her failed 2008 presidential campaign.

Most of Trump's Republican opponents supported amnesty in one form or another. Beginning with early attempts to pass so-called comprehensive immigration reform under President George W. Bush, the Chamber of Commerce/ *Wall Street Journal* wing of the GOP establishment began making an argument in favor of amnesty. According to their thinking, the Republican Party would fall into permanent minority status if steps were not taken to pander to the growing Hispanic population.

According to this theory, Hispanics residing legally in the U.S. don't care about the economy, health care, national defense, trade, schools or religious liberty. No, all they are concerned with is protecting illegal immigrants, their welfare handouts and their immunity from all criminal prosecution while simultaneously giving them a path to legal status and presumably even more advantages over the native, taxpaying, law-abiding population. The Beltway consultants pushing this theory imagined a fantasy world where Republicans caved on immigration and suddenly every "new American" voter with Mexican heritage would stampede to the polls to vote for their new amigos John McCain and Mitt Romney. Trump rejected that consultant con and won the nomination, and eventually the election, because he refused to ignore the rampant lawlessness that open borders had created.

In the run-up to the general election, the pundit class insisted that a massive surge in Hispanic voting would punish Trump for his immigration policies and rhetoric.

However, exit polling and other analyses show that Trump likely performed better among Hispanics than Mitt Romney had four years earlier. Trump's victory finally put to rest the establishment lie that the GOP would need to abandon its principles on immigration in order to remain a viable force in American politics.

Chapter Nine
Down the Stretch

AFTER TRUMP CLINCHED IN THE GOP NOMINATION, IT WAS TIME TO CHOOSE a Vice President.

The establishment voices who had opposed Trump's candidacy from the beginning now began to counsel him, much like Chuck Schumer offering free advice to Republicans on how to win elections. Major party figures, wealthy donors, and other connected Republicans advised Trump to pick a VP nominee who could serve as a moderating force on the campaign trail, while reassuring Republican voters. But most of the candidates the establishment pushed had crossed Trump at some point or another during the campaign. If there's anything we know now about Trump, it's that he values loyalty. And there were precious few big-name Republicans who had remained loyal to him throughout the rowdy primary campaign.

For Trump supporters, there was a worst-case scenario with any VP candidate. By now, even Trump's most ardent supporters had come to recognize the volatile nature of his campaign style. In his war against political correctness, Trump often overstepped traditional bounds and offended the gentle sensibilities of career politicians and their K Street coatholders. In the nightmare scenario his supporters imagined, Trump would nominate an establishment-type politician who would deliver an October surprise by bailing on the ticket when the fallout and blowback against Trump became too intense.

Such a betrayal, especially by someone from the GOP's genteel country-club class, was easy to imagine. So loyalty was paramount.

N.J. Gov. Chris Christie seemed like the natural selection. After dropping out early in the race, Christie had immediately endorsed Trump. His criticisms until that point had always been mild, gentle enough to be written off by either man as the casual banter you might hear from guys who grew up in the tri-state area. Christie quickly became a powerful ally of Trump's, regularly appearing on the cable news programs to advocate on his behalf. Christie connected Trump with his New Jersey-based network of donors and appeared with him many times throughout the campaign.

Most of all, Christie wanted the job, badly. His governorship had turned into, for lack of a better term, shit. He had few good options and vice president looked a lot more appealing than his back-up plan, grabbing the PM-drive gig on sports radio WFAN after Mike Francesa's retirement.

Former House Speaker Newt Gingrich was also in the mix. The pro-Newt side made a good argument. The savvy politician had adroitly maneuvered under a Democrat president to accomplish much during his leadership in Congress. Trump, as a political outsider, would need that kind of inside experience to successfully push his MAGA agenda through a stubborn and recalcitrant Congress. But Gingrich came with his own baggage. How many failed marriages could one Republican ticket carry? Plus, Gingrich's prickly personality, and his knack for producing sensational sound bites, which had served him well enough in his own presidential forays, threatened to upstage Trump in the media.

Other voices in the Republican Party insisted that Trump play identity politics. Trump lagged in support from minorities and women, they said, so why not put a minority or a woman on the ticket? Carly Fiorina, Oklahoma Gov. Mary Fallin and S.C. Gov. Nikki Haley, the Methodist daughter of Indian Sikh parents, were all brought up, but I doubt Trump ever seriously considered any of them.

Haley was out because she had done her best to deliver South Carolina to Marco Rubio. Fiorina and Trump were always oil and water, and neither the *Rolling Stone* story nor her alliance with Ted Cruz put her back on Trump's dance card. She is now an avid Never Trumper.

But beyond all that, identity politics was anathema to Trump. If he had cared about identity politics, he would never have entered the political arena and he would not have vanquished everyone in his path. Indeed, Trump's rejection of identity politics was the secret of his success. If you want to know what happened, *and Hillary this means you,* your answer must include Trump's rejection of identity politics.

Trump ended weeks of speculation on July 15, tweeting the announcement that Indiana Gov. Mike Pence would be his choice. The choice surprised many observers because Pence had endorsed Cruz prior to the Indiana primary. However, if you read between the lines, Pence's endorsement statement was carefully crafted. He praised Cruz and lauded his strict adherence to conservative dogma, but he avoided any attacks on Trump. Was Pence leaving the door open all along for his vice presidential candidacy?

For most Republicans, Pence was something of an unknown quantity. Throughout his career, he'd done little to court controversy. He'd spent six terms in the House before becoming governor of Indiana, but most Americans knew little of him.

Pence provided Trump with an experienced sidekick. He was also a steady hand, not prone to upstaging Trump in the way Christie or Gingrich might have, and he was a strong social conservative. He was an evangelical convert from Catholicism—in other words, he checked two important boxes. His son was a Marine—check another box. As he made the media rounds, it became clear that Pence was an excellent selection. He was calm, collected, and well-spoken. He was the yin to Trump's yang. He brought much-needed stability to the boisterous campaign. With Pence on the ticket, conservatives, especially his fellow evangelical Christians, could be certain that the Trump White House would stand up for religious liberty and the pro-life movement.

I liked Pence, too, but mostly because he was a former talk radio host.

Pence's most memorable line of the campaign came during his convention speech, and I remember it clearly.

"I've seen this good man up close, his utter lack of pretense, his respect for the people who work for him and his devotion to his family," Pence said of Trump. "And if you still doubt what I'm saying, remember, as we say back home, you can't fake good kids. How about his amazing children, aren't they something?"

You can't fake good kids—how true.

The Convention

Donald Trump didn't just win the Republican nomination, he executed a hostile takeover of the Grand Old Party. The chattering classes that began writing Trump's political obituary in June 2015 before he even finished his opening speech had been proven wrong.

All the might of the political establishment had coalesced against him during the primaries, yet he prevailed. Their dreams of a brokered convention were dashed. Never Trump was nevermore. Trump proclaimed victory over the Republican Party on July 21, 2016, at the Quicken Loans Arena in downtown Cleveland.

"Together, we will lead our party back to the White House, and we will lead our country back to safety, prosperity, and peace," he said. "We will be a country of generosity and warmth. But we will also be a country of law and order."

It was the beginning of a convention speech that would defy convention.

Earlier candidates used the moment to unite the Republican Party and appeal to the much-needed independent voters by tacking toward the center. In other words, they pandered and began with the switch part of a bait-and-switch.

Not Trump. He fully affirmed his continuing commitment to the MAGA platform he had elevated during the campaign and offered a grim but honest assessment of the present condition of the United States.

"If you want to hear the corporate spin, the carefully-crafted lies, and the media myths, the Democrats are holding their convention next week," he said. "But here, at our convention, there will be no lies. We will honor the American people with the truth, and nothing else."

Trump ripped into the Obama administration's criminal justice policies for prioritizing social justice over the safety and well-being of the American people. He called out the left's sickening kowtowing to cop-hating extremists. And he invoked the story of Sarah Root, a 21-year-old college graduate who was killed by a drunk-driving underage illegal immigrant in Nebraska. Far from tiptoeing around racially sensitive issues that his predecessors were loath to even mention, Trump confronted them with candor.

"I will tell you the plain facts that have been edited out of your nightly news and your morning newspaper: nearly four in 10 African-American children are living in poverty, while 58% of African-American youth are not employed," he said. "Two million more Latinos are in poverty today than when the President took his oath of office less than eight years ago. Another 14 million people have left the workforce entirely."

Then Trump turned to the state of international affairs. The current administration had done little more than dither as Syria descended into a hellishly failed state. Obama's Syria "red line" came and went. Meanwhile, Obama had encouraged Europe's calamitous open-borders response to the invasion of Mideast "refugees." All around the globe, U.S. weakness had spread instability and chaos. Before Obama and Hillary took the helm of American foreign policy, Trump said, the Middle East was at least under some semblance of control.

"Libya was cooperating," he said. "Egypt was peaceful. Iraq was seeing a reduction in violence. Iran was being choked by sanctions. Syria was under control.

"After four years of Hillary Clinton, what do we have? ISIS has spread across the region, and the world. Libya is in ruins, and our Ambassador and his staff were left helpless to die at the hands of savage killers. Egypt was turned over to the radical Muslim Brotherhood, forcing the military to retake control. Iraq is in chaos.

"This is the legacy of Hillary Clinton," he concluded. "Death, destruction and weakness."

The picture of the world Trump painted was bleak, not a single pastel in sight. But could anyone dispute it? The liberal pundits didn't even try to reckon with the facts of his assessment. Instead, they all read from the same talking points with identical buzzwords, characterizing his speech as 'dark' and gloomy—as if printing those adjectives would somehow undermine the truth of his words.

"Donald Trump's dark speech to the Republican National Convention," read the *Washington Post* headline. "Trump's Speech Casts U.S. in Dark Light," wrote the *New York Times*. "Donald Trump Offers Dark Vision of America," said CBS. Not to be outdone, the *New Yorker* titled its article, "Donald Trump's Dark, Dark Convention Speech." In other words, it was doubly dark.

The elite New York and Washington, D.C.-based media figures who had predicted Trump's demise hundreds of times before this day remained out of touch. From inside their cosmopolitan bubbles, the America Trump talked about was foreign to them.

The talking heads on the nightly news were insulated from the darker-than-dark tumult and disorder of which Trump spoke. They traveled in stretch limousines. They lived in doorman buildings and gated communities. Their children went to private schools. Their jobs, such as they were, were at non-profits, think tanks or Ivy League universities. They had trust funds and summer cottages on Nantucket. Affirmative action would never ever cost them a coveted slot—they were legacies, and the dean of admissions was only a phone call away. They had no experience with opiate addiction, and had never lost a loved one to heroin trafficked by illegal immigrants or to Chinese-made fentanyl delivered by the same foreign hands.

These elite media personalities had never been the victim of illegal-alien crime, nor had they conversed with the surviving loved ones. Their phony-baloney jobs were never threatened by visa programs that placed the interests of global corporations ahead of those of American workers.

Sure, they were familiar with the issues of urban poverty that had only been exacerbated by generations of Democrats. They had read about them in their college textbooks. But they were ignorant of the grinding, relentless and unforgiving reality of rural poverty.

For the elites, the Obama years had been anything but dark. But for the rest of us, the voters who propelled Trump to the nomination, his convention speech was exactly what we wanted: honesty in the face of media lies, and the courage to stand in the breach on behalf of the hardworking Americans who had been forgotten, or worse, shunned.

The Media Turns

The media's off-again, on-again love affair with Donald Trump ended once and for all when he accepted the GOP nomination—the same phenomenon John

McCain had experienced in 2008. Apparently, they hadn't known he was a Republican until he picked Sarah Palin as his running mate. Now, eight years later, the same network executives and anchors who had profited so handsomely for a year from the Trump-led ratings mania again came to their senses.

Yes, Trump brought eyeballs, and more readers and viewers meant higher revenues from advertisers. But some things were more important than profits. And so, as if a switch had been flipped, the media titans and their talking heads turned on the man who had driven their viewership to record levels. Nowhere was this change of attitude more pronounced than on MSNBC's morning show, hosted by Joe Scarborough and Mika Brzezinski.

Morning Joe, as they call it, was vapid TV prior to the 2016 GOP primary campaign. Scarborough, a former Republican member of Congress from Florida whose political career was undistinguished at best, offered similarly mundane insights into American politics. With his bizarrely oversized forehead, he resembled a grown-up version of the banjo boy in the movie *Deliverance*—a fact duly noted in many side-by-side "separated-at-birth" photo memes on the internet. He had previously fled Congress under, shall we say, questionable circumstances, after Lori Klausutis, a young intern, was found dead in his district office. Mika, the daughter of a foreign policy advisor to Jimmy Carter, didn't exactly pull herself up by the bootstraps. In hindsight, you can perhaps forgive Joe and Mika for running such a shallow and unentertaining morning show—considering they were simultaneously maintaining a clandestine and adulterous affair.

How could you expect them to provide entertaining and informative content when they were playing doctor with the shades drawn? As the old song goes, "Livin' here, lovin' there, lyin' in between."

When they weren't playing bury the brisket, Mika and Joe showcased some regular "experts," including Mike Barnicle—yes, the same Mike Barnicle who was run out of Boston journalism due to his penchant for routinely fabricating his columns in the *Globe*. Joe and Mika's regular guest panel also included Mark Halperin, a second generation far-left chattering skull who would later be exposed as a serial sexual abuser—a Harvard man, naturally.

During his primary run, Trump expertly leveraged *Morning Joe's* platform, flattering the narcissistic co-hosts with plaudits and praise, all the while using them to advance his own ends. MSNBC, ever the enemy of Republicans, enjoyed Trump's broadsides against his GOP opponents—all the better that they should occur on one of the network's programs. Trump delivered ratings and, in return, Joe and Mika served up softball questions. Joe and Mika, meanwhile, were flattered by Trump's attention, his apparent affection for them, and his willingness to phone into their dismal chat show several mornings a week.

Indeed, throughout much of the GOP primary, Joe and Mika were but supporting characters on their own show. Scarborough bragged to an audience in New York that he'd given advice to Trump heading into one of the primary debates. During an interview in February, Trump characterized Joe and Mika as "supporters," a claim the pair only tepidly denied.

Much like their own relationship, Joe and Mika's affair with Trump was carried on off the air as well. Joe, with his roots in a very different part of Florida, the Panhandle, nonetheless understood the Palm Beach club scene, and he was especially familiar with Trump's Mar-a-Lago. I personally witnessed Joe at the Mar-a-Lago bar one night that Christmas season of 2015. Was he a paying member or was he comped? That's a question for him to answer. I will say I didn't see him signing any checks but maybe he was running a tab.

Voicemail messages leaked to the now-defunct *Gawker* website further revealed the off-air coziness between the MSNBC lovebirds and the New York real estate mogul. In the undated message, Joe and Mika are heard thanking Trump profusely, unctuously.

"We are so, so grateful for everything, Donald, and we just want to call you and tell you how much it means to us," the obsequious Scarborough gushed.

However, the Mar-a-Lago access, the regular morning phone calls, the huge boost in ratings for an otherwise failing morning show—all that was not enough to earn *Morning Joe's* loyalty, or even their neutrality, once it became clear Trump was going to go one-on-one against MSNBC's anointed Democrat Hillary Clinton.

After months of shamelessly sucking up to Trump, Scarborough channeled his inner #NeverTrump and began assailing the Republican Party for letting Trump happen. As a recovering Trumpaholic, one of Banjo Boy's 12 steps was penning an op-ed for the *Washington Post* calling on the GOP to remove Trump from the top of the ticket.

"At long last," the erstwhile Trump bumkisser wrote. "Donald Trump has left the Republican Party few options but to act decisively and get this political train wreck off the tracks before something terrible happens."

By late August, Scarborough's Trump Derangement Syndrome was off the charts. The wannabe rock star released a music video attacking Trump, marked with the hashtag #AmnestyDon. The video was full of attacks on Trump and obvious jokes about the Republican nominee's private parts.

"From out of the west rode a soft and flaccid man, with fear in his eyes and a burnt orange tan," sang Scarborough. "He said he'd build a wall for us but then he up and ran. When the cowboys smell the dirty con of … #AmnestyDon."

The candidate responded in characteristic Trump fashion, taking to Twitter to point out *Morning Joe's* ratings and threatening to spill the beans on the vapid hosts' third-rate romances and low-rent rendezvouses.

"Some day, when things calm down, I'll tell the real story of @JoeNBC and his very insecure long-time girlfriend, @morningmika," he tweeted. "Two clowns!"

Hillary vs. Donald

The Democrats thought they and their alt-left media liegemen had maneuvered the Republicans into nominating the least viable candidate in a broad field of talent. Conservatives, however, had waited many years for a courageous candidate to rise up and confront Clinton. For decades, we had watched as the Clintons skated by on crime after horrific crime, protected by their fellow Democrats, and enabled by their media sycophants, some of whom had actually been on their payroll.

That was about to end.

Clinton's campaign strategy was apparent from her convention speech. She was going to tar Trump as misogynistic, racist, xenophobic, nativist, and whatever other nasty pejoratives she could crib from *Roget's Thesaurus*. Meanwhile, she would raise outrageous sums of money from her cronies on Wall Street to flood the airwaves with an unprecedented flood of negative ads against Trump. According to one post-election analysis, Clinton spent $211.4 million on TV and radio ads during the general election, with pro-Hillary outside groups chipping in another $103 million. Trump, in contrast, spent only $74 million. More than half of Clinton's ad buys were implicit or explicit attacks on Trump.

But all the 30-second spots in the world couldn't wash away the stench of corruption around Clinton. Although FBI Director Comey had exonerated her, sort of, she was still facing criticism from Republicans and a handful of media types—and she struggled to come up with a believable excuse for her behavior. Comey may have let her off the hook in a legal sense, but his press conference had damaged her in the court of public opinion.

In an interview with Fox News' Chris Wallace, Clinton was confronted with the fact that Comey had exposed her lies to the American people.

Wallace: After a long investigation, FBI Director James Comey said none of those things that you told the American public were true.

Clinton: Chris, that's not what I heard Director Comey say, and I thank you for giving me the opportunity to, in my view, clarify. Director Comey said my answers were truthful, and what I've said is consistent with what I have told the American people, that there were decisions discussed and made to classify retroactively certain of the emails.

What was she drinking? At no point had Comey said anything that would remotely suggest Clinton was truthful in her public statements. Comey made clear that Clinton had lied about her devices, about her servers, about the exchange of classified information, about the convenience of the clandestine arrangement. She had even lied about her lies—and now she was lying about the FBI Director's assessment of her lies! It was pure 200-proof distilled Clinton BS. Even the fact-checkers at *Politifact* and the *Washington Post*, loath to criticize Hillary in even the mildest terms, gave her statement a rating of "pants on fire" and "four Pinocchios."

After going more than 200 days without taking questions from reporters, Clinton finally relented in early August, offering remarks to the National Association of Black Journalists and the National Association of Hispanic Journalists. This was hardly a risk for Clinton.

The entire crowd of so-called journalists applauded her when she took the podium. She was given the opportunity to explain her untruthful comments to Wallace, but even in front of this credulous audience, the conniving Clinton again proved herself incapable of telling the truth. Asked about her remarks on Fox, Clinton said she may have "short-circuited"—an odd choice of words for a woman already suspected of being in failing health.

"I may have short-circuited it and for that I will try to clarify," she said. "I was pointing out in both of those instances that Director Comey had said that my answers in my F.B.I. interview were truthful."

While Clinton relied on carefully crafted, poll-tested advertising to attack Trump, the GOP nominee preferred to do the attacking himself. He wasted no time going after Clinton's character, her lies about the private server, and, occasionally, her policies. If anyone thought he was going to change, evolve, or moderate his positions for the general election, they were wrong.

At a rally in Windham, N.H. in early August, Trump took full advantage.

"She took a short-circuit in the brain," Trump said. "She's got problems," He also described her as "unstable," "unbalanced," and "totally unhinged."

"Honestly, I don't think she's all there," he added. "She's a liar. She is a horrible, horrible human being. She's incompetent and I don't think that you can even think of allowing this woman to become President of the United States."

The attacks only escalated from there.

Basket of Deplorables

Hillary Clinton's most devastating gaffe came during a fundraising speech to an audience of Beautiful People in New York City one Friday night in the early fall:

You know, to just be grossly generalistic, you could put half of Trump's supporters into what I call the basket of deplorables. Right? They're racist, sexist, homophobic, xenophobic—Islamophobic—you name it. And unfortunately, there are people like that. And he has lifted them up. He has given voice to their websites that used to only have 11,000 people—now have 11 million. He tweets and retweets their offensive hateful mean-spirited rhetoric. Now, some of those folks—they are irredeemable, but thankfully, they are not America.

To translate: Clinton told her wealthy New York donors that roughly 25 percent of the country were deplorable, irredeemable racists.

Hours after Hillary coughed up that outrageous insult, I was on the campaign trail in Hudson, Massachusetts, at the opening of Trump's statewide headquarters. When you run a daily talk show, you follow the news more closely than most people. Since Hillary delivered her nasty-woman slur on a Friday night when fewer people were paying attention to the news, I wasn't sure if many of the hundreds of Trump stalwarts at the rally knew yet about the "Deplorables" line. But they'd heard all right—loud and clear.

Voter after voter came up to me gleefully embracing the deplorable moniker. One Hispanic woman even approached me touting a handmade pin on her shirt: Proud to Be Deplorable. Men scrawled "Deplorable" on scratch paper and then used paper clips to attach it to the breast pockets of their shirts and coats. They were proudly embracing her insult. By the beginning of the following week, the Deplorable brand had gone mainstream. Social media users were inserting "Deplorable" into their user names. Conservative websites and talk shows, including my own, began marketing Deplorable merchandise. The shirts are still hot sellers online: Proud to be Deplorable, Proud Member of the Basket of Deplorables, Deplorable Lives Matter—the material was endless. And all of it speaks to the cultural cross-currents Clinton unleashed when she decided to insult one-quarter of the country.

As part of her don't-blame-me post-election book tour, Hillary herself maintains that the unsavory quip didn't cost her votes. But I saw with my own eyes how Hillary's scurrilous rhetoric inflamed a swath of the country that already had her number, bigtime.

At a rally in Jackson, Mississippi, Trump returned fire, capitalizing on Clinton's gaffe.

"Hillary Clinton is a bigot who sees people of color only as votes, not as human beings worthy of a better future," Trump said. "She doesn't care what her policies have done to your communities. She has no remorse. She's going to do nothing for Hispanics and African-Americans."

Collapsing on 9/11

Was Hillary Clinton physically fit enough to be president? It was a legitimate question considering the 69-year-old candidate's public health record.

Concerns over Clinton's health were first raised in December 2012 when Clinton, allegedly suffering from a "stomach virus," fainted and sustained a concussion. The State Department used Clinton's fainting spell to temporarily delay her first appearance before Congress, during which she was scheduled to testify about the Benghazi attack. When Clinton was finally well enough to come to Congress, she showed up wearing special glasses that are often used to treat double vision in patients who have suffered from severe head injuries.

After Clinton resigned from the State Department, she was not in the public eye for long stretches of time, so we don't know much about her health problems during the time when she was plotting her second campaign for president. However, emails released by the State Department suggested that Clinton's health problems were not limited to the slip-and-fall that preceded her first Benghazi hearing.

In the emails, her aides routinely discussed her sleeping habits and her health. It was always an open question whether Clinton would be awake in time for a phone call from a foreign diplomat. One email sent by top Clinton aide Jake Sullivan indicates that her staffers had conducted research into a drug that is used to treat Alzheimer's, Parkinson's and a few other major late-life disorders.

Sullivan noted that the drug in question—Provigil—is often prescribed to treat "excessive sleepiness in patients with Parkinson's, Alzheimer's and multiple sclerosis."

Sullivan added that Modafinil, another name for the drug, "gained attention in the medical community because it is the first effective stimulant with no significant potential for abuse. [I]t can be used for two to three day stretches at a time, with few known side effects and little risk of addiction."

That email only spurred speculation regarding Clinton's health—even if CNN and MSNBC ignored it.

Clinton's persistent cough on the campaign trail further inflamed questions about her health.

In February, Clinton was speaking at New York event when she had one of her first public coughing spells. She chugged some water and popped a lozenge, but her vocal chords refused to cooperate. She continued coughing for almost two minutes, as she tried to choke out the scripted lines in front of her.

At a rally in Cleveland on Labor Day, Clinton had a 20-second coughing fit that left her speechless, groping on the podium for a cough drop.

"Every time I think about Trump," she joked, "I get allergic."

Reporting Hillary's health problems was taboo in the alt-left media. The same newspaper columnists who had warned about John McCain's age and his history of skin cancer now lectured us that questions about a candidate's health were off limits. It was sexist, we were told, to suggest that the female candidate isn't healthy enough for the job—even if she's on her sixth 60-second coughing fit of the week.

That all changed, though, on Sept. 11 when Clinton collapsed on a sidewalk in lower Manhattan and had to be dragged into a van after leaving a memorial event at the site of the old World Trade Center.

At first, the CNNs of the world denied that Clinton had fallen. It was Fake News, they said, promulgated by the vast right-wing conspiracy. There was only one problem with this latest mainstream media fable: there was video, and this wasn't like the Zapruder film. You didn't need to watch it hundreds of times. You didn't need to study it carefully. One look and you knew what had happened. Clinton was not healthy. Not at all.

In the video footage, Clinton is seen stumbling into a van, flanked by several campaign staffers. At one point she collapsed and the staffers raced to prop her up, but not quickly enough. Clinton fell like a bag of potatoes and had to be dragged the rest of the way into the van.

Clinton's 9/11 collapse undercut several weeks of her campaign insisting that she was as healthy as a horse, that hairball cough notwithstanding. But her team nevertheless persisted in new, ever-changing spin. First we were told that Clinton had overheated and was severely dehydrated. Then that she had allergies. (You know how allergies kick up in the fall, right?) Then she had a cold. Then she had pneumonia. Then Bill Clinton later said she had the flu. We never learned the truth about Hillary's ailment, but the tumble damaged her credibility, even among the reporters who wanted so badly for her to win, or, as Monday's campaign talking-point put it, "power through." Everyone on MSNBC and CNN said exactly the same thing. Hillary was "powering through."

The First Debate

Trump's polling numbers had spiked following the RNC convention, but his lead was brief. Clinton enjoyed her own post-convention opinion-poll bounce, in part because of Trump's regrettable feud with Khizr Khan, a Muslim Gold Star father who had spoken out against Trump at the Democratic convention. Throughout August, Clinton led by 6-7 points, but Trump began to claw away at her lead heading into the first debate of the general election on September 26 at Hofstra University on Long Island.

Once Clinton entered the debate arena and took her place on the stage opposite Trump, no one could protect her. Finally, a bold and aggressive Republican would be able to confront Clinton with the scandals that were spoken of only on talk radio. Finally, she would be held to account for her decades of corruption. At least, that was what we hoped for. The first debate turned out to be a disappointment for Trump, owing in part to a well-timed release of opposition research which helped cast Trump as anti-woman.

Trump landed some shots, but Clinton was better prepared. Hillary ripped into Trump's unwillingness to release his taxes, suggesting, as Romney had earlier, that Trump had not paid any taxes, or that some other bombshell lurked in the documents.

"There is something he is hiding," she said.

Trump tried to box her in, suggesting half-jokingly that he would release his tax returns when Clinton released the 33,000 emails she had deleted from her private server. But Trump's attempt to rebut well-rehearsed lines of attack from his Democrat opponent did not resonate. Instead, viewers were distracted by Trump's repeated sniffing into the microphone. It was a matter of optics, but nonetheless important, like Richard Nixon's 5 o'clock shadow in the first debate against JFK in 1960. Social media obsessed over Trump's sniffing, with many prominent liberals suggesting that the teetotaler had snorted cocaine before the debate.

In response to his questions about her health and stamina, Clinton delivered her most damaging attack by invoking the case of Alicia Machado, a Venezuelan Miss Universe contestant.

"And one of the worst things he said was about a woman in a beauty contest," she said. "He loves beauty contests, supporting them and hanging around them—and he called this woman 'Miss Piggy,' then he called her 'Miss Housekeeping' because she was Latina."

She continued: "Donald, she has a name. Her name is Alicia Machado. And she has become a US citizen and you can bet she is going to vote this November."

Clinton's digital campaign was ready for the attack. They quickly released and publicized the video of Trump's 20-year-old comments about the beauty queen.

Trump was apparently caught off-guard.

"Where did you find this?" he asked.

It would not be the last time some ancient tape from the archives returned to haunt Trump.

Access Hollywood

If you ask me what was the worst day to be a conservative talk show host on the Trump Train, the answer is easy. It was Billy Bush Day, a Friday. For who knows how long, some producers or executives at NBC had been hanging on to the ultimate piece of opposition research—audio of the future Republican nominee talking vulgarly about his advances on women. It was a nightmare, a catastrophe. As soon as it was released, everyone understood what was about to happen.

The mainstream media would replay the clip. Every network would lead the nightly news with it. The 24/7 news channels, even Fox, would run it on an endless loop. Viral memes, videos, and hot takes would spread like wildfire across social media platforms. The left-wing groups would all issue their statements. Planned Parenthood would express outrage. The DNC would dust off their tired War on Women rhetoric. Screeching CNN pundits would blow Trump's comments out of proportion. By the end of the weekend, every voter in the country would have heard the tape.

The days following the Bill Bush tape were a tough, depressing time to be in talk radio. But it was certainly even tougher for GOP elected officials and candidates. "Grab 'em by the Pussy" became the only issue and every Republican candidate was hounded for statement. It was David Duke all over again, only worse, much worse.

Will you condemn that thing Trump said more than ten years ago when he was still a registered Democrat? Are you still going to vote for him now that he's been caught on tape bragging about "raping" women?

It was obnoxious on a number of levels.

First of all, Trump had no idea he was being recorded and was clearly trying to impress his interlocutor. He was bragging, laughing, trash-talking, cajoling. It was over-the-top. It was also pure Trump. Does anyone really think Trump, approaching 60 and married to a supermodel, was running around grabbing random women? Of course not.

But that didn't stop the Democrats from parading out a long train of women who alleged, with little or no evidence, that Trump had sexually assaulted them. One after another, women stepped forward, made evidence-free allegations against Trump, and then disappeared. Some filed lawsuits. Those were all dismissed. So where are those women now? Strangely, or maybe not so strangely, the media—and the Democrats—lost all interest in these alleged victims after the election.

Secondly, but importantly, the people most outraged by the Billy Bush tape were the same people who had shrugged off multiple credible accusations lodged against the husband of the Democratic nominee, former President Bill Clinton. Sure, Slick Willie wasn't on the ticket, but Hillary was a co-conspirator in covering up his sexual assaults. She ran the Bimbo Eruptions Unit when Bill was president. Her job was to shame and discredit whichever of Bill's paramours went public on a given day. Long before she was attacking Bill's victims as First Lady, she was working to ensure that a woman named Juanita Broaddrick didn't derail then-Arkansas Attorney General Clinton's political career. As I've said, I had the opportunity to speak with Broaddrick in person and on my show multiple times. I absolutely believe that she's telling the truth when she says that Bill Clinton brutally assaulted her in a hotel room, biting her lip before advising her, "Ya better put some ice on that."

And I also believe her when she says Hillary later approached and intimidated her into silence.

Finally, by far the most depressing aspect of the whole *Access Hollywood* affair was the pathetic response of Republicans. The lily-livered, spineless, front-running, fair-weather Republicans fled the U.S.S. *Trump* like rats off a sinking ship.

In a conference call that later became public, House Speaker Paul Ryan all but ordered Republican members of Congress to abandon Trump and even attack him if it would help them keep their seats.

According to Steve Bannon, even Chris Christie, his own New Jersey approval ratings hovering lower than whale excrement, bailed on Trump. In a *60 Minutes* interview following his ouster from the White House, Bannon told Charlie Rose that Christie was supposed to be at a campaign event that weekend and skipped out with no explanation. (That betrayal cost Christie a plum appointment in the Trump administration, according to Bannon.)

I'm not ashamed that I stuck by Trump throughout the Billy Bush disaster. Abandoning Trump like so many other members of the conservative media never even crossed my mind. It was simple: Nothing could come out of Trump's mouth that would somehow make the prospect of a Hillary Clinton presidency acceptable. Nothing.

As the newspaper columnists were writing yet another of their definitive obituaries of the Trump campaign, a man living in exile in the Ecuadorian embassy in the United Kingdom was preparing to unveil a cache of hacked emails that would once again upend what was already an unprecedented election.

Wikileaks

Julian Assange and his website, *Wikileaks*, were already major players in American politics. The vast archive of diplomatic cables Army intelligence analyst Bradley Manning handed them in 2010 put the organization squarely on the radar of the U.S. intelligence services—and of the U.S. political media. Four years later, CIA contractor Edward Snowden handed *Wikileaks* a massive trove of files that exposed the federal government's capacity to spy on almost any digital communication at any moment.

Americans were divided on the Snowden leaks. Some consider him a traitor, others a hero. But his actions ensured that by 2016, virtually every voter in America was familiar with Assange and an organization that would shake up the presidential election in ways that were unpredictable—and often hilarious.

Wikileaks didn't have a monopoly on publishing embarrassing, private emails from Democrat Party bosses and their underlings. Indeed, some of the more disruptive leaks came from the website *DCLeaks.com*. Of course, the mainstream media would have us believe this was a classic Russian operation, but they've never offered any evidence to support the allegation. If you ask me, there are still too many unanswered questions surrounding other DNC scandals to simply accept that the Russians did it. I'm talking of course about the murdered DNC staffer Seth Rich and the mysterious case of Imran Awan, the now-indicted Pakistani IT aide to then-DNC Chairwoman Debbie Wasserman-Schultz.

Wikileaks, on the other hand, consisting primarily of John Podesta's emails, were more likely than not the work of Russian hackers. At least, that's the conclusion of President Trump's CIA Director Mike Pompeo.

Regardless of how the emails entered the public domain, once they were there, they were fair game. Clinton and her allies would insist that it was unethical, un-American even, for journalists and political operatives to even glance at the emails. But imagine for a moment that the *Access Hollywood* tape had been hacked from an NBC server and posted to the internet. Does anyone think Hillary Clinton would have stood on principle and ignored it?

Much like Clinton's State Department emails, *Wikileaks* published large tranches of emails on a rolling basis. Every morning, reporters would wake up and check Twitter to see if the official *Wikileaks* account had announced a new batch of emails. Whenever they arrived, the race was on to find the next potentially explosive email.

The content of the emails themselves was not earth-shattering. Not compared to the emails Clinton sent her daughter and the Arab leaders on the night of the Benghazi attack. But the very existence of a hacked trove of emails became a major factor in the coverage of the race as Election Day neared. There was never a guarantee that Podesta's emails would reveal some disqualifying communication, but the potential was always there. And any time the news media spent talking about *Wikileaks*, which was precious little on the alt-left outlets, was time they weren't spending on the *Access Hollywood* tape. In that way, *Wikileaks* undoubtedly helped Trump yet again to navigate and exploit the treacherous 24-hour news cycle.

But just because the Podesta emails did not contain some smoking gun does not mean they weren't highly amusing for political junkies like me and my listeners.

John Podesta was a Democrat's Democrat. Raised in Chicago, he began his political career volunteering for George McGovern's unsuccessful 1972 presidential campaign. He worked for several Democrat members of Congress before setting up his own powerhouse lobbying firm, The Podesta Group, alongside his brother Tony.

In the Clinton administration, Podesta served as chief of staff for a spell. He was reportedly one of the first Clinton staffers to learn about Monica Lewinsky, a scandal which he was later chosen to "manage." When the Clinton administration ended, Podesta established the Center for American Progress, the nation's leading progressive think tank. He later joined the Obama administration as a counselor. In short, Podesta was a well-connected man at the center of Democrat Party politics for decades, which ensured that the phishing attack that ultimately exposed his emails would provide an unprecedented behind-the-scenes look at Democrat politics and the Clinton Crime Family.

The Podesta Emails

On the day that news broke that Clinton used a private email server during her tenure as Secretary of State, Podesta was involved in a flurry of emails aimed at damage control. Neera Tanden, who worked for Clinton's presidential campaign in 2008 and was then running the Center for American Progress, strategized with Podesta. Tanden and Podesta were key Clintonistas, but they were never at the heart of Clinton's State Department operation. Both operatives were stunned by Clinton's negligent handling of the server. While Hillary was publicly downplaying the significance of her private server, her campaign chairman and closest friends and aides knew all too well how disastrous the revelations would be.

"We've taken on a lot of water that won't be easy to pump out of the boat," Podesta wrote. "Most of that has to do with terrible decisions made pre-campaign, but a lot has to do with her instincts. Almost no one knows better [than] me that her instincts can be terrible."

In this case, as was almost always the case, Clinton's first instinct was to lie—a trait passed on to her staffers like a contagious virus. Podesta further complained to Tanden that the staffers who followed Clinton from the State Department to the campaign concealed details of the server from other campaign officials. Clinton's lawyer David Kendall, former staffers Cheryl Mills and Phillipe Reines "sure weren't forthcoming here on the facts here," Podesta wrote.

"Why didn't they get this stuff out like 18 months ago? replied Tanden. "So crazy."

The internal panic revealed in the Podesta emails undercut more than a year of narrative that the Democrats had worked to establish—the inevitability of Hillary, the most qualified candidate for president ever, etc. etc. Rather than the nonchalance that was their public stance, in their own words in the emails, they showed that they knew the private server was significant and damaging. As always, Trump was there to turn the dagger.

"If my people said the things about me that Podesta & Hillary's people said about her," he tweeted. "I would fire them out of self respect. 'Bad instincts'."

Then-President Barack Obama was also caught up in the leaks. The question, of course, was whether Obama knew that his Secretary of State was using a private, illegal home-brew server, likely jeopardizing national security. Publicly, Obama invoked an excuse he had used often during his presidency. He learned about the server "the same time everybody else learned it, through news reports." That was the public messaging. But privately, Clinton's people admitted that it was impossible that Obama was only now learning about the private email server.

Following Obama's disingenuous comment, Team Clinton went into spin mode.

"It looks like POTUS just said he found out HRC was using her personal email when he saw it on the news," wrote Clinton spokesman Josh Schwerin.

"We need to clean this up," replied Cheryl Mills.

"He has emails from her—they do not say state.gov," she wrote.

In other words, Obama was always aware of the secret server arrangement Clinton had established to protect her from the probing eyes of curious reporters.

But I was more interested in the exchanges between the liberals. The entire clique of Clintonistas was like a gang of catty high-school mean girls, mocking one another—and voters—behind their backs. There was real entertainment value here!

In a 2011 exchange, for example, Clinton's communications director Jennifer Palmieri mocked media magnate Rupert Murdoch for raising his children as Roman Catholics. John Halpin, a senior fellow at Center for American Progress, started the exchange.

"Friggin' Murdoch baptized his kids in Jordan where John the Baptist baptized Jesus," he wrote, adding that "the most powerful elements of the conservative movement are all Catholic."

Halpin derided the Catholic beliefs of conservatives as "an amazing bastardization of the faith."

"They must be attracted to the systematic thought and severely backwards gender relations and must be totally unaware of Christian democracy," he wrote.

Palmieri replied, "Their rich friends wouldn't understand if they became evangelicals," adding that Catholicism "is the most socially acceptable politically conservative religion."

And then there was the dispatch about needy Latinos.

The subject line of the Aug. 21, 2015, email from Podesta to Clinton read: "Needy Latinos and 1 easy call."

Podesta advised Clinton to reach out to the following needy Latinos: Federico Pena, the former secretary of energy and, later, of transportation under her husband; and Bill Richardson, the former New Mexico governor.

Podesta knew the call with Richardson wouldn't go over well with Clinton. The governor had burned the Clintons in 2008 by throwing his support behind Obama, earning himself a prime spot on the Clintons' infamous enemies list.

Podesta had arranged a call between Richardson and Bill Clinton, and Hillary wasn't happy about that.

"I had heard that you were upset that I encouraged a call between WJC and Richardson to bury the hatchet," he wrote. "Not withstanding the fact that [Richardson] can be a dick, it was worth getting him in a good place."

Podesta and Tanden were also critical of their candidate at times. In one exchange, Tanden expressed frustration that Clinton had referred to herself as a moderate.

"I mean it makes my life more difficult after telling every reporter I know she's actually progressive but that is really the smallest of issues," replied Podesta. "It worries me more that she doesn't seem to know what planet we are all living in at the moment."

Podesta's emails also introduced the country to spirit cooking. The leaks included an invitation from his brother to attend a "Spirit Cooking dinner" at the home of an "artist" known as Marina Abramovic. According to a book released by Abramovic in 1996, her recipes include breast milk, sperm, and urine. The spirit cooking invitation spurred dozens of conspiracy theories about Podesta's relationship with the occult, but Abramovic insisted the affair was "just a normal dinner."

The Wall Street Speech Transcripts

The closest thing to a bombshell found in the Podesta emails were transcripts of the speeches Hillary had given to major Wall Street banks. As was the case with the server, Team Clinton's public messaging on the Wall Street speeches did not reflect the private deliberations. While Clinton downplayed the speaking fees she took from banks and spun a nonsensical yarn about Wall Street hating her, Tanden expressed her concerns to Podesta. It didn't help, of course, that Bernie Sanders' main line of attack on Clinton concerned those Wall Street speeches—and the unreleased transcripts.

In a Feb. 7, 2016, email with the subject line "speaking at banks," Tanden suggested that Clinton should return the speaking fees.

"[D]ont shoot me but if we lose badly maybe she should just return the money. Say she gets the anger and moves on," she wrote.

"Feels a little like an open wound," she said, adding that left-wing canvassers were hearing more and more about the Wall Street speeches.

We had known about the speeches for months. Hillary had been paid very big money to talk for very short periods of time. According to an analysis by the Associated Press, Clinton made 94 paid appearances after leaving the State Department in 2013. She collected a total of $22 million, with a median speaking fee of $225,500. Almost every major business concern and trade group got in on the action. They did the right thing, as the wiseguys say.

Goldman Sachs paid her $675,000 for a series of three speeches. Bank of America handed her $225,000 for one speech. So did Morgan Stanley. And it wasn't just big American banks getting in on the action. Verizon Communications, Inc. paid her $225,000 for a speech, as did Mediacorp Canada, General Electric, Xerox Corp., and London Drugs Ltd. Even trade groups like the American Society of Travel Agents and the International Dairy-Deli-Bakery Association were willing to cough up Clinton's exorbitant speaking fee.

The question was obvious: What was in it for the banks, corporations and trade groups paying out the fees? Were these pay-to-play arrangements? Because they sure as hell looked like they were. Unfortunately for Sanders, he was already out of the race, campaigning for his one-time foe, when we learned that Goldman Sachs and others had been willing to pay hundreds of thousands of dollars to listen to the former secretary of state.

Months after leaving Foggy Bottom, Clinton gave a speech to an audience at a Goldman Sachs confab in South Carolina. This one bagged her $225,000. Lloyd Blankfein, the global financial firm's CEO, raised a question about what to do in Syria. "My view," Clinton said, according to the leaked transcripts, "was you intervene as covertly as is possible for Americans to intervene."

Clinton, who was attacked by the left-wing of her party for being too hawkish, then complained about the lack of secrecy these days. It's harder, she lamented, to pull off clandestine regime change because everyone wants to "tell their friendly reporters" what we're doing. Perhaps she was thinking about Libya and her own plans to tout the North African miracle that never was.

Publicly, Clinton was urging some vague multilateral solution to the Syrian Civil War. But privately, she was telling some of the most powerful financial leaders in the country that her aim was toppling the Bashar al-Assad regime. In other words, Clinton was telling her donors she would do to Assad what she had done to Muammar Gaddafi in Libya. What could possibly go wrong?

In a different speech transcript, Clinton revealed her private position on immigration and trade in the western hemisphere. Speaking to a Brazilian bank in 2013, Clinton said her "dream" is for "a hemispheric common market, with open trade and open borders."

What a gift to the Trump campaign!

All the Clinton people could do was scream about Russian hacking and cast doubt as to the authenticity of the emails. "Don't have time to figure out which docs are real and which are faked," Podesta tweeted.

Of course, none of them were faked.

Left-wing Media Exposed

The leaked emails were embarrassing for the Clinton campaign, but even worse so for the liberal journalists caught up in the data dump. *Wikileaks* showed how big-time reporters from POLITICO, the *New York Times*, and CNBC were the common nightwalkers of journalism, prostituting themselves out to their card-carrying fellow travelers in the Democrat Party.

For Glenn Thrush, POLITICO's ace political reporter, Podesta was basically his assignment editor.

"Can I send u a couple of grafs, OTR [off the record], to make sure I'm not fucking anything up?" Thrush wrote in an April 30, 2015 email to Podesta.

"Sure," replied Podesta.

Minutes later Thrush sent Podesta half his story. The balding, ink-stained wretch even added this revealing line: "Because I have become a hack I will send u the whole section that pertains to u Please don't share or tell anyone I did this Tell me if I fucked up anything."

There it was in black and white. Thrush's own words. "I have become a hack."

There was a time when such a revelation would have been the end of a journalist's career. Thrush's pretense of objectivity was gone. His partisan hackery was revealed for the entire world to see. Anyone who was paying attention could see that he was not honest broker of the news but was in fact a Democrat hatchet man, a cheerleader for Hillary—a hack indeed.

So what happened to Thrush? I wish I could tell you that he was drummed out of the journalism community and is now flipping burgers at a soon-to-be-automated fast-food joint. But the sad truth is, Thrush was promoted to the *New York Times* to lead the once-prestigious paper's White House coverage. He's still a partisan hack, but I'm not sure whether Podesta is available for copyediting. (In the fall of 2017, Thrush finally got at least some comeuppance—he was suspended by the *Times* for his serial sexual harassment of young women. He lost a big book contract—was going to write a memoir of his career as a paid stenographer for the Democrat party? And of course he checked into "rehab." They always do.)

The DNC emails also revealed that a colleague of self-proclaimed hack Glenn Thrush's at POLITICO, Ken Vogel, was an agent of the Democrat Party. Vogel, the chief investigative reporter for POLITICO since its founding in 2007, had come to the Arlington, Va.-based outlet from the *New York Times*. (It's a small world, isn't it?) And like Thrush, Vogel suffered no adverse consequences.

Indeed, the revelation proved to be a resume enhancer.

According to leaked emails, Vogel provided pre-publication copy of an April 30, 2016, story to Mark Paustenbach, the DNC's deputy communications director. The story was about joint fundraising agreements between the Clinton campaign and Democrat Party state committees. Unsurprisingly, the Clinton campaign was hogging cash and skimping out on promised donations to the state committees.

"Vogel gave me his story ahead of time/before it goes to his editors as long as I didn't share it. Let me know if you see anything that's missing and I'll push back," Paustenbach said in an email to Luis Miranda, an Obama administration alumnus who was running the DNC communications shop.

Obviously, letting the subject of a story edit your copy is more than a little unethical for a journalist. And it makes you wonder, how many other stories from this influential political reporter have prominent Democrats been allowed to see pre-publication?

Letting Democrats proofread your story before it goes to print is bad enough. But Dana Milbank, a syndicated columnist for the *Washington Post*, took it another step further.

Milbank actually let the Clinton campaign write columns for him!

For a Passover-themed column, Milbank decided to write about the "10 Plagues of Trump." But the overpaid hack couldn't be bothered coming up with his own list. So how did the Yale University graduate break his writer's block?

He crowd-sourced his plagues from the DNC!

The day before Milbank's column ran, the DNC's deputy communications director, Eric Walker, sent out a work order to the organization's research team. "Research Request: top 10 worst Trump quotes?" read the subject line. Walker added, "Milbank doing a Passover-themed 10 plagues of Trump."

When the column finally hit the *Washington Post*—and newspapers around the country—Milbank had used eight of the themes the DNC gave him.

Of all the alleged journalists who were outed by leaked Democrat emails, John Harwood is perhaps the most insufferable. Milbank, Vogel, Thrush—they were totally shameless hacks, but they were engaging in mutually beneficial transactions. They got access to the DNC, to Hillary, and in return Hillary and the DNC got to spread their campaign propaganda. But Harwood prostituted himself out to John Podesta as a volunteer campaign strategist and sucked up to the guy at every turn.

"I imagine," Harwood wrote in a December 8, 2015 email to Podesta, "that Obama feels some (sad) vindication at this demonstration of his years-long point about the opposition party veering off the rails."

The opposition party! Now, that kind of language would be okay coming from MSNBC's Rachel Maddow. We all know she's in the tank. She doesn't even hide it. But Harwood was allowed to moderate GOP debates. Regarding the "opposition party" going "off the rails," Harwood added, "I certainly am feeling that way with respect to how I questioned Trump at our debate."

You're Not Helping, Bill

If you're trying to answer the question of what happened in the 2016 election, the story begins in the 1970s in Little Rock, Arkansas, with an aspiring young Democrat by the name of William Jefferson Clinton. After graduating from Yale Law School, Clinton returned home for a gig as a law professor at the University of Arkansas. But he was not interested in academia. And so in 1974, Clinton made his first foray into American politics, running for a U.S. House seat then held by Rep. John Paul Hammerschmidt. Clinton had hoped to capitalize on the anti-Republican fervor sweeping post-Watergate America, but it was not to be. He lost that first race by a narrow margin, only to be elected attorney general of Arkansas two years later—and just one year after marrying Hillary Rodham Clinton.

Attorney General Bill Clinton's tenure as the top prosecutor of the Natural State was unremarkable—with one exception.

In April of 1978, Juanita Broaddrick (then known as Juanita Hickey) was a 35-year-old nursing home administrator from Van Buren, Arkansas, who met Clinton for the first time during his campaign for governor that year. One night during the campaign she was invited over to the Clinton headquarters in Little Rock. A few weeks later, Broaddrick found herself in the area for a nursing home conference, so she called the campaign to see if she could stop by. Clinton, she was told, would not be at the campaign office, but he was willing to swing by the coffee shop in the hotel where she was staying.

What started out as an innocent cup of joe ended with the aspiring governor of Arkansas violently raping the young nursing home administrator, according to Broaddrick, who first publicly acknowledged the attack in 1999.

That fateful day, the lobby of the Camelot Hotel began to fill with people, so Clinton suggested that the pair take their meeting up to her hotel room. In the hotel room, Clinton made small talk about a prison he intended to renovate should he win the gubernatorial election. Then, suddenly, he struck. He grabbed Broaddrick, forcefully kissing the married woman. She rebuffed his advances but he persisted.

Here's how Broaddrick described the attack in a Feb. 1999 interview with *Dateline NBC*:

Then he tries to kiss me again. And the second time he tries to kiss me he starts biting my lip … He starts to, um, bite on my top lip and I tried to pull away from him. And then he forces me down on the bed. And I just was very frightened, and I tried to get away from him and I told him 'No,' that I didn't want this to happen but he wouldn't listen to me…It was a real panicky, panicky situation. I was even to the point where I was getting very noisy, you know, yelling to 'Please stop.' And that's when he pressed down on my right shoulder and he would bite my lip. … When everything was over with, he got up and straightened himself, and I was crying at the moment and he walks to the door, and calmly puts on his sunglasses. And before he goes out the door he says 'You better get some ice on that.' And he turned and went out the door."

Broaddrick later recalled that after the attack, Hillary Clinton had approached her and told her not to worry about an unwanted pregnancy, because Bill was sterile after a childhood case of mumps. What a nice consolation!

According to Broaddrick, Hillary not so subtly implied that the aspiring power couple was grateful that she was dummying up about how her husband had used Juanita for his own unspeakable ends in that Little Rock hotel room.

In January 2016, Broaddrick tweeted, "I was 35 years old when Bill Clinton, Ark. Attorney General raped me and Hillary tried to silence me. I am now 73….it never goes away."

Broaddrick repeated those claims on my radio show during the campaign.

During the 1990s, Broaddrick's allegations were viewed with great skepticism. The media, already prone to protecting powerful Democrats like the Clintons and the Kennedys, had no physical evidence to support her claims, since she never reported the alleged attack to the police.

Bill Clinton's sexual predations continued as he ascended the ranks of the Democrat Party, culminating with his affair with a young White House intern by the name of Monica Lewinsky. Through the course of the Lewinsky investigation, Clinton's lurid sexual past would be aired before the public, notably in the form of Ken Starr's official report.

Clinton would ultimately become the second president in U.S. history to be impeached, after Andrew Johnson. The Senate failed to convict Clinton on the charges of perjury that he had so obviously committed. But the Lewinsky scandal marred his presidency and forever followed the First Lady who chose to remain by his side, viciously attacking anyone who dared suggest her husband had done anything untoward with women.

Bill's sexual attacks, and Hillary's complicity in the cover-ups, would haunt her presidential campaign to the bitter end.

The Clinton Foundation

The Clintons survived two scandal-plagued terms together, but they took separate paths after leaving the White House. Hillary went on to serve a lackluster eight years in the U.S. Senate, while Bill Clinton began laying the foundation of the most lucrative racketeering enterprise in American history, the Clinton Foundation, which would loom large over the campaign.

Once again, Bill would overshadow his wife.

Peter Schweizer's seminal book *Clinton Cash* was the first crack in the dam protecting the racket the Clintons had run under the guise of an international charity for more than a decade.

Schweizer, an editor-at-large for *Breitbart News* who also ran a right-wing think tank called the Government Accountability Institute, conducted painstaking research, connecting the dots in publicly available documents between massive donations to the Clinton Foundation and actions taken by Senator, and later, Secretary of State Clinton.

Schweizer's book was a genuine bombshell.

Clinton Cash showed how the Clinton Foundation, ostensibly a charity, effectively served as a vehicle for Clinton shakedowns across the globe. The foundation supported the Clintons' lavish lifestyle, providing them with private jets and international junkets. It also provided them with the means to reward their ever-expanding network of loyalists and hacks like Sydney Blumenthal, who was on the payroll for $10,000 a month. The foundation worked in tandem with the Clintons' other private sector activities, allowing Bill, and later Hillary, to collect those outrageously large speaking fees from Wall Street banks and other special interests.

Schweizer's reporting in *Clinton Cash* was carefully rolled out, with advance copies provided to both the *Washington Post* and the *New York Times*. With few exceptions, both liberal newspapers confirmed his reporting and in some instances expanded it into new, even more damning territory.

The most devastating allegation contained in Schweizer's book, and reaffirmed by the liberal press, involved a little known Canadian mining magnate, American uranium, and Rosatom, a state-run Russian nuclear firm.

In *Clinton Cash*, Schweizer reported that Clinton's State Department, along with other federal agencies, had approved the sale of Uranium One, a Canadian mining company, to Rosatom, a state-owned Russian nuclear company. Clinton was just one of nine members of the Committee on Foreign Investment in the United States (CFIUS), which is tasked with approving or rejecting transactions that may affect U.S. national security. However, Clinton was apparently the only CFIUS member whose husband and foundation benefited—to the tune of $145 million—from donations and speaking fees paid out by beneficiaries of the Uranium One sale.

The *New York Times'* reporting on *Clinton Cash* confirmed that Rosatom was taking over the Canadian mining company in a series of transactions from 2009 to 2013. Simultaneously, the Russians suddenly became quite eager to hear Bill Clinton speak. He travelled to Moscow in June 2010 for a $500,000 payday from a Kremlin-linked bank. Around the same time, the Clinton Foundation was the grateful recipient of multimillion-dollar cash infusions from parties that stood to benefit from the Uranium One sale.

According to the *Times*, the Clinton Foundation received $2.35 million from Ian Telfer, an investor who was chairman of Uranium One when it was acquired by Rosatom. It received another $31.3 million, plus a $100 million commitment for future contributions, from Frank Giustra, whose mining company had merged with Uranium One. Giustra, who was a political unknown before the Clinton Foundation came under close scrutiny, would turn out to be a key player in the Clinton Foundation racket.

Giustra had become close to Bill Clinton through the activities of the Clinton Foundation. Clinton had the connections and the profile; Giustra had the money and the private jet. The pair were fast friends by the time Hillary Clinton became Secretary of State, which led the Obama administration to attempt to impose new standards of transparency on the foundation. To serve in the cabinet, Clinton would have to publicly release the names of all donors to the Clinton Foundation.

For donors who preferred secrecy, that would have been a major problem.

But with Giustra's help, the Clintons set up a Canadian branch of the Clinton Foundation racket that allowed them to avoid the standards of transparency called for by the Obama administration. The Giustra-led Canadian arm of the Clinton Foundation allowed the Clintons to continue accepting anonymous "donations," including from foreign entities, while Hillary oversaw major aspects of U.S. foreign policy, including questionable sales of American assets to alien interests.

Ten months into the Trump Administration, the Uranium One deal came under renewed scrutiny, when reporters working for *The Hill* revealed that the Obama administration had uncovered substantial evidence of corruption. According to *The Hill*'s reporting, the FBI accumulated a wealth of evidence, including documents and eyewitness accounts, that officials within the Russian nuclear industry were engaged in an elaborate scheme involving bribery, kickbacks, extortion and money laundering aimed at consolidating the Kremlin's control of the U.S. atomic energy market.

Despite the FBI's red flags, Clinton and the other CFIUS members voted to approve the transaction.

Clinton insisted throughout the campaign that the foundation was on the level. It was a life-saving enterprise, fighting AIDS in Africa and helping Haiti recover from a disastrous hurricane. But everywhere the Foundation went to help, it seemed, a payoff awaited the Clintons. Just ask the Haitians! Bill was appointed by the U.N. to oversee relief efforts. Suddenly Hillary Clinton's brother Tony Rodham got a gold-exploitation permit from the Haitian government—the first one issued in a half-century. To paraphrase the old country song, the Clintons got the gold, the Haitians got the shaft.

As instructive as Schweizer's book and subsequent reporting were on the subject of the Clinton Foundation, the most revealing look at how the Clintons operated their network of pseudo-charities and private sector consulting firms comes from leaked emails from one of their top confidantes. In a memo made public by *Wikileaks*, Doug Band, a senior aide to Bill Clinton, lays out in a business-like fashion how the Clintons, despite years as "public servants," had become fabulously wealthy.

Band called the memo: "Bill Clinton, Inc."

The memo bristles with Band's resentment of Bill and is clearly his pitch to spell out just how instrumental his own firm, Teneo, had been in setting up the state-of-the-art racket that was the Clinton Foundation. In the leaked memo that was circulated among Clintonistas, Band described how the Clinton Global Initiative, a subsidiary of the Foundation, worked hand-in-hand with his Teneo to ensure that Bill got paid. Teneo was a Clinton subsidiary of sorts, and employed Hillary's closest aide Huma Abedin, who pulled down a six-figure salary from the firm even as she earned a check from the State Department. According to Band, Teneo was responsible for directing more than $50 million in "for-profit activity" to the former president, with another $66 million in future contracts.

The memo outlined in great detail how the Clinton Foundation was leveraged to simultaneously enrich both Teneo and Bill Clinton. Major banks would make a contribution to the Clinton Foundation, but then they would pay an additional fee, negotiated by Teneo, for Bill Clinton to give a speech.

They called these payments speaking fees, but does anyone really think a Bill Clinton speech is worth $900,000? No, these weren't speaking fees. These were investments—investments in the potential political favors that the family would be able to offer in the future to large corporations, foreign governments, and whoever else was on Teneo's clientele list. And these payments often came with access to the former president. Coca Cola, for example, got a face-to-face meeting with Clinton at his home in 2009 after the soda company shelled out millions to the foundation.

The Bill Clinton, Inc., memo once and for all laid to rest the notion that the foundation was only about helping starving children in Africa. It exposed the profit-driven motives of the power-mad couple who were, as Hillary infamously remarked, "dead broke" when they left the White House.

Although Bill Clinton could probably have managed a decent protection racket without his politically ambitious wife, the handsome speaking fees he enjoyed would have been smaller without the *quo* part of a *quid pro quo*. And it was Hillary, first as a Senator, then as a Secretary of State, and later as the presumptive Democratic presidential nominee, who could provide the payoffs interested parties sought.

The Clintons' insatiable greed on one hand and their political ambitions on the other were a source of great stress for their political advisers. Consider their dealings with the King of Morocco. In one of the leaked email exchanges obtained by *Wikileaks*, Huma Abedin all but admits that Hillary Clinton was involved in a pay-to-play arrangement with Morocco. The email exchange occurred around the time Clinton was preparing to make official her presidential run, and it showed that her aides were becoming increasingly anxious about the Foundation's acceptance of foreign donations—even if, publicly, they downplayed the Clintons' lucrative relationship with Moroccan King Mohammed IV.

The question Team Hillary was confronting was whether the former Secretary of State should attend a Clinton Global Initiative event in Marrakesh. Abedin was insistent that Clinton attend. Her presence at the powwow "was a condition for the Moroccans to proceed" with a major gift to the Foundation.

"So there is no going back on this," Abedin wrote in an email.

She pressed the financial case for sending Clinton to Africa. The meeting "was HRC's idea, our office approached the Moroccans and they 100 percent believe they are doing this at her request. The King has personally committed approximately $12 million both for the endowment and to support the meeting. It will break a lot of china to back out now when we had so many opportunities to do it in the past few months. She created this mess and she knows it."

On the other side of the argument was Robby Mook, Clinton's baby-faced gay campaign manager.

"We really need to shut Morocco and these paid speeches down," Mook wrote to Podesta in February 2015. Hillary ultimately skipped the Marrakesh conference, but Bill and Chelsea showed up—they stayed in one of the Moroccan King's palaces.

That wasn't the last time the Clintons' Morocco connection would come back to bite them.

On the last day of October, just days before Election Day, the *Daily Caller* reported that Hillary Clinton had done two major favors for Moroccan interests during her time as Secretary of State, as the Foundation was accepting up to $28 million from the King.

Not only did those favors benefit a foreign country, they also undermined American interests.

The first favor related to the Florida-based Mosaic Company, which operates the largest phosphate mining facility in the U.S. As it happens, Morocco contains 75 percent of the world's estimated phosphate reserves. Exporting the mineral, which is a key ingredient is most fertilizers, accounts for up to 35 percent of Morocco's total exports. Additionally, the bulk of that mining is conducted by OCP, a state-owned enterprise. If you're at all familiar with the Clintons' m.o., you can probably see where this is headed…

In 2011, Environmental Protection Agency administrator Lisa Jackson tried to shut down Morocco's leading rival in the global phosphate industry, Mosaic Company, with a slew of regulatory measures. The EPA used Homeland Security aircraft to survey Mosaic properties in the U.S. in search of environmental problems and even threatened the Florida company with punitive Super Fund penalties. Jackson's war against Mosaic worked to the obvious benefit of Morocco. Its $28 million donation to the Clinton's paid off handsomely.

But wait, there's more.

Jackson joined the Clinton Foundation's board of directors two years later, months after leaving the EPA.

The exposure of the Clinton Foundation as a massive racketeering enterprise aimed at enriching the Clintons was a seminal event in the 2016 presidential election. The foundation was like an octopus, with tentacles of corruption reaching into virtually every aspect of the Clintons' political lives—and the federal government. As more and more of Hillary's activities as Secretary of State somehow became entwined with major Clinton Foundation donors, everything she did became suspect. The foundation became an unparalleled political liability that Clinton could never successfully defend, because it was indefensible.

Although the Clintons had always insisted that the foundation would continue to operate if Hillary won the presidency, they eventually admitted that it would be shuttered. Since her loss, the Clinton Foundation has lost interest in helping any victims of natural disasters, even American citizens in Houston, Florida, and Puerto Rico who were devastated by hurricanes in the fall of 2017.

Something's changed for the Clintons. What could it be?

The Clintons' Women

Throughout the campaign season, political analysts had wondered whether Donald Trump would use Bill Clinton's sordid past as a serial sexual predator against Hillary. There was never any doubt in my mind. As early as April 2016, Trump had used his Twitter account to call Hillary one of the "all time great enablers"—a not-so-veiled jab at Clinton's complicity in her husband's extramarital—and extralegal—sexual exploits. That signaled that Bill's history of sexual licentiousness was fair game, and Trump's attacks on the Clintons culminated in one of the most unique presidential debate tactics in American history.

Prior to the second presidential debate in St. Louis, two days after the release of the *Access Hollywood* tape, the Trump campaign announced a surprise press conference, which would take place 90 minutes before the debate began. When the political press entered a small conference room, seated before them were five people. In the middle sat Donald Trump flanked by four women: Juanita Broaddrick, Kathleen Willey, Paula Jones and Kathy Shelton.

Like Broaddrick, Willey and Jones were victims of Bill Clinton's sexual depravity.

Jones was a former Arkansas state employee who accused Clinton of sexually harassing her while he was governor. According to Jones, Clinton propositioned her and exposed himself in a Little Rock hotel room. Jones kept quiet about the story until 1994, when David Brock, then a hatchet man for the right wing, published her account in the conservative *American Spectator* magazine.

Jones filed harassment charges against Clinton on May 6, 1994—two days before the statute of limitations expired for such charges—seeking $750,000 in damages. More than four years later, Clinton settled with Jones for $850,000.

Willey was a White House aide who alleged in a 1998 interview on *60 Minutes* that Bill Clinton had sexually assaulted her in 1993, shortly after the suicide of her husband. According to Willey, Clinton approached her during an Oval Office meeting, kissed her, groped her breasts, and forced her hand onto his genitals. Clinton denied the allegation, claiming, according to Monica Lewinsky, that he would never attack a woman with small breasts like Willey. Ultimately, Special Counsel Ken Starr determined not to press charges over the Willey incident, owing to discrepancies in the various accounts of the attack Willey had given.

Kathy Shelton, unlike Jones, Willey and Broaddrick, was a victim not of Bill but of Hillary.

For at least a quarter of a century, Clinton had always sought to portray herself as the champion of women and girls. I was never quite sure what that meant, but she repeated it at every opportunity. Practically speaking, being a champion for women and girls involved, for Hillary, defending unrestricted abortions and taxpayer funding for Planned Parenthood. But the case of Kathy Shelton cast Clinton's claims of championing women in an entirely different light.

Shelton was 12 years old when a 41-year-old family friend allegedly lured her into his car, violently raped her, then abandoned her on the side of the road. In 1975, Clinton was the court-appointed attorney for Thomas Alfred Taylor, the accused rapist. Taylor faced 30 years to life in prison, but Clinton's exploitation of a legal technicality prevented forensic evidence connecting Taylor to the crime from being used in court. So the child molester was permitted to plead down the charge to "unlawful fondling of a minor."

In an affidavit submitted to the court, Clinton wrote that Shelton was "emotionally unstable" and had a "tendency to seek out older men and engage in fantasizing"—an early look at what would become the Clintons' "nuts and sluts" defense that they used against any women who accused Bill of sexual misconduct. If the facts of the case did not offer an accurate enough glimpse into Clinton's character as a young public defender, audio obtained by the *Washington Free Beacon* painted a chilling portrait of a young Hillary's thinking at the time she was defending a child rapist.

In the mid-1980s, Clinton made comments about the trial in an interview with Roy Reed, an Arkansas newspaper reporter. The long-forgotten interview only came to light when *Free Beacon* reporters dug around the dusty Clinton archives at the University of Arkansas. In the audio recordings, Clinton recounts her initial involvement in the case.

"The prosecutor called me a few years ago, he said he had a guy who had been accused of rape, and the guy wanted a woman lawyer," said Clinton. "Would I do it as a favor for him?"

Clinton had previously recounted some details of the case in written accounts, casting the decision to represent Taylor as difficult and ethically challenging.

The audio recording told a different story.

"It was a fascinating case, it was a very interesting case," Clinton said, describing the rape of a 12-year-old girl.

"I had him take a polygraph, which he passed—which forever destroyed my faith in polygraphs," she added with a maniacal laugh.

But now it was payback time in St. Louis for the women the Clintons dismissed as nuts and sluts. Donald Trump, the Clintons' erstwhile friend and campaign contributor, whose wedding Hillary Clinton had attended a decade earlier in Palm Beach, had assembled a living museum of the Clintons' decades-long abuse of, and careless disregard for, women. Juanita Broaddrick told me later that when she and the other women sat down in the conference room with Donald Trump, they had no idea he was about to open the doors and bring in the national media to interview them. But they were not intimidated by the reporters, most of whom were openly cheerleading for Hillary. The women spoke in concise TV-ready soundbites.

Jones: "I'm here to support Mr. Trump because he's going to make America great again ... I think they should all look at the fact that he's a good person and he's not what other people say he's being, like Hillary."

Willey: "I think we can bring peace to this world and I think Donald Trump can lead us to that point."

Broaddrick: "Actions speak louder than words. Mr. Trump may have said some bad words, but Bill Clinton raped me and Hillary Clinton threatened me. I don't think there's any comparison."

Shelton directed her words at Hillary.

"I just want to know, you've got a daughter and a grandbaby. What happens if that daughter of yours, if that would have been her [who was assaulted at age 12]? You would have protected her. You don't know me, so I'm a piece of crap to you ... Who cares about me, as long as you can win your first case as an attorney?"

Broaddrick, Jones, Willey, Shelton—all together as Trump's guests of honor for the debate. It was amazing. And if you have any doubt about the impact it had on the Clintons, just look up at the video of Bill Clinton's expression upon seeing his assembled victims, filing into the auditorium to watch the brutal oratorical throwdown.

Before we get into the debate itself, a rhetorical question: Can you imagine Jeb Bush, Ted Cruz, John Kasich or Marco Rubio pulling off a stunt like this? I didn't think so.

But even apart from the stunt—which none of his Republican challengers would have had the testicular fortitude to execute—Trump won the second debate going away. He'd learned his lessons from the first one-on-one televised showdown, and he came prepared.

Anderson Cooper set the tone for the debate early on.

"You bragged that you have sexually assaulted women," he snidely asked. "Do you understand that?"

A more neutral moderator would have asked Trump to respond to the allegations made against him following the release of the *Access Hollywood* tape. But this is CNN we're talking about. The Clinton News Network. This is Anderson Cooper, a gay blue-blooded New York socialist socialite. So rather than ask the question a journalist might ask, Cooper essentially told Trump: You're an admitted rapist, right?

Trump stood his ground.

"No, I didn't say that at all, I don't think you understood what was said. This was locker room talk. I'm not proud of it, I apologized to my family, I apologize to the American people, certainly I'm not proud of it..."

Cooper interrupted: "Just for the record, though, are you saying that what you said on that bus eleven years ago, that you did not actually kiss women without consent or group women without consent."

"I have great respect for women, nobody has more respect for women than I do—

Cooper: "So, for the record, you're saying you never did that?"

"—I was embarrassed by it, but I have tremendous respect for women..."

Cooper interrupted again: "But have you ever done these things?"

After Cooper's third attempt to cast Trump as a rapist, based on his private boasts to Billy Bush, Trump turned the tables.

"If you look at Bill Clinton—far worse. Mine are words, and his was action. His was—what he's done to women... there's never been anybody in the history of politics in this nation..."

Given who was in the audience, Trump didn't need to finish his thought. If you had been paying attention, you knew he was right. Hillary had managed to remain married to a serial sexual predator, but now she—and her surrogates who were "moderating" the debate—were trying to argue that Trump's flippant remarks to a D-list media personality were disqualifying.

Trump capped his cinematic performance with a vow to his supporters:

"I didn't think I'd say this, but I'm going to say it, and I hate to say it," he said, staring at Hillary. "But if I win, I am going to instruct my attorney general to get a special prosecutor to look into your situation, because there have never been so many lies, so much deception…"

Clinton underestimated the appetite for her prosecution among the debate audience.

She responded: "It's just awfully good that someone with the temperament of Donald Trump is not in charge of the law in our country—"

"Because you'd be in jail!" Trump interrupted.

The crowd laughed and cheered.

Chapter Ten

Carlos Danger

As much as Bill Clinton's sexual predatory behavior influenced the course of U.S. politics, no American pervert had a greater impact on the 2016 presidential election history than Anthony Weiner, former Democrat Congressman from New York City. Weiner, the husband of Clinton's right-hand woman, Huma Abedin, fell from grace in 2011. But the sad story of his lewd and lascivious lifestyle would not be fully understood until five years later, in 2016, when his uninhibited sexual proclivities triggered a criminal investigation that would send shockwaves throughout the American political system.

Few outside of New York now remember that Anthony Weiner wasn't always a laughingstock. Prior to his initial errant tweet, Weiner was a rising star in the Democrat Party. Beginning in 1999, Weiner had served as a Congressman from the New York district once represented by his mentor, Chuck Schumer. He served seven terms in the House, re-elected time and again by more than 60 percent of his district's voters. He was celebrated on MSNBC for his bombastic floor speeches, in which he unabashedly assailed the Bush administration and, later, his Republican colleagues in Congress. His strident advocacy of left-wing causes and his caustic attacks on the GOP made him a darling of liberal America.

In 2010, Weiner cemented his place in the pantheon of modern Democrat heroes, marrying the woman sometimes described as Hillary's "surrogate daughter" in a civil ceremony presided over by Bill Clinton.

One year later, Weiner tweeted out a picture of his penis, setting in motion a chain of events that would lead to his ouster from Congress and, ultimately, to the demise of Hillary Clinton's political career.

Amid the fall-out from the X-rated tweet, Weiner was harangued by the late Andrew Breitbart, who had obtained a copy of the quickly deleted picture of Weiner's private parts. Weiner denied that he was the man pictured in the tweet, going so far as to suggest that a political opponent might have hacked his account to frame him. Or perhaps it was a doctored photo—regardless, it wasn't him! But Breitbart made it his life's mission to expose the congressman and send him forever into ignominy. Weiner continued to deny the accusations and levied scurrilous attacks against the conservative blogger.

In the end, however, Breitbart prevailed. In the face of mounting evidence, Weiner was forced to admit that the initial tweeted image was him.

"I have not been honest with myself, my family, my constituents, my friends and supporters, and the media," Weiner said at a press conference in New York. "To be clear, the picture was of me, and I sent it."

Weiner even apologized specifically to Andrew Breitbart.

Weiner resigned from Congress but by April 2013 he was back in politics, running for mayor of New York City. Throughout the campaign, Weiner faced skepticism from voters, but he was leading in the polls to succeed Michael Bloomberg right up until the moment a website called *The Dirty* revealed a whole new series of sexts, many of them only weeks old.

Thus did America meet Carlos Danger.

Carlos Danger was the *nom de guerre*—or was it *perv*?—that Weiner used after his Congressional downfall. The rehabilitation was not going well. It turned out Carlos Danger was sexting various women online, including Sydney Leathers, the young woman who helped expose Weiner for the second time by selling her story to the U.K.-based *Daily Mail*.

Unfortunately for Clinton and the rest of the Democrat Party, Weiner's contribution to American political history wasn't over—and neither was Sydney Leathers'.

On August 28, 2016, the *New York Post* dropped a bombshell on the Clinton campaign: Carlos Danger was up to his old tricks. The husband of Huma Abedin had been caught yet again texting unsavory images to random women on the internet. And it was worse than before: the new images showed an aroused Weiner lying half-naked in bed with his toddler son sleeping next to him. The *Post* ran the R-rated photo on the front page.

Abedin announced immediately that she would be separating from her horny husband. But there were more shoes to drop.

On September 21, the *Daily Mail* in London revealed that the recipient of Weiner's scandalous sexts was a 15-year-old girl from North Carolina. The *Daily Mail* only learned of the scandal after Sydney Leathers encouraged the teenager to sell her salacious tale to the British tabloid for a handsome sum. Regardless of its provenance, the story was heavy with political—and legal—implications. The New York Police Department and the FBI began criminal investigations of Weiner's online activities.

The investigation into Carlos Danger's recidivistic cyber-philandering dragged on with little fanfare until the cops discovered a laptop of his containing a new trove of previously unrecovered Hillary Clinton emails. For FBI Director Comey, the newly uncovered emails threatened to undermine his decision the previous July to broom the criminal investigations into Clinton's use of a private email server. And so on a Friday afternoon 11 days before America went to the polls, Comey sent a letter to Congress that would rock the campaign.

Here's the money quote from Comey's Oct. 28 letter: "The FBI has learned of the existence of emails that appear pertinent to the investigation."

Translation: The FBI was re-opening the investigation into Hillary Clinton's use of a private email server.

Comey's letter was in a long series of "October surprises" that have rocked recent American presidential elections.

In October 1964, President Lyndon B. Johnson's long-time aide Walter Jenkins was arrested and charged with disorderly conduct with another man in the restroom of a YMCA in Washington, D.C.

Jenkins was "hospitalized" and closeted FBI director J. Edgar Hoover sent him a bouquet of flowers and a touching get-well-soon card. Eight years later, at the White House, national security advisor Henry Kissinger delivered an October surprise for Richard Nixon—that the president was very near to his goal of ending U.S. involvement in Vietnam.

"We believe that peace is at hand," the legendary diplomat told the American people.

More recently, in October 2000, Republican candidate George W. Bush's 1976 drunk driving arrest surfaced. A defense attorney in Maine confirmed to a reporter that the Republican nominee had been busted for driving under the influence in Kennebunkport, and Bush confirmed the report after it was revealed.

But Comey's October Surprise may have been the most significant one yet, thanks to the nature of the revelations and the advent of social media. Hillary Clinton's obviously criminal use of a private server was once again dominating the news.

How far would this new investigation reach? What squalid secrets were stashed on Weiner's laptop? How many of the 33,000 Hillary emails could be recovered by the FBI's forensic sleuths? What new scandals would the American people be signing up for if they elected another Clinton?

I remember these tumultuous days vividly. On the day that the Comey letter dropped, I was broadcasting alongside Ann Coulter from the Kowloon restaurant in Saugus, Massachusetts. The news that Clinton might yet pay for her high crimes and misdemeanors brought cheers not only to Ann and me, but to the crowd of Trump supporters gathered to watch the show. It appeared that maybe, just maybe, the Clintons would finally get some justice and that we deplorable, irredeemable bitter clingers were catching a lucky break.

No one could have predicted that Weiner's perversions would eventually lead to the downfall of the Clinton empire—no one except Donald Trump.

On Aug. 3, 2015, Trump had tweeted the following: "It came out that Huma Abedin knows all about Hillary's private illegal emails. Huma's PR husband, Anthony Weiner, will tell the world."

How's that for a prophecy?

Clinton responded to the news the only way a Clinton knows how, which, if you've been following this story so far, means she lied. Comey was the great savior of the Democrats after the press conference on July 5 in which he advised Obama's corrupt attorney general not to press charges against Clinton. But he was about to get a severe media makeover thanks to the Clinton media smear machine. No longer was Comey the last honest man in Washington, D.C.—now he was a partisan hack, just another cog in the vast right wing conspiracy that had always been responsible for every indignity Hillary suffered.

Hillary's lying commenced. Comey's letter, she said, was delivered only to Republicans! This was supposed to support her conclusion that he was a Tea Party hatchet man. But anyone who looked at the letter could plainly see that Sens. Diane Feinstein (D-Calif.) and Patrick "Leaky" Leahy (D-Vt.) were cc'd on the letter, along with a number of other Democrats from a host of congressional committees.

The next day, long after millions of Americans had seen that the letter had gone out to the Democrats in Congress, Hillary continued peddling her latest Big Lie.

"We've made it very clear that, if they are going to be sending this kind of letter that is only going originally to Republican members of the House, that they need to share whatever facts they claim to have with the American people."

Some analysts, such as *FiveThirtyEight*'s Nate Silver, believe the Comey letter cost Clinton the election. I disagree. What cost Clinton the election was the long chain of unethical, corrupt and illegal behavior that forced an FBI Director to re-open a criminal investigation into her conduct days before a presidential election.

Post Script: In September 2017 Weiner pleaded guilty in federal court in New York to one count of transferring obscene material to a minor—sexting an underage girl. He was sentenced to 21 months in prison.

Weiner is now imprisoned at Federal Medical Center Devens in Ayer, Massachusetts. His release date is scheduled to be May 14, 2019. His Bureau of Prisons number is 79112-054.

Chapter Eleven

Election Night

AFTER SIGNING OFF THE RADIO FOR THE LAST TIME BEFORE ELECTION DAY ended, I made my way down Route 128 to the Trump campaign's victory "celebration" in Braintree. I'd been booked by the state campaign weeks earlier as the "host" or "master of ceremonies" or something, but I figured it would be a short night. I was neither cheerful nor optimistic, and listening to Fox's dire projections on Florida as I drove down didn't improve my mood. But I figured I owed it to my listeners to show up and commiserate with them at the very least. Little did I know that I and millions of other Americans were about to experience what the *ABC's Wide World of Sports* used to call "the thrill of victory and the agony of defeat." And the thrill of victory would be so much sweeter because we'd all been braced for the agony of defeat.

Election Day began like any other. Voters in Dixville Notch, N.H. headed to the polls at midnight to cast the first presidential votes of the day—4 for Hillary Clinton, 2 for Donald Trump, 1 for Gary Johnson, and a single write-in for Mitt Romney. It was an inauspicious start, but Dixville Notch's long-term track record of political prognostications is about as accurate as Punxsutawney Phil's weather forecasts.

When the polls finally started to close across the country, I was sitting in the function room of F1 Boston with a handful of Trump loyalists. I noticed that there were more waiters, bartenders and busboys in the room than... "celebrants." As the old saying goes, "Success has a thousand fathers, and failure is an orphan." Early on the Trump victory party in Braintree looked like the New England Home for Little Wanderers.

When the earliest polls closed, the Associated Press called the race in Indiana and Vermont. Vermont was Bernie Land, and Clinton would have taken it even if every Bernie Bro was too stoned to vote. Indiana's 11 electoral college votes went to Trump. No surprises there, considering Trump's vice presidential running mate was the popular governor of the Hoosier State. John McCain had lost Indiana in 2008, but it went Republican for Mitt Romney in 2012, for Bush twice, and had never supported Bill Clinton.

We were off to a good start.

Andrea Mitchell reported live from the Clinton headquarters at 7:30 pm EST. She was still smiling and didn't look like she'd hit the cash bar yet.

"This is the night that Hillary Clinton has been waiting for!" she said. You just knew Andrea had her broken-glass-ceiling monologue ready to go, once her heroine reached the magic number of 270.

Polls had just closed in Ohio—too close to call. North Carolina—too close to call. West Virginia, coal country, goes to Trump. Trump led, 24 to 3.

By 8pm, Trump and Clinton were neck-in-neck in Florida. The election analysts were mulling over county-level turnout data. Polls in the Panhandle, in the Central time zone, closed an hour later, which meant Trump could expect a late rush of votes from that traditionally conservative part of the state. On NBC, they weren't in full blown panic mode yet. But something tells me the Clinton whiz kids in downtown Brooklyn were planning on a blowout in Florida—that was the vibe I'd gotten from Fox an hour earlier on the drive down. With 75 percent of the vote counted, the Sunshine State's 29 electoral votes remained up for grabs.

James Carville was in the middle of some folksy down-home Cajun explanation when Lester Holt broke in: Trump wins South Carolina—9 electoral votes.

"The night is still early," Holt assured the audience.

Polls closed in Pennsylvania—too close to call. New Hampshire—too early to call.

Then a slew of states came in with unsurprising results: Alabama for Trump—9 electoral votes; Connecticut for Clinton—7 electoral votes; Delaware for Clinton—3 electoral votes; the District of Columbia for Clinton—3 electoral votes; Illinois and Maryland, both to Clinton—20 and 10 electoral votes, respectively; Massachusetts for Hillary—11 electoral votes; Mississippi for Trump—6 electoral votes; New Jersey for Clinton—14 electoral votes; Oklahoma to Trump—7 electoral votes; Rhode Island to Clinton—4 electoral votes; and Tennessee to Trump—11 electoral votes.

Clinton now led Trump, 75—66. It was beginning to look like the night was going to play out as so many experts thought it would. But by 9pm, pivotal swing states like Florida, Virginia, and Pennsylvania remained in play.

As 9 pm approached, NBC got some field reports. Katy Tur, a dim-witted ex-girlfriend of Keith Olbermann who had been one of Trump's media foils throughout the campaign, looked tired.

"I've spoken to a high-level source in the Trump campaign," said Tur, "who says they believe it is going to go down to the wire in Ohio."

In Brooklyn, the first cracks in the Clinton Team were spreading.

"They're getting a little nervous in Michigan because the Democratic areas of Detroit and Flint are not showing the kind of vote they'd like to see," Andrea Mitchell reported from Clinton headquarters.

The clock struck nine in the east and another slew of races were called: New York's 29 electoral votes went to Clinton and Texas' 38 electoral college votes went to Trump, no surprises there. Then Kansas, Louisiana, Nebraska, North Dakota, South Dakota, and Wyoming—all to Trump for a total of 25 electoral votes. Trump had pulled ahead—137–104.

With 91 percent of the vote in, Florida was still too close to call. Ditto for Ohio, where the margin at 9pm was fewer than 3000 votes. And in North Carolina, with 68 percent reporting, the margin was less than 400 votes.

Those tight margins thrilled Trump voters—and it only got better.

Back to Andrea Mitchell.

"There's gotta be some fingernail biting right now," Holt said to her.

"You're absolutely right," she said. "First of all, Virginia was something they were so confident in. They've got Terry McAuliffe as the governor, they've got Tim Kaine as a senator, as the running mate.

"They actually took money out of Virginia, advertising, they were that solid, they thought, in Virginia. That is not good news for them."

And the Old Dominion wasn't the old lady's only problem.

"Michigan's making them nervous," Mitchell added. In other words, the glass ceiling was still intact.

As the 10 pm marker approached, Trump still maintained his lead over Clinton by 33 electoral votes. The mood at the Trump victory party in Manhattan was jubilant.

"Folks, this is a night about the battleground states," said Holt. "We knew it would be but it is far closer than any imagined."

Michigan, Florida, Ohio, North Carolina, Pennsylvania, New Hampshire— all still too close.

"A lot of drama here this night," said Holt.

Trump takes Missouri—10 electoral votes.

Before 10 pm, Ohio was called for Trump—18 electoral college votes.

Romney lost Ohio. McCain lost Ohio. Bush won Ohio twice.

The last time someone won Ohio and lost the presidency was Richard Nixon in 1960. (And we all know how Joe Kennedy and Momo Giancana, of *Kennedy Babylon* fame, stole that election.)

Trump now led, 168–109.

But that wasn't the worst news for Clinton.

Chuck Todd, the longtime Democrat Senate aide now parroting the DNC's talking points on NBC "News," didn't think Florida was going well for her. That wasn't how it was supposed to be; Hillary was supposed to dominate in states with large Hispanic populations and major cities.

"And I think North Carolina is trending Trump here," said a glum Todd.

At 10:10, CBS' Dan Rather tweeted: "Nearing cardiac arrest time for team Clinton. She trails in FL + VA. Early indications in Michigan are enough to give them heebie jeebies."

Virginia came in with some hope for Clinton, tossing its 13 electoral votes to the Democrat. But Trump's win in North Carolina—15 electoral votes—followed soon after. At 11:30 pm, the Associated Press called the state of Florida for Trump—29 electoral votes.

Then a rush of states called: Utah for Trump—6 electoral votes; California for Clinton—55 electoral votes; Hawaii for Clinton—4 electoral votes; Idaho for Trump—4 electoral votes; Oregon to Clinton—7 electoral votes; Washington State to Clinton—12 electoral votes; and Iowa to Trump—6 electoral votes.

Trump continued to lead—228-209. For the first time, we could all see him within reach of that all important 270.

Georgia, the long-time red state Clinton had hoped to turn blue, came in for Trump—16 electoral votes.

244-209—now the liberals were really sweating. The gray spaces on the map were dwindling, with Pennsylvania, Maine, Michigan, and Wisconsin and more still in play.

"At the Clinton headquarters, long faces and tears," reported Lester Holt. He then ran down through the remaining too-close-to-call states, and Trump had a slight edge in all of them.

Midnight came and went.

New Hampshire, Pennsylvania, Michigan, Minnesota, Wisconsin, Arizona and Maine—still all too close.

On CNN, the realization was slowly setting in.

"They were coming to this event for what they thought would even be an early night watching Hillary Clinton being elected as the first woman president," said CNN's Brianna Keilar. "And now they are confronting the reality that they could be walking out of here not knowing, or even expecting that Donald Trump will be president."

CNN anchor Wolf Blitzer kept throwing his coverage over to John King and his magic high-tech electoral map. There was, Blitzer insisted, still a path to victory for Clinton. "If she wins North Carolina," Blitzer said, before King interrupted him to note that Trump had already won North Carolina.

With Trump at 248 electoral votes, the math was looking darker and darker for Clinton. Her last best hope was sweeping Michigan, Wisconsin, Minnesota, and Pennsylvania.

First Michigan went for Trump. Pennsylvania and Wisconsin later fell during his acceptance speech.

At 1:56 am, the *Daily Mail* called the election for Trump. The Fleet Street Brits are always a step or two ahead of our lamestream American media these days. The *Mail* was followed in rapid succession by the AP at 2:31 am, Fox News at 2:40 am, and the *New York Times* at 2:41 am.

Minutes after the *Times* called the race, Clinton made the phone call to Trump to concede.

Over at CNN, Blitzer was still desperately trying to resuscitate Clinton's dying campaign. He was shocked when Dana Bash interrupted his analysis to inform him that Clinton had conceded.

The Clinton News Network was the last of the alt-left media to throw in the towel, but it finally did so at 2:48 am.

According to reporting after the fact, Clinton did not want to make the concession call. It was only after President Obama called her and encouraged her to do so that she had her aides place a call to Trump Tower. And even after that, with a crowd of disillusioned loyalists wondering what was going on, Clinton refused to address her supporters and publicly concede. In the wee small hours of the morning, it was John Podesta who drew the short straw and had to go downstairs to the ballroom to tell the crowd to go home.

"This is an historic night," said Vice President-elect Pence. The crowd roared. "It is my high honor and distinct privilege to introduce to you the President-elect of the United States of America, Donald Trump."

"Sorry to keep you waiting," Trump said. "Complicated business!"

"I've just received a call from Secretary Clinton," said Trump.

Roars from the crowd.

"She congratulated us—it's about us—on our victory," Trump said. "And I congratulated her and her family on a very, very hard-fought campaign. I mean, she—she fought very hard."

It's All Over Now, Baby Blue

"You're awake, by the way," said Maddow on MSNBC. "You're not having a terrible, terrible dream. Also, you're not dead and you haven't gone to hell. This is your life now. This is our election now. This is our country."

Richard Engle, NBC correspondent, as Hillary's hopes faded: "Well, let's just cut to the chase assuming, and that's what we're talking about, that he does win. People I'm speaking to think it's absolutely catastrophic."

Ana Kasparian from the *Young Turks*: "I have no respect for women who voted for Trump. And the reason why is because—look, I don't think you're a single-issue voter, I think you're dumb. I think you're fucking dumb."

Van Jones: "People have talked about a miracle. I'm hearing about a nightmare…You have people putting children to bed tonight, and they're afraid of breakfast."

"We went into the night knowing there was a chance Trump could win," PBS *NewsHour* anchor Judy Woodruff said. "But all the smart people said it was not going to happen."

"I was talking with people on both campaigns and I was getting the same prediction from Team Trump that I was getting from Team Clinton—which was that Hillary would end up with a few more than 300 electoral votes," CNBC anchor and *New York Times* columnist John Harwood said.

John Dickerson, like Harwood a second-generation Democrat operative employed by an alt-left network, said senior Republican senators called him before the election to say, 'Here are the things Hillary Clinton is going to have to do to reach out to Republicans.'

"The premise was that she was going to win," the distraught Democrat Dickerson deadpanned.

Hugh Hewitt, a Mitt Romney follower who voted for Trump, said: "I didn't see it coming. Anybody who says they did, I think they're lying."

"America is crying tonight. I'm not sure how much of America, but a very significant portion. And I mean, literally crying," said Lawrence O'Donnell of Harvard and MSNBC.

"Everybody is crying and so upset and it is the end of their world," said Mika Brzezinski.

"This is a different earth than it was 24 hours ago," mourned Comrade Chris Matthews.

"Is there a doomsday plan?" Maddow asked.

Martha Raddatz was choked up, on the verge of tears, although she would later deny it.

"From slavery to Nazism," said MSNBC analyst Jonathan Alter, "We have faced challenges before to who we are as a people."

"History is put on hold, yet again," said Mitchell, whom Hillary Clinton had called her favorite reporter. Damn that glass ceiling . . . .

"I may be moving to Canada," tweeted Snoop Dog. "Fuck this shit."

The *Boston Globe's* Annie Linskey later told CNN that she only popped into the Clinton victory party to grab a couple of quotes for her 'Clinton Wins' story.

"When I got there, the Clinton people were just so happy," she said. "The biggest smiles.

"All I needed were two or three happy quotes. Just a little graf of happiness, because we assumed she was going to win." It was just more fake news from the *Boston Globe*.

Pundits and Pollsters

The election of Donald Trump wasn't just a reckoning for the political establishment. November 8, 2016 also shook the pollsters, pundits and chattering classes. The so-called experts, the people who are paid handsomely to predict election outcomes, got this one all wrong.

Take Nate Silver. He's America's top polling guru—or should I say he *was*.

Silver became the Billy Beane of political polling in 2008 when he figured out that if you averaged the polls of swing states and based your Electoral College predictions on that, you would get a pretty accurate prediction of who was going to win the presidential election. Since nailing the 2008 election, he's enjoyed some fame. He even managed to snowball his success that year into a gig as Editor-in-Chief of ESPN's *FiveThirtyEight*, a political blog, and as a special correspondent for ABC News.

But he and his 538 team really blew the 2016 election. As one caller to my show joked after the election, the pollster was demoted to Nate Bronze.

On June 16, 2015, Silver's website, *FiveThirtyEight.com*, published its first story discounting Donald Trump. "Why Donald Trump Isn't A Real Candidate, In One Chart."

Harry Enten wrote:

"At *FiveThirtyEight*, we like to celebrate outliers. LeBron James's Cleveland Cavaliers may end up losing in the NBA Finals, but James's performance has been outlandishly good. In the same vein, I want to congratulate Donald Trump, who reportedly will declare today that he is running for president… Trump has a better chance of cameoing in another *Home Alone* movie with Macaulay Culkin—or playing in the NBA Finals—than winning the Republican nomination."

Enten was doubly wrong. LeBron won Cleveland its first NBA championship and Donald Trump won the Republican nomination, slicing through a historically large field of candidates like a hot knife through butter. (And by the way, LeBron's celebrated endorsement couldn't deliver Ohio, or Florida, for Hillary Clinton.)

But wait, there's more.

On July 16, 2015, Enten gave us "Two Good Reasons Not to Take The Donald Trump 'Surge' Seriously".

"In reality, the broad, shallow nature of Trump's support suggests it's due mostly to near-universal name recognition," wrote Enten, "thanks in part to being in the news more often than the news anchors."

At the time, everyone thought ¡Jeb! Bush was the frontrunner. People were getting ready to watch the son and brother of former presidents run against the wife of a former president who was herself a former secretary of state.

A few days later, Silver personally weighed in, dubbing Trump a troll.

"In the long run—as our experience with past trolls shows—Trump's support will probably fade," Silver smugly said. "Or at least, given his high unfavorable ratings, it will plateau, and other candidates will surpass him as the rest of the field consolidates."

In August 2015, Silver discounted Trump's surge in the polls. Likening Trump to Pat Buchanan, Mike Huckabee, Herman Cain, Michele Bachman, and the Rick Santorum of 2012, Silver gave Trump just a two percent chance of winning the Republican primary. Two percent!

Despite his expertise in the field of polling, Silver oddly discounted polls showing Trump gaining support. Again, in August 2015, he wrote that Trump was winning the polls at the cost of the nomination. Seriously.

He tweeted:

Media: Trump's doing great!

Nerds: No. Those polls don't mean what you think.

Media: A new poll shows Trump doing great! Proved you wrong!

The headline on his corresponding blog post read, "Donald Trump Is Winning the Polls—and Losing the Nomination." This time around, Silver compared Trump to Joe Lieberman, Rudy Giuliani, and Rick Perry. Trusting these polls, he wrote, is like "projecting a major league pitcher's numbers from high school stats."

That blog post also contained a sentence that I'm sure Silver would like to take back:

"In the case of presidential primaries, indicators such as endorsements and support from party elites tend to be more reliable indicators of eventual success."

Endorsements? Party elites? Clearly Silver and his crew of eggheads didn't have a clue why Trump so easily triumphed in the GOP primaries.

Silver's professional analysts are paid to study politics. They spend their days looking at polling and examining voter turnout models. It is their job to accurately analyze and predict election outcomes. And they blew it, but they weren't the only ones.

On Election Day, the *Real Clear Politics* polling average had Clinton winning Michigan by more than three percentage points and Pennsylvania by almost two. The RCP average had Clinton winning Wisconsin by six and a half.

Minutes before midnight, Silver acknowledged that the Democrats' best hope if Trump won Wisconsin was a 269-269 tie.

Larry Sabato, a University of Virginia political scientist who often appears on cable news networks, also blew the call.

On November 7th, he published his final "Crystal Ball." The political fortune teller gave Clinton 322 electoral college votes and Trump 216.

How did all of these experts get it so wrong? How did all the very smart people who have devoted their lives to understanding, analyzing and forecasting politics screw up so badly? And why do they still have jobs?

Poor Dick Morris. The Clintons' old pollster went to work for Fox News in 2012 and predicted that Mitt Romney would win—easily. He didn't and Morris paid the price—Rupert Murdoch kicked him down the stairs.

So what was the difference between Morris and Silver, Sabato et al.?

Morris is a conservative.

Chapter Twelve
Picking Up the Pieces

AFTER THE ELECTION, HILLARY CLINTON PUBLISHED A MEMOIR. THE TITLE, *What Happened*, was meant as a statement, a teaser as to the content. She would explain to the world how she lost, or, in her view, how the presidency was stolen from her—for a second time. The truth is, Clinton still doesn't know what happened. So the title would have been better posed as a question—*What Happened?* And if you're asking the question, the simplest answer is, well, you happened, Hillary.

We can forever analyze the economic factors that led people who voted twice for Obama to fall in behind Trump in Michigan, Pennsylvania, and Wisconsin. We can talk about how rapid globalization, the off-shoring of manufacturing jobs, and the rise of the internet created the sweeping social changes that tipped some swing states in favor of Trump. We can speculate about the over-reaching cultural authoritarianism of the PC Police on the left. We can even entertain the historical theories about electoral pendulums swinging this way and that after two presidential terms. We can get pedantic with our analysis, but at the most basic level, the single biggest factor in the election, apart from Trump, was Hillary Clinton.

And Clinton lost because she is a bad person.

Clinton is a congenital liar. Her first and last instinct is always to lie, and her only north star is the quest for power and money, not necessarily in that order. From her early days shaming Bill's rape victims and laughing as she got a child rapist off on a legal technicality, to her ethically-challenged days staffing the Watergate committee and her time in the White House slut-shaming Bill's bimbos, Clinton was and is an utterly immoral and amoral human being. This is a woman who was complicit in her husband's serial sexual harassment and assaults. A woman who lied to the parents of American heroes murdered by terrorists in Benghazi, and then had the audacity to call them liars. Volumes could be written about Clinton's lies, but for now we'll have to settle for just a chapter.

In the late 1970's, with Bill Clinton serving first as attorney general and then as governor, Hillary tried her hand at cattle futures trading with the help of a former executive at Tyson Foods—the largest employer in Arkansas—and the farm firm's outside counsel. According to financial records, Clinton made a profit of $98,540 from an initial investment of just $1,000 in less than one year of trading futures. Even for seasoned Wall Street pros, such returns were—and are—unheard of. It would be like buying a computer one day, and inventing Google the next. Her commodities trading would come under scrutiny after she moved into the White House. She told the press that her amazing success betting on cattle futures could be attributed to having studied an obscure column in the *Wall Street Journal*.

But Clinton didn't just lie about the unethical ways she enriched herself. She also lied about stupid, trivial things like her name.

In April 1995, Clinton found herself in Nepal as part of a goodwill tour of Asia. Nepal is the location of the world's tallest peak, Mt. Everest, and it was there that Clinton got to meet Sir Edmund Hillary, the New Zealand native who first climbed Everest in 1953.

"At an airstrip in Katmandu, Nepal—just after an overnight tiger safari and just before her departure for this poverty-ridden pocket of South Asia," the *New York Times* reported, Mrs. Clinton shook hands with the then 75-year old Sir Edmund Hillary.

Clinton told the old man that her mother had been so enthralled by his adventures that she named her daughter Hillary after him.

There's only one problem: Clinton was born years before Hillary summited Everest and gained world fame.

Clinton also lied about easily disprovable things. Like sniper fire in Bosnia, for example.

In 1996, Clinton made a trip to that war-torn land. In her 2008 campaign, she puffed up the harrowing visit, claiming that she "landed under sniper fire" and had to run for cover. Journalists quickly produced video tape of her calmly walking off the plane with her young daughter Chelsea to a warm welcoming ceremony at the Tuzla airport.

Clinton also lied about her family roots.

In a 2015 speech in Norwalk, Iowa, Hillary tried to spin a yarn that was just too politically convenient. At a time when immigration was becoming a hot campaign topic, Clinton decided to remake herself as the offspring of an immigrant family.

"All my grandparents, you know, came over here, and you know my grandfather went to work in a lace mill in Scranton, Pa., and worked there until he retired at 65. He started there when he was a teenager and just kept going. So I sit here and I think well you're talking about the second, third generation," she said. "That's me, that's you."

As Andrew Kaczynski of *BuzzFeed* news pointed out, Clinton's claim that all of her grandparents immigrated to the U.S. was incorrect. According to census and military records available through *Ancestry.com*, Clinton's paternal grandmother Hanna Jones Rodham was born in Pennsylvania; her maternal grandmother Della Howell was born in Illinois, and she married Edwin Howell, also born in Illinois.

Then there were the political expedient lies about Islamic terrorist attacks that began long before Benghazi.

Clinton told NBC's *Dateline* that her daughter Chelsea Clinton was right next to the World Trade Center towers when the planes hit on Sept. 11, 2001. Years later, Chelsea told her story to *Talk* Magazine, recounting that she was watching TV in a friend's apartment when the attack happened.

As her primary opponent, Bernie Sanders learned all too well about Clinton's penchant for tall tales.

He was the victim of myriad dirty Clinton tricks. Of course Clinton claimed she never ran negative ads against Sanders. That was a lie. She also lied about Sanders' support for Obama's clean-power plan. And she lied repeatedly throughout the primary campaign when she insisted that Wall Street was spending money opposing her candidacy. She even attacked Sanders for failing to help with HillaryCare in the 1990s, which Sanders quickly rebutted by producing photos and video of him standing behind her as she lobbied for the bill.

Clinton deceptively claimed the U.S. solar industry employs more Americans than the oil industry. She falsely stated that ISIS was using clips of Trump condemning Muslim terrorism in their recruitment videos. She lied about the gun industry, complaining that it was "the only business in America that is wholly protected from any kind of liability." She falsely asserted that hedge fund managers "pay less in taxes than nurses and truck drivers."

Clinton isn't the first liar to make a career in politics. She is, however, very, very bad at politics. She has none of the natural instincts that her husband has. It was apparent that she did not feel our pain. And on the campaign trail, she was more prone to gaffes than even Joe Biden.

Clinton's pandering was often grotesque and racially tinged. In the South, she would drop her Gs and begin speakin' with a twangy accent, throwin' in the occasional "y'all" and sometimes even appropriating old African-American sayings.

"I don't feel noways tired," she told a crowd in Selma, Alabama in 2007.

In April of 2016, Clinton joined *The Breakfast Club*, a morning show on one of New York's top hip-hop radio stations. Clinton was asked what one item she always kept in her pocketbook.

"Hot sauce," she replied.

"She's pandering to black people again," one of the hosts joked.

"Is it working?" she asked.

The campaign would later carry on with the tale, insisting that everywhere she goes, Clinton carries Ninja Squirrel, a hot sauce sold at Whole Foods—where else would she shop, or claim to shop? Whole Paycheck, of course.

"And we continue to carry chili flakes and jalapenos around," Clinton spokesman Nick Merrill added. As then Milwaukee County Sheriff David Clarke said at the time, Clinton might as well have told the black radio hosts that she always carried a watermelon in her purse.

In another instance of racial pandering, Clinton joined New York City Mayor Bill de Blasio at a fundraiser known as the Inner Circle. Each year, politicians show up and embarrass themselves with lame jokes. Clinton and de Blasio went a step further.

The Mayor was the star of a skit meant to play on the hit Broadway musical *Hamilton*. He did some painful rapping before Clinton walked out as the surprise guest. Clinton thanked de Blasio for endorsing her earlier in the year. That endorsement was noticeably belated, considering he ran her first Senate campaign.

"Took you long enough," said Clinton.

"Sorry, Hillary," he said. "I was running on CP time."

CP Time, of course, stands for "colored people time," an idea that plays on stereotypes regarding the punctuality of black people.

The racist crack was so obviously scripted that there was no way Clinton didn't know it was happening in advance. "SKIT FOR BRAINS" read the *New York Daily News* tabloid headline the next day, with a picture of a glassy-eyed de Blasio nearly busting out of his suit, with Clinton next to him in her latest General Mao-style pantsuit.

As a Democrat, Clinton needed to observe the strictures of political correctness, which sometimes turned normal, everyday expressions into scandals. For example, Clinton assured CNN's Jake Tapper that she would be able to handle Trump's outrageous attacks against her because she was used to dealing with men who were "off the reservation." Later that night, her campaign walked back the comment because it was offensive to Native Americans.

"@HillaryClinton meant no disrespect to Native Americans," tweeted a campaign spokeswoman. "She wants this election to be about lifting people up, not tearing them down."

The most destructive Clinton gaffe was undoubtedly her pledge to destroy the economic foundation of many Appalachian communities.

"We are going to put a lot of coal miners and coal companies out of business," Clinton said at a CNN town hall in Columbus, Ohio.

This was another classic Kinsley Gaffe. Clinton was actually telling the truth. She shared the progressive delusion that wind mills and solar panels are advanced enough to make coal-fired power plants obsolete. Like Obama, she planned to use the jackboot of the EPA to crush the coal industry. The remark stood in stark contrast to Trump's pledge to get the EPA off the backs of the fossil fuel industry. Conservatives quickly capitalized, blasting the short video clip across social media.

Clinton tried to walk back the damaging line the only way she knows how: with more lies. At a meet-and-greet with West Virginia voters, an unemployed coal miner pressed Clinton on her pledge to close down mining. "I do feel a little bit sad and sorry that I gave folks the reason or the excuse to be upset with me," Clinton told the man.

"I just wanna know," the miner said, "how you can say you're gonna put a lot of coal miners out of jobs and then come in here and tell us you're gonna be our friend."

"I have been talking about helping coal country for a very long time," Clinton said, adding that her remark had been taken out of context.

"I didn't mean that we were going to do it," she lied.

Clinton lost the coal-mining state of West Virginia to Trump by more than 40 points. She may know that her anti-coal position cost her votes in West Virginia and parts of Ohio, but she certainly doesn't know why she lost so many other states. In her post-election memoir, Clinton dodges blame like she dodged sniper fire in Bosnia.

Here's the current list of forces, factors, institutions, and people Clinton has blamed for her loss: The FBI, James Comey, the Russians, Putin, anti-American forces, low-information voters, people assuming she'd win, bad polling, Obama (for winning two terms), people wanting change, misogynists, suburban women, the *New York Times*, TV network executives, cable news, Netflix, Democrats not making the right documentaries, Facebook, Twitter, *Wikileaks*, fake news, content farms in Macedonia, Republicans, Bernie Sanders and Democrats.

In short, virtually everyone and everything but herself.

Chapter Thirteen
America First Again

A COLD, PATCHY DRIZZLE WAS DRIFTING OVER THE POTOMAC RIVER AS President-elect Donald Trump walked to the podium overlooking the national mall. Standing before legions of admirers, Trump placed his left hand on a pair of Bibles—his personal copy and the Lincoln Bible—as Chief Justice of the Supreme Court John Roberts led him through the same oath of office every American president before him had sworn. It was a historic day, the culmination of a long and bitter fight to wrest control of the country back from the political elites. And if those elites thought that Trump was going to moderate or soften his message because of the office he now held, they were wrong.

Trump's inaugural address was an unprecedented assault on the Beltway status quo and what would soon come to be known as "the Deep State."

"Today's ceremony has very special meaning," said Trump. "Because today we are not merely transferring power from one administration to another, or from one party to another—but we are transferring power from Washington, D.C. and giving it back to you, the American people.

"For too long, a small group in our nation's Capital has reaped the rewards of government while the people have borne the cost," he said. "Washington flourished—but the people did not share in its wealth. Politicians prospered—but the jobs left, and the factories closed. The establishment protected itself, but not the citizens of our country.

"That all changes—starting right here, and right now, because this moment is your moment: it belongs to you. It belongs to everyone gathered here today and everyone watching all across America.

"This is your day. This is your celebration," he said. "And this, the United States of America, is your country.

"At the center of this movement," Trump said, "is a crucial conviction: that a nation exists to serve its citizens. Americans want great schools for their children, safe neighborhoods for their families, and good jobs for themselves.

"But for too many of our citizens, a different reality exists: Mothers and children trapped in poverty in our inner cities; rusted-out factories scattered like tombstones across the landscape of our nation; an education system, flush with cash, but which leaves our young and beautiful students deprived of knowledge; and the crime and gangs and drugs that have stolen too many lives and robbed our country of so much unrealized potential.

"This American carnage stops right here and stops right now."

The alt-left media instantly dismissed the speech with one word, the same adjective they'd used to brush off his nomination acceptance speech in Cleveland seven months earlier: "dark." On the stage, former President George W. Bush turned to Hillary Clinton and pronounced his verdict: "That was some weird shit."

More than a year has passed since the most transformational presidential election since 1980. So where do we stand?

Trump's West Wing

The first question Trump had to answer after winning the presidency was who he would bring with him into the White House. When staffing the West Wing, loyalty is key, and during the campaign, many of the establishment hands who would have been at home in any other Republican White House had disqualified themselves with their relentless attacks on Trump. The federal government was teeming with Obama-era holdovers and career hacks who would seek to undermine Trump at every turn. The last thing he needed in the White House was friendly fire.

Trump's first major staffing decision was as pragmatic as it was symbolic. He picked RNC Director Reince Priebus to serve as his Chief of Staff and former Breitbart CEO Stephen Bannon to serve as Strategic Advisor. The positions would be co-equal, with Priebus managing the day to day operations and Bannon controlling the broader political strategy. The choice of both men was a clear message to both the GOP establishment and the populist wave Trump rode to victory.

On the one hand, Priebus was an establishment suit. His presence in Trump's administration indicated at least some respect for the traditional way of doing business. On the other hand, Bannon's high-level post ensured that Trump's inner circle would have at least one force resisting the inexorable pull of the Swamp. Both men would depart the White House within the first few months. It was obvious from the beginning having two allegedly co-equals in charge wouldn't work. As Johnny Martorano used to tell me, in the Mob, even if you only have two wiseguys on a crew, one of them has to be the boss. Winter Hill or the White House, the same principle applies, and as the new administration began, there was a third player vying for the President's ear—his son-in-law, Jared Kushner.

No one knew at the time of course, that Bannon would soon become a one-man wrecking crew, leaking indiscriminately, badmouthing and backstabbing the president and his family, and generally attempting to suicide-bomb the Republican party before and after his eventual firing from the White House in August 2017.

Nor did anyone understand that before the end of 2017, Trump's first National Security Advisor, retired Gen. Michael Flynn, would please guilty to lying to the FBI. Flynn had served as Director of the Defense Intelligence Agency under Obama before becoming a major critic of the administration. During the election, Flynn was a stalwart Trump ally—lending his gravitas to a campaign that often seemed sorely lacking in foreign policy experience. However, Flynn's tenure as Trump's NSA was brief—the briefest of all his cabinet selections—as Flynn was forced to resign by February 13. His resignation followed reports that he had lied to Vice President Pence regarding the nature of his post-election communications with Sergey Kislyak, the Russian Ambassador to the U.S. Flynn's apparent deception of Pence was all the more problematic given the outbreak of unsubstantiated Russian conspiracy theories that were beginning to obsess Trump's opposition.

For press secretary, Trump selected former RNC spokesman Sean Spicer. Spicer was the voice of the Republican Party during the fall campaign, and he was often compelled to make statements critical of Trump in this official capacity. Gaffes and inaccurate statements marred Spicer's tenure behind the podium. In an April 12 briefing, Spicer compared Syrian dictator Bashar al-Assad to Adolf Hitler, insisting that Assad's behavior was somehow more heinous or evil than Hitler's.

"I think when you come to sarin gas," he said, "[Hitler] was not using the gas on his own people the same way that Assad is doing."

Spicer's trouble behind the podium provided endless fodder for late-night shows. *Saturday Night Live* used Melissa McCarthy to parody the press secretary several times. Eventually, the Palin effect kicked in, and Spicer became a running joke. By the end of July, Spicer was gone.

Kellyanne Conway, the fiery GOP pollster who so effectively defended Trump in her television appearances, especially after the *Access Hollywood* October surprise, was rewarded with the position of Senior Counselor. Of the original team Trump assembled, she is the only top advisor still working in the White House.

For Attorney General, Trump chose Alabama Sen. Jeff Sessions. I loved this pick. As a former U.S. attorney and former state attorney general, Sessions had the prosecutorial credentials. And, considering he was the only U.S. Senator to endorse Trump, he had proven his loyalty. After a pitched confirmation battle, Sessions assumed office—and then the trouble started.

One of Sessions' first actions in office was recusing himself from all investigations related to Hillary Clinton and the Trump campaign, including the ongoing investigations into Russia's election-related activities. While many lawyers defended Sessions' recusal from an ethical perspective, Trump was not pleased.

Following the appointment of Special Counsel Bob Mueller, Trump became enraged with his attorney general. According to the *New York Times*, Trump berated Sessions in the Oval Office and told him he should resign—an experience Sessions later told close associates was the most humiliating of his political career. Sessions reportedly provided Trump with a resignation letter, but Trump declined to accept it after his advisers convinced him that Sessions' departure so early in his presidency would only cause more problems—namely, another bruising Senate confirmation fight.

Although Trump expected his AG to shield him more from investigations that began under the Obama administration, Sessions did institute important reforms, especially the prosecution of illegal aliens. Under his predecessors, the DOJ was loath to admit that any heroin dealer or gang-banger was a foreign national; now, the official press releases include the immigration status of criminals in the headlines. Just in New England, illegal aliens are busted every week for illegal re-entry, opioid trafficking, or gang-related offenses. Trump promised a restoration of law and order, and Sessions is delivering.

If Trump's pick to run the Justice Department was natural and predictable, his choice for Secretary of State was a bit more unusual. In mid-December, Trump announced his nomination of ExxonMobil CEO Rex Tillerson to run the State Department. From Trump's perspective as a businessman, Tillerson's pick made sense: The man was responsible for running a global corporation with more than 83,000 employees, while the State Department has just over 30,000 employees on the payroll.

Tillerson's nomination was pragmatic in a sense, but also puzzling for Trump's biggest supporters. Although the Texas energy executive had always been a Republican, his policy views were a bit of a mystery. When he was CEO of ExxonMobil, the company announced its support for a carbon tax—a longtime pipe dream of the environmental left. And Tillerson's support for the Trans-Pacific Partnership was a matter of extensive public record. Ditto for many of the so-called free trade agreements Trump had criticized on the campaign.

Although Tillerson's confirmation faced resistance from Sens. Marco Rubio and John McCain, the Senate confirmed him on a 56–43 vote. Since taking over in Foggy Bottom, Tillerson's relationship with Trump has been rocky. As Tillerson has worked behind the scenes to build relationships with his peers, Trump's boisterous foreign policy pronouncements, often emanating from his Twitter account, have left his Secretary of State scrambling to get on the same page. Tillerson has also faced rumor after rumor that he would be departing early from his post, rumors that Trump had only fed by suggesting in media interviews that Tillerson may not be with him for the duration.

Trump's pick to run the Treasury Department was even odder than his choice for State. He picked Steve Mnuchin, a Goldman Sachs alumnus who later operated several hedge funds and even dallied in film producing. Politically, Mnuchin was something of an independent. Although he supported capitalism and free markets, he had donated to Al Gore, Hillary Clinton, John Kerry and Barack Obama. But he was an early supporter of Trump's.

After attending Trump's victory party the night of the New York GOP primary, Mnuchin got a call from the Republican frontrunner asking if he would serve as Trump's national finance chairman. Mnuchin accepted the job, and after serving on the transition team, he welcomed the chance to run Treasury.

Then there is James Mattis, the Secretary of Defense. In 2016, more than a few conservative columnists and bloggers floated "Mad Dog" Mattis as a potential vice-presidential nominee. His appeal was obvious. Mattis led Marines in the first Gulf War and served as a commanding officer of the 1st Marine Expeditionary Brigade in Afghanistan. In Iraq, Mattis commanded the 1st Marine Division during the 2003 invasion. He was promoted through the ranks into leadership positions, eventually serving as Commander of the U.S. Central Command under Obama.

Mattis' distinguished record of service made him eminently more qualified for the post than his two most recent predecessors, Leon Panetta and Chuck Hagel. *Marine Corps Times*, for example, called him the "most revered Marine in a generation." But what really endeared conservatives to Mattis was his colorful commentary about the nature of war and the American armed services.

In the lead-up to the invasion of Iraq, Mattis offered this advice to his Marines: "Be polite, be professional, but have a plan to kill everybody you meet."

And this is the advice he had for the Iraqis after the initial success of the invasion: "I come in peace," Mattis recalled telling them. "I didn't bring artillery. But I'm pleading with you, with tears in my eyes: If you fuck with me, I'll kill you all."

Mattis' alpha-male mentality was just what the Defense Department needed, after spending the Obama years contemplating the best way to provide transgender bathrooms on our nuclear submarines.

"You go into Afghanistan, you got guys who slap women around for five years because they didn't wear a veil," Mattis told a San Diego forum in 2005. "You know, guys like that ain't got no manhood left anyway. So it's a hell of a lot of fun to shoot them. Actually, it's a lot of fun to fight. You know, it's a hell of a hoot. It's fun to shoot some people. I'll be right upfront with you, I like brawling."

For Secretary of Labor, Trump initially chose Andrew Puzder, the CEO of SKE Restaurants, which operates the Hardee's and Carl's Jr. restaurants. Puzder was an impeccable pick who rose to the attention of conservatives through his op-eds in the *Wall Street Journal*, in which he eviscerated progressive arguments in favor of a higher minimum wage. And Puzder served as a surrogate for Trump, including on my own radio show. But the very characteristics that made Puzder such an excellent pick to run a government agency put a target on his back.

The Democrats mounted a concerted effort, publicly and privately, to derail Puzder's confirmation. It began with behind-the-scenes delays with his paper work and questions over his potential conflict of interests. But then it spilled over into public, with Democrats alleging that Puzder mistreated his workers. Another knock they had on Puzder? He supported the inevitable automation of menial jobs, like being a cashier at Carl's Jr. The attacks on Puzder peaked when it was revealed that he had employed an illegal immigrant as a house-keeper. On the eve of his confirmation hearing, Puzder withdrew his nomination. Puzder was eventually replaced by Alexander Acosta, a former member of the National Labor Relations Board and a former U.S. attorney in Miami. (And no relation to CNN's Jim Acosta, whom the President sometimes called out personally as "Very Fake News.")

Fake News

In the immediate aftermath of the shocking loss, Hillary Clinton and her team of Brooklyn-based pajama boys began making excuses for the biggest upset since Super Bowl III. Ultimately, they would settle on Russia, Vladimir Putin, and election hacking, or collusion, or meddling, as the prime driver of the unexpected defeat. But there was another culprit they blamed: Fake news.

In their minds, well-written—but entirely made-up—stories on the internet were hugely influential. You probably saw some of these stories if you perused the internet for news during the campaign. All it took was a teenager with a laptop in Macedonia who could create a website and write a news story. The sites had newspaper-style names—*NewChristianPost.net*, *TrueNewsDaily.com*, or *USConservativeToday.com*. And the articles were scandalous: George Soros paying anti-Trump protesters $3,500 a month! Proof Surfaces That Obama Was Born In Kenya! Pope Francis Forbids Catholics From Voting For Hillary! Bill Clinton Sex Tape Just Leaked! And because they were scandalous, they spread like wildfire across social media.

According to Hillary Clinton, these pieces of click bait prevented her from winning the White House. That's a bit of a stretch, considering Trump was also targeted. Regardless, bemoaning fake news became a major part of Clinton's post-election alibi as her supporters were asking, What happened?

But the fake news talking point backfired—big time.

"Fake news played a role in this election and continues to find a wide audience," reported MSNBC's Brian Williams, who knows more than a little about fake news.

You can't make this stuff up! Williams, of course, was demoted from NBC *Nightly News* to an unwatchable program on MSNBC following the revelation that his entire career was built on fake news. Williams had spun Clintonesque lies about his feats of bravery during the Iraq War and his harrowing coverage of the carnage during Hurricane Katrina. He was quite literally one of the poster boys of fake news—one of many. And he wasn't the only one lecturing the rest of us about the danger of Macedonia content farmers. Dan Rather, who infamously used *60 Minutes* to publish fake memos in 2004 casting George W. Bush's military service as a fraud, also investigated anti-Hillary fake news.

So while Clinton thought she'd latched on to a good excuse by blaming fake internet news, the rest of us heard people like Williams and Rather promoting her excuses and broke into fits of laughter.

Conservatives had been dealing with fake news for decades—and not just stupid stories on the internet. We had to endure multiple networks and major newspapers pushing ideologically driven fake news. Naturally, the fake news moniker the Clintons created was swiftly applied to the mainstream media networks and personalities that had slobberingly backed her candidacy. The Democrats stopped talking about fake news, but the fake news didn't go away. It only continued as liberal media outlets became overwhelmed with Trump Derangement Syndrome—TDS.

The fake news phenomenon has taken its toll on what was once called mass media. According to a Zogby poll in November 2017, 48 percent of American adults believe the alphabet networks and big newspapers—CBS, ABC, NBC, *New York Times*, *Washington Post*, *Los Angeles Times*, et al.—are untrustworthy.

Unsurprisingly, there is a partisan split. Two-thirds of Democrats trust Brian Williams, Dan Rather and their fellow fabulists, while 69 percent of Republicans do not.

We're one year into his presidency, and Trump now finds himself bedeviled by fake news. Most of the time, anti-Trump fake news stories are based on just one anonymous source or alleged source. There was the report from NBC that Tillerson called Trump a "moron." Then there was the report that Trump wanted to increase the U.S. nuclear arsenal ten-fold. Then there was Trump's trip to Japan, during which CNN falsely claimed that Trump didn't know Japanese automakers have American plants. And that "gaffe" came right before Trump allegedly overfed Prime Minister Shinzo Abe's koi fish. Time and again, the networks and newspapers have produced thinly sourced, garbage stories all aimed at undermining Trump.

But the biggest piece of fake news was, of course, the dodgy dossier.

Golden Showers Dossier

Nine days before Trump's inauguration as the 45th President of the United States, *BuzzFeed* news published a shocking document that made outrageous and unverified claims about the soon-to-be-president.

The dodgy dossier, as it would come to be known, had circulated among media outlets well before election day. *Mother Jones'* David Corn, in the days before he was outed as yet another alt-left serial sexual predator, referenced the document somewhat vaguely. And Sen. Harry Reid, ever the dirty trickster, had alluded to it in pre-election interviews.

In the fall of 2017, House investigators discovered that Fusion GPS had cut checks to four Beltway "journalists" at the same time it was shopping the dossier around in 2016. As this book went to press, Fusion GPS was still refusing to release the names of the four "journalists."

As election day neared, however, no media outlet dared to publish the salacious, unverified claims. But two months later, when the news broke that FBI Director James Comey had presented the document to President-elect Trump at their first meeting in Trump Tower, suddenly the dossier was newsworthy, regardless of its veracity. So *BuzzFeed* put the entire document online and CNN took it from there.

We now know that the dossier was the product of Fusion GPS, an opposition research firm run by former reporters from the *Wall Street Journal*. Fusion GPS's work was funded initially by the conservative website *Washington Free*

Beacon. But when Trump secured the nomination, Clinton's campaign and the DNC picked up the contract. After Clinton's campaign attorney Marc Elias paid Fusion GPS, the firm contracted with Christopher Steele, a British former MI6 agent who had specialized in Russian operations.

The Steele dossier included a number of outrageous claims. Putin had, Steele claimed, been cultivating Trump for five years, part of a far-reaching effort to get him elected president and sow division within the West. The dossier admitted that Trump had, for some inexplicable reason, declined "sweetener real estate business deals" in Russia, but asserted that he had accepted intelligence from the Kremlin, "including on his Democratic and other political rivals." Without evidence, Steele claimed that the Trump campaign was in constant communication with agents of the Russian government.

But the most scandalous claim of the dossier involves the so-called golden showers. According to Steele, his sources in Russia claimed that Donald Trump went to a hotel in Moscow in 2013 and rented the same Ritz Carlton room once occupied by Barack and Michelle Obama. So strong was Trump's hatred for the Obamas, the dossier asserted, that Trump paid Russian prostitutes to urinate on the bed the Obamas supposedly slept on. The implication, of course, was that Putin had video of Trump engaging in this lurid behavior and that Trump would be susceptible to blackmail by a foreign adversary as a result.

The accusations were ludicrous. Trump was a well-known germaphobe. Prior to the presidential campaign, the man rarely shook hands with people. Only someone suffering from severe Trump Derangement Syndrome could read the dossier and swallow it as truth. But none of that mattered. The media believed that Trump was an evil man, so there was no claim about his past or his character that could be discounted, facts and common sense be damned.

BuzzFeed first posted the dossier, but it was CNN that really lent credibility to this piece of anti-Trump fan fiction. Jake Tapper, a longtime associate of the Clinton crime family, got the ball rolling. In his serious voice, Tapper explained the breaking, exclusive news that he had uncovered with the help of Jim Sciutto, formerly of the Obama administration, Carl Bernstein, of Watergate fame, and Evan Perez. For weeks on end, CNN cited the dossier as conclusive proof that the Trump campaign had colluded with Russians in order to defeat Hillary Clinton.

Neil Gorsuch

Throughout his tumultuous campaign, Trump faced various antagonists from the right. Trump was not conservative enough for them; he hadn't paid his dues; he wasn't ideologically pure. However, nothing eased their concerns about Trump's ideological purity like his reaction to the sudden death of Supreme Court Justice Antonin Scalia. Even before Scalia's death it had seemed likely that Obama's successor would get to appoint at least one Justice. Had Clinton won, the older liberals on the bench would have retired, knowing that they would be replaced by younger orthodox leftist mandarins. But with Scalia's seat now vacant, conservatives faced the prospect of seeing the entire ideological balance of the Supreme Court skewing left for a generation or more.

Trump understood that conservative voters cared deeply about the Supreme Court, and he used the vacant seat as a tool of persuasion. Months after Scalia's death, Trump, with the help of the conservative Heritage Foundation, published a list of potential nominees to the court and vowed to nominate someone from that list.

Throughout the campaign, Trump repeatedly brought up the Supreme Court to rebuke any of his critics on the right. And it was a convincing argument: Trump might be crass, but do you really want Hillary Clinton putting some 35-year-old ACLU attorney on the highest court?

Trump's Supreme Court gambit would not have been possible without Senate Majority Leader Mitch McConnell. McConnell had never been a darling of the right. He was the epitome of the establishment Republican. He could always be counted on to defend the status quo, to protect business as usual.

But when Obama nominated liberal judge Merrick Garland to the court, McConnell didn't blink. He refused to even hold confirmation hearings for Garland. It was a bold move. I'm sure that countless Beltway consultants told McConnell that obstructing Obama's court pick would lead to electoral disaster in 2016, but they were wrong. McConnell's decision not only gave Trump a critical tool for his campaign, but it also preserved the conservative tilt of an entire branch of the federal government.

As promised, President Trump delivered what will likely become one of the most lasting legacies of his presidency. Trump chose a stalwart conservative legal mind to replace Scalia on the Supreme Court: Neil McGill Gorsuch. A former clerk for Justice Anthony Kennedy, Gorsuch sat on the U.S. Court of Appeals for the Tenth Circuit in Colorado. His establishment credentials were impeccable: Columbia University, Harvard University Law School, and Oxford. Throughout his career, Gorsuch demonstrated a knack for clear and concise legal opinions in the tradition of textualism and originalism. In other words, he applied the law as written, rather than as he wished it was.

Gorsuch's nomination to the Supreme Court thrilled Republicans and his confirmation hearings showed exactly why. In the face of mind-numbingly stupid criticisms from idiots like Democrat Sen. Al Franken, another soon-to-be-outed sexual predator, Gorsuch was unflappable. He defended his past rulings and demonstrated a strict fidelity to the rule of law. The Democrats didn't lay a glove on him. Gorsuch was confirmed in April, by a 54–45 vote, with three Democrats voting in favor.

Trump vs. The World

On foreign policy, Trump's record of accomplishment has been a blend of striking successes and odd deviations from his promises of America First. Much as he promised on the campaign trail, Trump found his General Patton in Secretary Mattis. And just as he vowed, Trump got the lawyers and bureaucrats off the backs of the war-fighters.

The results were stunning, especially when it came to ISIS, the blood-thirsty Muslim terrorists Obama had blithely dismissed as "the j.v. team."

During the feckless Obama era, the junior varsity rose to power and conquered vast swaths of territory in the Middle East. From its headquarters in Syria and Iraq, the group dispatched mercenaries to carry out attacks in Belgium, France and Germany. The Muslim death cult inspired many more attacks just through their slick use of online propaganda. What always made ISIS different from other terror groups like Al-Qaeda was its early move to capture Raqqa and expand the territory under its control. The Taliban in Afghanistan had territory under its control, but the group was nothing more than a ragtag band of illiterate tribal goatherders. ISIS, on the other hand, declared its intention to establish a true Islamic State. Holding territory, including valuable factories and oil fields, gave ISIS power, money and an allure that helped it recruit foreign fighters.

Obama, meanwhile, openly admitted that he lacked a strategy to deal with ISIS.

Fewer than 10 months into the Trump administration, here's a headline from, of all places, the *New York Times*: "ISIS Fighters, Having Pledged to Fight or Die, Surrender en Masse." Coalition forces have crushed the Islamic State. And now, the biggest question involving ISIS is what to do with all the loser terrorists who are now fleeing the Mid East, returning to the West, and swearing up and down that they were just cooks and clerks. ISIS-aligned terrorists certainly live on in cells across Europe and North America, but the vaunted Islamic Caliphate has lost its stranglehold on Iraq and Syria.

The first major test of Trump's America First foreign policy came in Syria. Following reports that Syrian dictator Bashar al-Assad was planning to use chemical weapons, Trump ordered a limited missile attack on an airbase where the attack was supposed to originate. The raid was successful, and Assad has not used chemical weapons since, but it raised questions among Trump's supporters about how the airstrike fit into his oft-proclaimed non-interventionist policy.

If the MAGA train was somewhat divided over the wisdom of the Syria strikes, it was decidedly less so over the use of an epic conventional explosive to wipe out a terrorist cave network in Afghanistan. The strike drew blazing headlines owing to the nature of the bomb used, the GBU-43/B Massive Ordinance Air Blast Bomb (MOAB). Nicknamed the Mother of All Bombs, the MOAB is the largest non-nuclear bomb in the American arsenal. And its effect on a cave system in Nangarhar province, near the Pakistani border, was devastating.

In the first year of his presidency, Trump has managed the annihilation of ISIS and the crippling of Al Qaeda, but he has also brought a renewed focus to another, even more serious geopolitical threat: North Korea and its arsenal of nuclear weapons. Although the deployment of the MOAB accomplished its near-term objective of killing cave-dwelling terrorist savages, many foreign policy observers viewed the strike as something of a warning to Kim Jong Un, the pudgy dictator of North Korea.

As in so many other areas of politics and policy, on the Korean peninsula Trump inherited a total mess. Beginning with Bill Clinton, U.S. policy with regard to North Korea had been one of appeasement and neglect. The Clinton administration thought they could work with Kim Jong Il to prevent the regimes' nuclear weapons program from expanding. Under the terms of Clinton's so-called "Agreed Framework" with North Korea, the United States would provide the rogue nation with cash and supplies, including 500,000 barrels in crude oil annually.

In addition, Clinton's agreement called on the U.S. to provide North Korea with light-water nuclear reactors, the idea being that the Norks could continue building a peaceful nuclear program while abstaining from developing bombs. If that sounds familiar, it's because John Kerry negotiated a similar agreement with Iran.

"This is a good deal for the United States," Clinton said in a White House address. "North Korea will freeze and then dismantle its nuclear program. The entire world will be safer as we slow the spread of nuclear weapons."

Kim Jong Il never respected the agreement. The influx of aid from America allowed him to bring the Korean people out of a devastating famine, while at the same time he continued to develop his clandestine nuclear weapons and ballistic missile programs.

The Bush 43 administration was as hapless as Clinton's. Following 9-11, the foreign policy energy of the new administration was dedicated almost exclusively to combating Islamic terrorism in Iraq and Afghanistan. Bush included North Korea in his famous Axis of Evil speech and his official policy toward the dictatorship called for regime change. However, the Bush era sanctions were ineffective.

In 2003, Kim announced that his country possessed a nuclear bomb. The U.S., along with China, Japan, Russia, and South Korea, attempted to get North Korea back to the table for diplomatic talks. But it was all a show. In October 2006, the rogue regime successfully tested its first nuclear bomb.

The Obama administration worked only behind the scenes to undermine North Korea. According to a *New York Times* article published after the 2016 election, the Obama administration had engaged in a campaign of industrial sabotage against the North Koreans, infiltrating the supply chain of missile products to ensure that its scientists were using faulty parts in their missiles. That *Times* article portrays Obama as some kind of secret agent who was single-handedly stopping the advance of Kim Jong Un's missile program, but it was mostly fake-news agitprop peddled to the *Times*' fellow travelers by Obama's Deep-State stooges—a subtle attempt to rewrite history and make it look as though Obama hadn't followed Clinton and Bush in ignoring one of the most serious geopolitical crises of the new century.

President Trump has not shied away from confrontation with North Korea, moving carrier groups and Air Force assets into the region while increasing test runs of nuclear-capable bombers. In his first address to the United Nations, Trump tore into Kim Jong Un.

"No one has shown more contempt for other nations and for the wellbeing of their own people than the depraved regime in North Korea," he said. "It is responsible for the starvation deaths of millions of North Koreans, and for the imprisonment, torture, killing, and oppression of countless more.

"We were all witness to the regime's deadly abuse when an innocent American college student, Otto Warmbier, was returned to America only to die a few days later. We saw it in the assassination of the dictator's brother using banned nerve agents in an international airport."

Trump drew headlines for mocking Kim, calling the tyrant "Rocket Man" and insisting that the young leader's continued development of ballistic missile technology was a suicide mission for himself and his destitute failed state.

"The United States has great strength and patience," Trump said, "but if it is forced to defend itself or its allies, we will have no choice but to totally destroy North Korea."

Trump vs. Congress

President Trump's relationship with Congress has been rocky, to say the least. House Speaker Paul Ryan, a notorious critic of Trump's and a man who counseled his House colleagues to abandon the GOP nominee following the release of the *Access Hollywood* tape in October 2016, made early attempts to rebuild his relationship with the president. But Ryan's shortcomings as a legislative leader have severely hamstrung the president's agenda in Congress. Sam Rayburn he ain't.

Nowhere was Ryan's failure of leadership more apparent than the Affordable Care Act, more commonly known as Obamacare. After filling out his cabinet and getting Gorsuch confirmed to the Supreme Court, Trump set his sights on the long-sought-after goal of repealing Obamacare. With Republicans in control of both branches of Congress and the White House, repealing the onerous failed health care law should have been a slam dunk. After all, Obamacare sparked the 2010 Tea Party revolution that put the House under GOP control for the last six years of the Obama administration. The calamitous federal health care law even contributed to Republican wins in 2012 and 2014. It was the central issue on which Republicans from Arizona to Massachusetts campaigned throughout Obama's entire presidency.

In the seven years after Obamacare's passage the GOP House passed no fewer than 50 repeal votes. But once Trump arrived in the White House, when the elected Republicans finally had the opportunity to *actually* repeal Obamacare, they choked.

As dreadful as Ryan was on Obamacare repeal, he at least engineered the passage of some semblance of a repeal bill, however flawed it was. But in the Senate McConnell could not succeed in putting a bill on Trump's desk. This, however, had more to do with Sens. John McCain, Lisa Murkowski and Susan Collins. While the two female senators were just concerned with keeping Planned Parenthood and Medicaid funded, McCain's complaint was more personal. After clashing with Trump throughout the campaign, he was loath to give Trump anything resembling a victory. McCain became the pivotal nay vote that sank the first health care reform effort.

The Congressional failure on the Obamacare front was pathetic. After seven years whipping the health care law in their campaign rhetoric and media appearances, the wonks on the right had failed to produce any replacement legislation. Trump devoted the early months of his presidency, and what little political capital he had, to repealing Obamacare, and the GOP majority in Congress let him down, although the tax-reform bill passed in December 2017 included a provision repealing the "individual mandate"—the fine for not having coverage. In itself, that knocked the financial underpinnings out from under Obama's disastrous Rube Goldberg scheme, and the president quickly bragged that Obamacare was on its last legs.

Reshaping the judiciary has gone mostly unnoticed, but it may be Trump's most important first-year accomplishment. After eight long years of Obama stacking the federal judiciary with liberal law professors, community "advocates" as well as assorted other Kool-Aid drinking apparatchiks, self-identifying victims and perpetually aggrieved members of protected classes, Trump set about reversing the tide. His picks might not all be Gorsuches and Scalias, but neither are they Kagans or Sotomayors. The plan, hatched by Trump's White House Counsel Donald F. McGahn II, has been wildly successful. Nearly one year into his presidency, Trump had appointed a dozen appellate judges, the most this early into a presidency since Richard M. Nixon.

Stopping Hillary

Trump's greatest victory came on Election Day—the final flushing of Clintonism from American politics. Trump could repeal Obamacare, pass Reaganesque tax cuts, and oversee three more years of high GDP growth, and I still think putting the Clinton Crime Family out of business will forever be regarded as his greatest contribution to the United States of America.

I continue to believe that Donald Trump was the only Republican who could have defeated Hillary Clinton. His visceral connection with voters in the critical states of Michigan, Ohio, Wisconsin and Pennsylvania was something no other GOP candidate would ever have been able to manage. The Obama voters who crossed over to vote for Trump would never have done so for Jeb Bush.

Without Trump, Republicans would have ceded the White House to Hillary Clinton and the Democrat machine. That would not only have cemented every executive and legislative connivance of her Democrat predecessor, it would also have tipped the balance of the Supreme Court irrevocably. Clinton would have replaced Scalia with a radical leftist. Justice Ruth Bader Ginsburg, knowing she would be replaced by a fellow traveler, would have taken not-so-early retirement. Perhaps the same could be said of Justice Anthony Kennedy. Forget about health care and taxes. Clinton's impact on the Supreme Court would have been more transformational to American politics than anything accomplished on Barack Obama's watch. Her promises to overturn *Citizens United* and in essence repeal the Second Amendment would have gone from hyperbolic campaign rhetoric to reality and that would have meant the eventual end of the American experiment, sooner, rather than later.

Instead, we have finally, a government committed to a policy of America First… again!

Thank you, POTUS.

EPILOGUE

PRESIDENT DONALD J. TRUMP WAS WORKING THE ROOM AT MAR-A-LAGO.

It was the evening of Dec. 27, 2017, a beautiful moonlit evening in Palm Beach, temperatures in the low 70's, not a cloud in the sky.

Twenty-two months earlier, at a pre-primary rally at a golf club in South Carolina, Trump had made his supporters a promise.

"We're going to win so much, you're going to get tired of winning," he said. "You're going to say, 'Please, Mr. President, I have a headache. Please, don't win so much. This is getting terrible!'"

That was one Trump prediction that hasn't come true. No one has yet gotten tired of winning, least of all the 45th president of the United States.

I was dining at the club with my family and some friends. Earlier that day, a national reporter for the *Washington Post* had emailed me, asking me about the ambience at Mar-a-Lago when the president is in town. So when I got a chance to speak to Trump, I told him what the reporter was looking for and asked him if he wanted me to share anything with the *Post*.

"Tell them," he said, "that I am relaxed and enjoying myself and I'm in a very good mood because I've just had the most successful first year of any president in American history."

He'd been saying the same thing all day, first while playing 18 holes at his Trump International Golf Course in West Palm Beach, and then later, as he stopped by Fire Station 2 on the Dixie Highway to talk to the firefighters on duty.

"Country's doing well," the president told the jakes. "How are your 401(k)'s doing, pretty well?"

CNN was apoplectic. They quickly posted a piece "fact-checking" his statements at the fire station.

"The stock market," Trump had said, "hit a new high 84 times since we won the election on November 8th of last year."

Yep, CNN grudgingly acknowledged, that was true. And that really bugged the alt-left media. The *Boston Globe*, for example, had run a fake-news headline in April 2016, predicting dire consequences for the economy if Trump won.

"Markets sink as trade wars loom."

At least the *Globe* could claim that headline was a parody. The day after the election, November 9, Paul Krugman, an "economist" for the *New York Times*, grimly assessed Trump's upset by saying, "If the question is when markets will recover, a first-pass answer is never."

Now Trump's enemies were sullen and silent as the market hit record new highs day after day after day. Even the *Wall Street Journal*, owned by Trump's friend Rupert Murdoch, couldn't quite accept the reality of the booming bourses. Its year-end headline: "Record Run Defies Skeptics."

Not to mention Trump haters.

At the fire station, Trump told the firefighters: "You have a big, big beautiful ship that we're turning around."

Specifically, he mentioned the tax cuts he had just signed into law—"the legislation of all legislation that's the biggest there is."

And cutting regulations—"We have the all-time record for stopping ridiculous regulations, and we're very proud of that record."

Of course, CNN sniffed that no one had ever kept records of cutting regulations, so there was no way to measure which president was number one.

At the firehouse, the president didn't even get into foreign policy. ISIS had been routed, and now demonstrations were breaking out across Iran against the hardline mullahs and their brutal theocracy. One reason for the Iranian turmoil was that the Persian economy was in a tailspin, in large measure because of the low oil prices worldwide. And once again, Trump could take credit.

After eight years of foot dragging by Obama, Trump's administration had signed off on final construction of the Keystone XL pipeline to bring more shale oil from Alberta to Gulf refineries. Meanwhile, the Dakota Access Pipeline had been in operation for only six months, and oil production in North Dakota had already grown by 78,000 barrels in a day just between September and October. The more energy the U.S. produced, the less hard Western currency went to OPEC... and to the savage Muslim terrorists that Iran and the oil-exporting Arab states financed and egged on.

After months of doom-and-gloom headlines about his abysmal popularity, Trump had gotten a post-tax bill bump, and at year's end, his favorable-unfavorable ratings in at least one poll were 46–53—exactly the same numbers Obama had at the end of his first year in 2009.

No wonder the well-heeled crowd at Mar-a-Lago seemed in such good spirits that evening. Trump was in his comfort zone. Four of his children, and nine grandchildren, had flown into PBI for the holidays. The conservative media were well-represented at the club that evening, including Fox News hosts Laura Ingraham and Jeanine Pirro, Newsmax CEO Chris Ruddy, and radio talk-show host Michael Savage.

Richard LeFrak, one of Trump's fellow billionaire developers from Queens, was mingling in the crowd. So was Bernie Marcus, the co-founder of Home Depot. Sitting at Trump's table were Ike Perlmutter, who had sold Marvel Comics to Disney for $4.4 billion in 2009, and Steve Wynn, the casino owner who would soon resign as finance chairman of the Republican National Committee in the wake of a major decades-long sexual-harassment scandal.

As I surveyed the pleasant surroundings, a few lingering doubts nagged at me. Could the Trump revolution weather the 2018 midterms? Could Trump win reelection in 2020? What if 2016 had been just the final gasp of the old America? History is replete with one-hit wonders, and I was considering the parallels between some of them and Trump. Oliver Cromwell, for example, was a game changer for a while, until he wasn't.

What if Trump turned out to be the modern Louis XV—*apres moi, le deluge.*

After me, the deluge.

Actually, though, that evening at Mar-a-Lago I was thinking more about yet another historical figure—one of the later Roman emperors, Julian I, better known as Julian the Apostate. Just as Trump had shed his liberal Democrat background, so Julian renounced the Christian religion that even his royal parents had embraced in the fourth century AD. (Or should I use the new PC designation—CE, meaning Current Era, as opposed to AD—Anno Domini, Latin for the Year of Our Lord?)

Anyway, Julian became emperor on what was basically a platform of "Make Rome Great Again."

This is the description of Julian the Apostate in *Wikipedia:*

"He believed it was necessary to restore the Empire's ancient Roman values and traditions in order to save it from dissolution. He purged the top-heavy state bureaucracy, and attempted to revive traditional Roman religious practices...."

Sound familiar? Merry Christmas!

Like Trump, Julian the Apostate was not without his critics. Some ancients complained that he was "excessively anxious for empty distinction," and that his "desire for popularity often led him to converse with unworthy persons."

Julian's reign only lasted two years; he died after being wounded in a quixotic campaign against the Sassanid empire in Persia. Fifteen years later the Roman army was destroyed at Adrianople by the Goths, and less than a century later, the western Empire itself was history.

If the Democrats were to retake the White House in 2020, these Trump years might be come to be regarded by history as but an interregnum. Trump himself might turn out to be nothing more than a footnote, like Macbeth, "a poor player that struts and frets his hour upon the stage, and then is heard no more."

As I was leaving Mar-a-Lago that evening, I waved good night to the president. He called me over to his table, and I noticed Michael Savage sitting across from him.

"When I die, Howie," Savage said, "you're going to inherit my radio show."

"Really?" I said. "So when are you going to die?"

Then Trump said to me, "Howie, what are we going to do about voter ID?"

This remains one of his obsessions, and I can understand why. It's why he set up a voter-integrity commission, since disbanded, to try to put an end to the endemic Democrat fraud that now takes place during elections. He's still angry that he lost New Hampshire to Hillary by 2736 votes.

I told him about the post-election investigation of the thousands of voters in New Hampshire who had taken ballots in 2016 under the state's same-day registration law. Trump always gripes about voters being bussed in from Massachusetts, but the larger problem is in the college towns—Durham, Hanover, Plymouth and Keene especially—where the out-of-state students turn out in droves. According to state law, anyone claiming New Hampshire residence, which you must in order to get a ballot, is required to obtain a Granite State driver's license within 60 days.

On November 8, 2016, 6540 people took a same-day ballot in New Hampshire. By August 30, 2017, only 1014 of them had gotten New Hampshire drivers' licenses.

"That's over 5000 people who voted who don't live in New Hampshire," I told the president. "How much did you lose New Hampshire by—3000 votes?"

"I didn't lose New Hampshire," he corrected me. "I won it!"

What about Sen. Kelly Ayotte, I asked? She lost her seat by 1017 votes. That election was definitely stolen.

"I still think she could have won, though," I said, "if she'd just shown up at your election-eve rally with you and Mike Pence and John Sununu in Manchester."

Trump shook his head. "You know when she lost? When she issued that 6 am statement Saturday morning denouncing me, saying she wouldn't vote for me. Remember that?"

Now we were back to the *Access Hollywood* tape. Like Paul Ryan and Chris Christie, Ayotte had jumped ship instantly, but Ayotte did it with even more virtue-signaling than any of the other RINOs. She piously said she could not tolerate "assaults on women," then added, "And I want my daughter to know that."

Trump shook his head as he recalled Sen. Ayotte's desertion under fire.

"And then after the election," he said, "I get a call from your friend, Mitch McConnell—"

Now Trump was pointing his finger at me. "Your friend—"

"My friend?" I said. "What did I do to deserve that?"

Trump continued: "McConnell says, I think you should appoint Kelly secretary of defense. I said, 'I don't think so.'" Trump shrugged. "But she did all right taking Gorsuch around to meet all the senators."

He paused for a second.

"But really, Howie, what are we going to do about this voter ID problem?"

I told him that after the new Republican governor, Chris Sununu, took office in January 2017, the GOP-controlled legislature in Concord finally began tightening up the fraud-ridden same-day voter-registration system. But the reforms weren't nearly strong enough to put an end to all of the abuses that the Democrats had been promoting.

"I had Gov. Sununu on my show after he signed the bill," I told the president, "and I asked him why the bill was so weak, and he said it was because they were afraid that if it were any stronger, some judge would throw it out as unconstitutional."

Trump frowned and shook his head.

"Why," he said slowly, "is everybody so afraid of judges?"

One of the women at the table piped up. "You're the president, you can do something about judges!"

Yeah, that's what FDR thought too. Trump didn't say anything. Maybe he was thinking what I was, that yes, perhaps he can do something, but it will take years to undo two terms of Obama's appointments of one doctrinaire leftist after another to the federal bench. Four years might be a good beginning, but even two terms won't be long enough to completely reverse what Obama did to the rule of law and order.

As I drove home, I remembered again what Trump had said at that rally in South Carolina where he told the crowd that they were going to get tired of winning, and that they would eventually implore to slow down and say, "Please don't do so much."

This is what Trump said he would reply to them:

"I'm going to say, 'No, we have to make America great again!' You're gonna say, 'Please.' I say, 'Nope, nope. We're gonna keep winning.'"

So that's what really happened. We won, and now we must keep on winning. The alternative is too horrible to contemplate.